Love's Pivotal Relationships

The Chum, First Love, Outlaw and the Intimate Partner

Richard Alapack

authorHOUSE®

AuthorHouse™ UK Ltd.
500 Avebury Boulevard
Central Milton Keynes, MK9 2BE
www.authorhouse.co.uk
Phone: 08001974150

First published by AuthorHouse 7/16/2007

ISBN: 978-1-4343-1904-3 (sc)
ISBN: 978-1-4343-2452-8 (hc)

Printed in the United States of America
Bloomington, Indiana

This book is printed on acid-free paper.

Love's Pivotal Relationships:

The Chum, First Love, Outlaw and Intimate Partner

Richard Alapack

Contents

INTRODUCTION

"In those matters seemingly removed from love the feeling is secretly to be found, and man cannot possibly live for a moment without it."[1] Pascal's words of wisdom remain valid as long as the human heart shall beat. As part of the longest love-letter ever written, Søren Kierkegaard also insists that love is the foundation of life, its mainspring. Without it, the heart beats hollow. He also warns us: "To cheat oneself out of love is the most terrible deception. It is an eternal loss for which there is no reparation, either in time or in eternity."[2] Loving demands risking a "leap." Every love-jump requires courage, too. Because why? Our very life might depend upon it, that's why. Alfonso Lingis writes, "We are never more... open to being so easily hurt, as when we give ourselves over in love to someone, never more vulnerable than when we are in love."[3] Equally strongly, he affirms the glory of humans. Willing we risk. "There are games in which what one loses, if one loses, is completely disproportionate to what one wins, if one wins. One stands to lose everything."[4] Lingis insists that gambling all for love is the chance we both crave and dread. Do we not "feel a kind of indifference," he asks, "and even disdain for someone who has never... played the

1

fool by loving someone who was only toying with him or her!"[5] So it comes to pass that with frightful earnestness we do seize the "moment": "Don't we really think that the one thing to regret in life is not to have dared, that the one thing we will never regret is to have made fools of ourselves for love?"[6] This theme is a main one, is it not, to make the old jukeboxes and the new iPods keep playing? "I'm not above selling my soul for love and if that's what it cost, then take the price tag off."[7] "I'd rather have love for just one hour, than have the world and all its gold."[8] According to Nietzsche, we reveal our core self while answering the question "who" in our life we have loved until now.[9] Ultimately, not how many have I loved matters… or how much I love someone… but how well I love her. That matters.

Legion is the perspectives on love. Some views are merely mundane; some phrases sear our consciousness; other words touch us with their beauty. When asked in his old age what constitutes maturity, Freud answered succinctly to love and to work. He also wrote, "We must begin to love in order that we may not fall ill, and must fall ill if…we cannot love."[10] Teilhard de Chardin maintains "Love alone is capable of uniting human beings in such a way as to complete and fulfill them, for it alone takes them and joins them by what is deepest in themselves."[11] The comedienne, Lily Tomlin, quips, "If love is the answer, what is the question?"[12] Esther Vilar documents the way women mask venality, manipulation, and exploitation as love: "Man… fights for his life and calls it love…. To a woman love means power, to a man enslavement."[13] In the name of science, a Dutch psychologist trashes as merely self-delusional the human experience of true and lasting love. To that skepticism, Kierkegaard provides an incisive rejoinder: "Only he who abides in love can recognize love. One must believe in love, otherwise one will never become aware that it exists."[14] It exists alright, the song-bird moans: "It is the heart that kills us in the end."[15] About the end, Lord Alfred Tennyson gives us a gem: "It is better to have loved and lost than never to have loved at all."[16] And Virgil pens the classic line, "Omnia vincit amor," "love conquers all."[17] Not for nothing does the great Persian poet, Jalal al-Din Rumi, urge humility whenever treating precious love-themes. In the world's longest poem about longing for lost love, he writes:

Whatever I try to say
Explaining love is embarrassing!
Some commentary
Clarifies, but with love silence is clearer.
A pen went scribbling along, but when it tried
To write love, it broke. If you want to expound on love,
Take your intellect out and let it lie down
in the mud. It's no help.[18]

When we get down to brass tacks, these solemn, cynical, or unbridled optimistic attitudes about love are merely "suffocatingly subjective" -- in the apt phrase of C. S. Lewis. About love and its derangement, it suits instead to let the phenomenon speak. Rumi puts it precisely, "Inquire of love itself. Ask the Lovers about 'Loverhood'."[19] Asking requires that our hearts be as stout as they are warm because sometimes the answer cuts like a knife:

In the slaughterhouse of love, they kill
Only the best, none of the weak or deformed.
Don't run away from this dying.
Whoever's not killed for love is dead meat.[20]

The vibrant nerve that quickens all the studies of this book is listening. I have paid attention to the experiences expressed by flesh blood and bone individuals and felt the pulse of their lives. My studies are "soul stories."[21] The phenomena within them concern us all: friendship, one's first or big love, an outlaw relationship, and one's intimate partner. Since narratives carry the cargo of these themes, the freight is not the rational-pragmatic material contained in scholarly books, journals, self-help books, pop psych works, or TV psychologist-personalities that dispense love-sex advice. What do I mean? In a nutshell, within my book the familiar buzzwords go missing: "cognitive," "behavioral," "logical," "useful," "objective", "empowering," "how-to-do-it." Absent too, are the familiar linear-boxed formats, charts and arrows, graphs, keywords, and long lines of important points set apart by bullets. For all their merit, surely such conventional words, phrases, and stylistic devices are of limited value. Surely, they do not exclude an alternative way of focusing upon love. I use instead stories filled with "heartlines" as cargo.

Still, at the outset it fits to offer a brief legitimization for a book of heartlines. Simply and straightforwardly, the findings that appear in mainstream psychological texts are behavioral-technological statements generated by quantitative methodologies from the perspective of presumed neutrality and distance. The concepts of normative orthodox psychology, therefore, are abstractly frozen (out of time) and arbitrary (out of any particular place). What is called "psychology" is more accurately a "behavioral technology." In order to communicate authentically psychological…psychological findings, I use story as the superior mode. Stories, parables, and narratives integrate the heart and head. Stories relate the small elegant details, the "little nothings" that make all the difference in life and love, in grief and joy, in war and death. Stories present the total picture not isolated, fractured pieces. Starting with "the moment,"[22] a parable traces the progression of events into a full blown relationship.

For example, two people cross paths as they approach from opposite directions. Their eyes lock. In an eye-blink, they are drawn to each other. Verve punctuates the "moment". Spontaneously, they veer in order to encounter one another. The unplanned eye-contact converts into a meeting as they swerve again and "accidentally" touch. After they "bump into" each other, they trade email addresses or cellular phone numbers while sitting and sipping some java. With a half-apology, they brush legs under the table. Perhaps while saying "good-bye," they hug one another. After parting, both feel that their "hour" has come. They take contact and continue to communicate. And so the "chance" meeting builds into friendship or a romantic relationship. Eventually, the two might co-create their peculiar larger network of social bonds including in-laws and children.

There are no theoretical recipes for this upbuilding; "tips" from the how-to-do-it books help the adventure minimally. Each story is as unique as the individuals' fingerprints. Doubtlessly, we can identify patterns and structures. But in a radical sense, it is "one-in-a-row-every time."[23] Often, as Kierkegaard drives home to us, it is "once only."

Narratives about these personal moments communicate the emotional atmosphere, the context, the setting, the temporal process, the concrete details, and the web spun between human beings -- all who partake of peculiar gender, race, color, creed, and age. Passion and tenderness emerge both undisguised and comprehensible. Put slightly differently, the common parlance of everyday life has shifted in this millennium. As a society today, we are moving away from the rational-dualistic-pragmatic way of thinking that had dominated since the dawn of modernity. Nowadays, we use as criteria of relevance that any matter under consideration be "on the ground" and assessed from the perspective of "the end of the day." These are not words from ideological positivism. They emerge from existential phenomenological thinking that had been running parallel to the mainstream during the 20th century, albeit underground. The main chore of the book, however, is not to expound theory or elaborate method but to present findings about love's pivotal relationships. Beyond the artificial conventions of narrow, one-dimensional, superficial, rational science, the poet Keats taught us the authentic braid of knowledge:

> *Beauty is truth, truth beauty—that is all*
> *Ye know on earth, and all ye need to know.*[24]

From the existential standpoints of Søren Kierkegaard and Frederick Nietzsche, the braid includes the researcher's own self-reflective search or psychological autopsy. I make myself my first subject of these studies. This disciplined act of bringing to the surface and reflecting on my own experiences has two consequences. Firstly, it is prophylactic. It puts out of play my own biases about the relationships, sets aside my personal assumptions, or suspends them (the technical phenomenological term is "bracketing"); in consequence, the bracketing authorizes me to use my experiences as a springboard for generalizing about the phenomenon. The knowledge in this book is personal, engaged, concerned, and earnest. I draw my portraits equally with heart and head. I stain them with tears of joy, anger, and sorrow; I mark them with passion and tenderness. What is the heart? Is it a physiological pump only? By no means! Or is it exclusive subject matter for the poet and songwriter? No, again. The heart is the mind warmed. Warmth generates beautiful and true knowledge. Knowledge that is relevant to life and love is not only answerable to *static norms* or *known standards* but equally to dynamic values and standards of beauty. Beauty is strict certitude in the realm of the *valuable* and hence of the *valid*. Beauty is as important to knowledge as conceptual judgment. Knowledge that is pertinent to life and love balances *norm* and *worth*. If these heartlines do not jump-start your thinking about your relationships while you read them, then in my task I have failed; if these heartlines do not provoke dwelling upon your feelings and memories, my writing falls dismally short.

CHAPTER 1

First Best Friend or Preadolescent Chum

Our friendships we cherish. What in life is more precious? William Shakespeare has penned the all-time classic line about cherishing ones friends: "Grapple them to thy soul with hoops of steel."[25] In one of the loveliest and most unique chapters in American psychiatry, Harry Stack Sullivan names our best friend our "chum" and calls the chum relationship a "miracle."[26] Within chronological preadolescence, someone out of my peer-group or sphere of contacts emerges as special. For the first time, another becomes as important to me as me. The "I" gives way to the "We." The two friends become actually or symbolically "blood" brothers or sisters.

The designating words change over time. A woman used to refer to her best friend as her "bosom buddy." Soldiers in World War II, for whom covering for each other in a foxhole was critical, affectionately tagged each other "asshole buddies." Sagas of "sidekicks" characterize the lore of the American west. Brother, sister, pal, true friend, mate, bro, bubba, or comrade! Ah, the lifeworld vocabulary is rich. It catches

7

the closeness, the sense of solidarity, and awesome trust. It captures the flavor of "true blue," the parable on friendship that follows soon.

Mainstream developmental psychology makes "prosocial behavior" its theme and thus writes shallower about friendship. It suits to chant early in this book my severe criticism of mainstream writing on matters of the heart. Our contemporary preoccupation with skills, strategies, and pragmatics reduces our affections to a superficial, one-dimensional level. The aim of this text, contrariwise, is to capture the phenomena of love in depth and with all their richness.

Friendship is much more important than manifesting social competence. Chums also tame each other: they make each other "real." The miracle is profoundly serious. The chumship is the first budding of love. As such, it foreshadows mature love. In Sullivan's words, the first best friendship is "the most health inducing" event that happens in our tender preadolescent years. In whatever way an individual had been "warped" in childhood, the chum relationship undoes it. It especially establishes and solidifies trust. The partners do everything together, share all, keep no secrets, and wear no lock on tongue or heart. It is also a relationship untroubled or "unencumbered" by the issue of sexuality. The gender of the person pales in significance to the person of the person.

Simultaneously, with gain comes vulnerability to pain. The nascent love renders the growing youngster at risk for unprecedented hurt. Before loving your first best friend, you might have known aloneness, rejection, or abandonment. Now for the first time, you know loneliness and longing. Likewise, a chum relationship gone wrong or "bad" creates a horrendous sense of rejection that rips trust to shreds. Here comes "true blue," a narrative on the chum. Reflections follow that spell out these ideas in detail and elaborate Sullivan's interpersonal approach.

True Blue

"The worst solitude is to be destitute of sincere friendship."[27]
Francis Bacon

It was a miracle. I never thought that anyone was going to like me much less love me. Unlike the other boys my age, I wasn't "into" sports. When it came to physical activities, I was a klutz. Moreover, about the fate of the local university or professional teams, I could care less. Even today, whenever I hear the words "Hawks" or "Falcons," my first association is to birds of prey. So the guys and I had nothin' to say to each other. They scorned and ostracized me.

At schoolwork I was a whiz. Brains, however, were not popular in my school except at exam time, when a major project was due, or when the guys wanted to copy my homework. They'd talk to me then and even invite me to their houses. Plain as the nose on my face, they were just using me. I paid no mind to it. Sure, it hurt. But shucks, it was better than being a cipher. In quiet despair, I went along and helped 'em with their schoolwork. Nevertheless, I never pretended that they liked me,

9

Did I do cartwheels home or walk the short distance on my hands? On that blessed day, Sir, it was one of two occasions in my life that I have been able to fly!

Your upper lip, Sir, is surpressin' a sneer. You doubt, don't you, that I truly rose into the air? Sakes alive! When Jesus was heaven-bound, the Evangelist St. Luke done told us the Lord soared and ascended to the Father. Do you think I exaggerate? I pity you, Sir, if you have not experienced a moment in your life when you had wings on your feet and your over-full psyche was poppin' out of your body. Nobody can translate accurately the Words of the New Testament or the life of the human psyche into the dead and abstract language of science.

What difference did the encounter make? When Rima entered my life, I felt like nothin' more than a satellite to all the well-meaning but misguided grownups. The gang of my peers, who were at the age of becoming socialized, ostracized me. In my diary, I called the process "turning into well-trained monsters." You can hear can you not, that the time for me was bleak? The creatures I was trafficking among did not seem real. Consequently, I did not feel real either. I did exist but I wasn't living.

Believe it or not, I had discovered existentialism in my pre-teen period. At first, I only read secondary sources, texts that construct boxes and then distort great thinkers by stuffin' 'em in 'em. Shoot, by picking up a few interesting phrases I had started to refer to myself as "a ghost in the machine." Later on, I read the brilliant and beautifully written original texts. You can never forget Søren Kierkegaard once you've had the guts to face death and despair. You'll always remember Fredrick Nietzsche, after you have followed him into his lonely mountains. I had already met loneliness and godforlornness, so it was no skin off my teeth to read these gentlemen. Nietzsche's wilderness is one marvelous place. There, it is possible to shriek.

Often, I needed to shriek....

Maybe the word "dawning" describes best my introduction to the human race. I don't believe in creation in the Biblical sense. However, meeting this girl in the midst of a Southern spring rain... doing cartwheels and hand-stands...then starting to glow... beginning to ascend... anticipating seeing fresh tears... and falling in love -- that was the dawning of my life. Peering through the soft summer raindrops, my eyes fell upon one drenched blue cotton dress. In consequence, my yesterdays receded forever into ancient history. In one magic moment of pure zany play, I watched a girl's beautiful face deliberately distort itself grotesquely and as a result my Old World once and for all went away. I could not have been more transmuted if Scottie from *Star Trek* had beamed me up into another galaxy. I do believe in a transfiguration and ascension. Maybe I believe in creation after all. I surely believe in the Miracle.

The next day, under the warm Southern sun, she told me about her daddy's dying. We were practically strangers, if you only count the minutes we had spent in each other's company. Nevertheless, she was flat out sobbin' like there was no tomorrow. I was crying over her crying. I was cryin' like there were no days-before-yesterday.

At first, doubtlessly she was surprised I was boohooin'. Shucks, all she could see was a short, pudgy kid who for all she knew was just a jock in disguise…doing some fancy cartwheels and showing one pretty nifty piece of hand-walking. The look in her eyes soon told me she switched on the same second sight she had used yesterday to decipher my topsy-turvy ways. She understood that my heart was much bigger than my short frame. Me! I couldn't think of a thing to say. Although my heart was geared to her emotions, I was in the situation well over my vocabulary. That's why, even if you wait until the cows come home, you'll never hear me say that words are everything.

I reached out my right hand to let her fresh tears roll onto my index finger. That night in my diary I wrote that it was like touching holy water.

She reached out and took my left hand and squeezed it tight. "Let's walk," she said. Assuming my compliance, she added, "Hey! How 'bout we go to the Dairy Queen?" I just nodded. Then I said, "I'll get me a Breeze, a Reese's Peanut Butter Cup Breeze." She let out a giggle. "I'll get me a Dutch Chocolate Blizzard, a large size Blizzard!"

Off we go. It was a forty-minute walk into town. The long dirt road was clay and the color of blood in a vein. Far off to the right toward the horizon, I could see puffs of white in the field -- a reminder that King Cotton used to abide in our town. I could hear the wind blowin' softly through our Georgia Pines. The landscape seemed alive to me, electrified and gorgeous. I was findin' myself in "hog heaven."

For me, that walk could have lasted forever. We might as well have been walking down the Yellow Brick Road. She and I with hand in hand... with her standing a head taller than me... she, talking up a storm... me, giving back mostly monosyllabic utterances. If I had not known already that the world had begun yesterday, I would have sworn that it began right there and then.

I could always feel Rima's emotions as if they were my own. That was the other area in which I was a step ahead of my peers. Before she and I became friends, being emotional was no asset. I was considered a "sensitive" child which carried the connotation "delicate" which my peer group translated into "sissy" and "cry baby." Even my daddy, who loved me like the Rock of Gibraltar, never understood why I didn't like fishing, detested hunting, and could care less for competitive sports. He understood even less my absolute preference for beautiful things like music and books, rainbows, and sunsets.

I learned to confine my emotions to the written word. No doubt, that had a lot to do with starting to keep a diary when I was less than eleven and one-half years old. Actually, it was reading the Anne Frank's *Diary*[28] that sharpened my pencil. By the time I had finished the first few pages of Anne's journal, I was half in love with her. Her simple spontaneous ability to express raw experience touched me deeply and prompted me to follow in her footsteps. My life was as confined as was her existence, cooped up in the small Amsterdam Annex. Likewise my peers' actions, like Anne's Nazi Gestapo, threatened to destroy my very soul. So I began to stain the terrifying blank pages. I also imitated Anne by using my diary the way she used her "Kitty." It served as my "friend"...until my real friend came along.

Rima was almost fifteen years old and thus had a couple of years on me. For all her impish ways, her guilelessness, and effervescence, she was built like the proverbial "brick shithouse." She looked like she should have been on the latest cover of *Sixteen Magazine*. To my eyes, she should have been on the cover of every magazine. I wanted to place her beautiful face everywhere. In point of actual fact, eventually I plastered photos of her all over my bedroom, ones showing the entire spectrum of her moods. I exaggerate. I never witnessed the entire spectrum of her moods. They were infinite. And that is no exaggeration.

My mamma raised her eyebrows the first time she walked into my Picture Gallery of One. She liked to question me to death 'bout my new interior decoration, but instead she rolled her eyes as only a Southern mother can and didn't say a word. Probably she just pondered the sight in her heart the way Jesus' Mother Mary did in the New Testament after they found the twelve-year-old boy in the Temple, teaching the "old dogs" of Jerusalem some new... New Testament tricks.

It was the sixth of August, during the dog days of summer. Rima and I had been friends a whole three months. She launched a surprise:

"I have to warn you about me. Some things you gotta know 'fore you decide to be my friend forever."

I lapsed into mono-syl-la-bi-bur-bia. "OK.... Sure... Shucks.... Shoot." What could I say? She could 'av told me she was a serial killer or that she had come from beyond the grave and it would have made no difference to me. I already loved her more than my life itself.

"I'm flat out weird, she said. My shrink told me I'm a 'lateral thinker'."

"What's that?" I asked.

"It means that I don't think in straight lines," she replied. "I got a mighty strong penchant for seein' only spirals."

Stupidly, I questioned, "Is that all?" The phrase "lateral thinking" sounded a tad too serious to tag her preference for circles, cycles, and crooked lines. Reading D. H. Lawrence had taught me -- remember I was a voracious reader back then -- there are no such things in nature as straight lines.

"I can't see squares either."

The way she paused prompted silence. Then, she giggled. "Of course, you gotta take what I say about straight thinkin' with a grain of salt and a mite bit of dill weed seed too 'cuz I ain't very logical either!"

I loved listening to her laugh and watching her mouth twist and flap. She had a very expressive mouth that choreographed her words. Continuing her litany, she added,

"He also said that I'm never 'literal'. I don't define things. I talk in metaphors. He's says that's why print' near nobody understands me."

I knew all this by then and wondered why she was sayin' it.

"And 'they' even say that I'm not 'interested'."

Not sure what she meant, I asked, "How's that?"

"I'm not domesticated to information technology. Cyberspace bores me. And I ain't ever itchin' to use email."

"I thought that I was the only kid who detested virtual reality," I exclaimed, telling her the Gospel truth: "You're jus' like me!"

"What don't you like about cyberspace, Glowy?" she asked.

Since we were two peas in a pod, I figured she thought together we could understand how come we were so different. I replied, "It's simulated, Rima. And everything's mediated."

She squealed, "Hey, hold on! Gimme a break, Glowy. I don't read those books with fifty dollar words!"

"'Simulated' jus' means fake. It's the opposite of pretend. Technology deletes emotions. It's scared of 'real' imaginin' too. Technology pretends that 'make believe' is just 'pretending'. That's all."

"Sakes alive! Everybody knows that technology is just a fake." She sounded cocksure. "And luv kin always crash a computer!"

I know that there is no technical explanation for the strange power love has upon computer technology, but in my heart I knew she was right. Then she asked me,

"Why do most people prefer the computer, Glowy?"

"Folks like to be entertained, Rima. Nowadays, they hanker after quick results. The computer gives a colorful illusion of efficiency. Shucks, if you were domesticated, you'd be tellin' me that your computer expedites everything!"

"Ain't it the truth?"

"Heck no, using the computer jus' wastes your precious time. On the face of this entire earth, nothing's more unreliable than computer technology. My nickname for it is 'the illusion of efficiency'."

She giggled, "Well, what does that other word, 'meter-maiden mean'?"

My voice chiseled an angry edge: "'Mediated' means that instead of meeting a real flesh and blood person, ya meet a phony!"

"What'ch ya drivin' at, Glowy." she answered. "Er you fixin' to tell me a cyborg ain't 'real'?" She was grinnin' from ear to ear.

"That's the point precisely!" I said, picking up on her peculiar logic. "Ya' get brainwashed into believin' you're nothin but a robot. Next thing you know, you're anonymous." I paused to let my emotions subside. "A cyborg isn't 'real'! But there are a peck 'av cyberpunks out there. And they're so de-tached that they're scary!"

She egged me on: "Go ahead on, Glowy. Keep talkin'."

"The Internet is manipulation and control. It's part of the Panopticon. This philosopher named Jeremy Bentham concocted a way to make us all the time controlled by makin' us all the time visible."

"Lawrdy, mercy, Glowy," she squealed. "A pan-y ole opticon!" What kind of trash er you tellin' me?"

"Shoot," it's just a word. This guy designed an architectural structure so to make sure power never ceases to function. I ain't pullin' your leg! Visibility is a trap, Rima."

She could tell that talkin' about the Panopticon riled me.

"What does the Pan-y-opticon have to do with luv or friendship?"

"We're just isolated objects of information under the Panopticon and also under the bell-shaped curve. We're jus' observed, diagnosed, slotted, and stuffed into boxes. That's why people nowadays only have friends for the sake of convenience, Rima, disposable friends. People hav'ta scrounge to make true friends."

"A bell-y shaped curve too! Laward, mercy! Those books you're readin' sure sound hi-lar-i-ous!"

"I don't know," I said. "It all fits together in my head. You log on and make contact, but nobody knows who you are. 'They' don't know who they are either. People go online and just start shaping their personalities and fabricating roles. It's all seduction and hoax. 'Impression management' some books call it. 'Polishing your statue' I call it. It's artificial, the complete opposite of pretending."

She laughed and said, "You know more -ed words and -ion words, Dr. Glowworm, than Mister Webster hisself!" Then, she sounded perplexed. "Do you know anybody who believes that a body ain't for 'real'?"

"Sure. Now that it's summertime, my schoolmates spend most their day going online, playing computer games, or cycling through MUDs. They tell me they create parallel lives. I want to shout, 'Get yer self just one life and make it real'! But what's the point? They already hate me."

In a mellow tone, she said, "Thems be hurtin' words, Glowy."

"You bet! Nobody cares about what'ch feel in your heart. Everybody's got a hundred 'virtual friends' and a thousand 'cyber friends'..."

She waited while I paused.

"Nobody ever wanted to be my friend. Nobody cares about having a 'true blue friend.'"

"I detest email, too." She chimed in. "After you hit your mouse, it gets very lonely. It's dis-em-bodied." She delayed a bit, gave out a little squeal. "I got that word from my shrink. I think it means that friendship on the Net comes without 'heartlines' attached!" With dead seriousness, she continued. "Miracles are an endangered species, too. You and me er print' near saying the same thing 'bout fake!"

"How do you mean?" I asked, intrigued by her leap of logic.

"Shoot! The eyes are real. Our eyes talk. But we' ain't never taught in school how to read the eyes. All they teach us are social skills. Even my shrink began with plans fer me to learn strategies." Then she giggled, "Till he discovered that I have lateral thinking!"

"You're right," Rima," I said. "Learn how to network and learn prosocial behavior! All they're interested in teachin' us is adjustment and conformity."

Her voice got mellow again: "You and me... Our friendship... it's 'true blue,' ain't it? We're more than just...of use to one another... ain't we?"

"Sure. You bet! I thought you knew that. Shucks! We have done tamed one another, Rima!"

"It'd kill me if it wasn't the Gospel truth," she said with incredible vulnerability. Then she picked up her earlier thread. "True friends hug too, and touch. That's the embodied part." She tossed her curls back and laughed, "I'd rather that we tamed each other than we be do-mesticated to technology!" Then she shifted focus: "Real friends smell too."

"To me, you smell like honeysuckle," I blurted out.

"Shucks, you must really like me," she said, "If-in I smell that strong and pur-ty!" Then she said, "Give me a big hug, Glowy! I gotta go fetch my kid sister from her ballet class." As she walked away, she turned and hollered, "Thanks for telling me about the pan-y-ole opticon and the fat belly curve!"

Rima and I were together every blessed day, without fail. Either she came over to fetch or I called on her. Mostly, we'd just pass the time of the day. After a while if some folks would see one of us alone they'd say, "Where's your other half?" She was always bragging on me, too. Her warm and bubbly presence made a body feel good just being near her. On a bone-chilling December day, she said,

"Do you like reading all those books about the world's biggest Giant?"

"Who?" I asked, wondering to what this was leading.

"No, silly!" she squealed, "not 'who' but 'what'. I'm askin' ya' 'bout technology. Why you always reading about a big fat 'what'!"

"A kid must understand technology, Rima, not just play games with it. Technology is pervasive. It affects everything, especially friendship." When she didn't say anything immediately, I continued, "Actually, I read about everything. Even my teachers can't understand some of the books that come naturally to me to enjoy. One teacher keeps giving me complex stuff like a book by a guy named Heidegger. That's how I come to grasp the essence of Technology. Mr. Hawkins said, 'I can't make head or tails out of this, and it might be beyond the grasp of your comprehension. Do you want to wrassle with it?' I knew he knew I'd understand it. But he was jus' using the mentality of sport, you know, 'tackle it,' 'wrestle with it', 'be aggressive' to motivate me."

"You never said nuttin' 'bout him before."

"He don't ever say much. I think he's interested in me 'cause he's done got sweet on my momma. So he don't get personal with me at school jus' in case he ever takes up with her. Folks here 'ud gossip."

"If-in he mashes a big crush on her, they'll wag their tongues sure as shootin'," she answered. "You be hearing whispers sizzling from end to end of this town." Then she added, "But at least he's in your corner."

"Yeah, most of my other teachers seem flat-out hostile concerning my reading."

"They must got the ole green-eyed monster big time. En-vy! And they mus' be stark ravin' threatened ta' boot."

"Kin you say more about that?" I asked, seeing that she had a better grasp of this predicament than I did. I had concluded they were mediocre. I didn't suspect envy.

"Shucks, they don't understand you. That's bad 'nough because sure as shootin' they would like to. Then you kin understand books they can't figure out, and they can't understand that either! It belittles 'em, Doctor Glowworm! Hey, you're a triple threat!" Then she roared with laughter.

"What's so funny?" I asked.

"Well, maybe you should play football 'cuz you're a boss-A triple threat."

I looked at her, amazed, as if she had come from Outer Space. With that sentence, she hit one of my most crooked nerves and straightened it as simply as tossing her curls. Once and for all, this particular talk terminated my envy of all the 'star-studded' jocks whose 'running, throwing, and kicking,' helped them to negotiate mainstream culture with ease but with no understanding.

It was on Christmas Day that she started a conversation that undid my most severe warping. We had exchanged presents. She bought me *The Little Prince*; I gave her *The Velveteen Rabbit*. We both cracked big smiles over having bought each other's Kahlil Gibran's *The Prophet*. After we congratulated each other on having such good taste and hugged each other in thanks for the gifts, Rima insisted on reading from the book:

> *Your friend is your needs answered*
> *He is your field which you sow with love and*
> *reap with thanksgiving,*
> *And he is your board and fireside.*
> *For you come to him with your hunger,*
> *And you seek him for peace...*
> *And let there be no purpose in friendship*

Save the deepening of the spirit
For love that seeks aught but the disclosure
of its own mystery is a net cast forth: and
only the unprofitable is caught...
...it is his to fill your needs, but not your
emptiness...[29]

"You bring the fullness out of me," I said, in response.

She squealed in obvious pleasure, and opened *The Velveteen Rabbit*. "Listen to this, Glowy!"

'What is REAL?' asked the Rabbit one day... 'Does it mean
having things that buzz inside you and a stick-out handle'?
'Real isn't how you are made,' said the Skin Horse. 'It's a thing
that happens to you. When a child loves you for a long, long time,
not just to play with, but REALLY loves you, then you become
Real'.
'Does it hurt?' asked the Rabbit.
'Sometimes,' said the Skin Horse....When you are Real you don't
mind being hurt....It doesn't happen all at once....You become.
It takes a long time. That's why it does not happen to people who
break easily, or have sharp edges, or who have to be carefully
kept. By the time you are Real, most of your hair has been
loved off, and your eyes drop out and you get loose in the joints
and very shabby. But these things don't matter at all, because
once you are Real, you can't be ugly, except to people who don't
understand.'[30]

"Nothing hurts," I said. If I lost you, that wouldn't hurt either. It would kill me."

Rima came close and looked straight into my eyes," Death is the only thing that can separate us, Glowy. Only death."

A few weeks later when we were back to school, she surprised me again.

"You're pretty smart, Doctor Glowworm, ain't ya'?"

"I reckon so. They say I'm gifted," I answered, half-heartedly.

"Really! Who?"

"The psychologists," I replied. "That just proves how stupid grownups can be."

"What do you mean?"

"Befor' you came along, I didn't have a single solitary blessed friend in the whole world, but I've been walking around for years being tagged as gifted."

"How did it happen?" She had the easiest way of digging for information than anybody on the face of my earth.

"Before my parents divorce I got sent for psychological testing. After I finished fixing his blocks and puzzles in what was, I guess, some kind of record time, I 'fessed up: 'I don't have any friends.' I was only eight years old. I didn't even have my diary yet and I was really lonesome. During that year, the arguments and fights between my mom and daddy had turned very ugly. They were too preoccupied to pay too much mind to me."

"What did the psychologist say to ya?"

"Not much. Jus' said that we'd come up with some strategy to help me make friends. Then he wrote down in the report that I was gifted." My voice got its angry-edge again: "How can a livin' body have no friends and be singled as superior? It's plumb stupid!"

She got real quiet. "You are gifted you know. You're a precious gift to me. And that's Gospel. Gimme me a Bible 'cause I'd swear on a stack of 'em!"

In a heartbeat, I started to cry. I was boohooing at first. Then the tears came in buckets. They came from a reservoir that must have been 20,000 leagues deep. She sat down beside me, put her arm around my shoulder, and pushed my head into the space between her shoulder blades and the elevated conical-shaped bumps of her multi-colored sweater. And she hummed to me the lyrics of Sinead O'Connor's haunting lullaby:

> *See the child... with the golden hair... Scorn not his simplicity...*
> *see how he stands alone and watches children play a children's*
> *game... simple child... He looks almost like the others yet they*
> *know he's not the same... Scorn not his simplicity... but love*
> *him all the more.*[31]

Rima's love poured out of her and through me. I felt something heal inside of me as she held me, as if she had put back together again the broken heart of Humpty Dumpy.

My tears had a history. When I started telling you about this, I must have sounded pretty cavalier about being a social isolate as a kid. But I did care about my predicament. It was living hell. I didn't belong or fit in anywhere, either in my peer group, at school, or in the church. I was considered an angry hot-head.

My stepfather, in particular, used to pull my trigger a lot. He knew how to get my goat. I think he enjoyed goading me into pitching a fit. Then, he would sit back, criticize me, and call me a "klutz." You can tell immediately that he wasn't too bright or original 'cause that's what print'near everybody else called me. Or when he wanted to rub it in that I was the kid and he was the grownup, he'd use anal phrases like, "You ain't finished shittin' yellow yet." Or to show me that he had the power, "I've got you where the chicken's got its eggs." But I knew that his Polish Aunt used to say the same things to him. So I knew he was nuttin' but a copycat with no imagination.

I suppose he knew how to do his job. But the only thing I ever saw him do with confidence was guzzle beer. No, I take that back. He was a professional couch potato, too, who would confidently watch sports on TV by the hour.

When I became pre-teen, he'd ask me when I was going to do anything "useful." Most of the time, I'd stand there holding my tongue. He'd say, "See, you want to cuss me out but you're too stubborn to say it! Little angelic baby boy wouldn't say 'shit' if he had a mouthful." When I'd finally blow my top, he'd call me a "little devil" berating me because I couldn't control my temper.

One day while egging me on to another tantrum, his speech slipped. He called me by my mom's name. It hit me like a ton of bricks. He was using me to express his anger at her. I didn't understand why. I figured she wasn't givin' him enough was the reason, although I didn't have a clue to what "it" was and what would be enough. Shucks, I only knew enough to know that there was some kind of a "thing" between a man and a woman; but I didn't have a clue as to what it is.

Anyhow, it just clicked. Hurting me was the best way for him to hurt her. I couldn't figure out how that was going to help him to get more of whatever he wanted out of her. Come to think of it, it still doesn't make good horse sense.

Finally, I let loose. I said I wanted to cut his heart out; I wished that he'd drop dead. I shouted that I would do him the favor and put him out of his misery! Of course, I didn't know his 'real' misery. I just always felt his cold contempt.

Looking back I actually feel sorry for him. Maybe if he had had a true blue friend when he was young, then he would have known how to treat my mom. Maybe then, he could have charmed the pants off her anytime he wanted.

I wish that I had more contact with my real dad 'cuz I knew he loved me. But the blood between him and my mom wasn't only bad, it was explosive. I had witnessed the worst of it before they finally split up. After I started to keep a journal, I wrote about it. I named it Psychological TNT. Banal, I know. But don't forget, I was not even twelve years old yet. And I had not met Rima.

Actually, I had gotten double framed early. They branded as too sensitive, reclusive, and book-worm-ish, and at the same time they called me angry-explosive. I read those words off a psychological report when one of my behavioral therapists was flirting with the receptionist before our session. I etched them in my diary along with the rest of my life. If Rima had not come to me, those notebooks of scribbles would be all that would have been left of me.

Nobody knew what to do with a sensitive-volcano back then. Of course, they don't know what to do with sensitive volcanoes these days either. They did then what they do now. They lined up a parade of doctors and therapists and sent me to shrinks. It was surely the proper thing to do. I would have done the same thing for me if I were in their shoes. What were they going to do instead? Prescribe a miracle? Shucks, even I never imagined the Mystery that would bring me her.

They did allow me to vanish into my imagination. Books and music kept me sane until I started writing my diary. Both kept me going until Rima came along. They let me know a vibrant world was out there with 'real' people. It kept alive the hope I might find that world.

The Little Prince put the finishing touch to my healing. From the day I read it, about my past I had no resentment and no regrets. I put the past back into the past where it belongs. Antoine Saint-Exupery's depiction of the friendship between the Fox and the Prince is my favorite passage in all of literature. You remember don't you, Sir, my voracity for books? It's what opened me to meeting Rima, that's for sure. You and everyone who you know should read the tale.

The little prince lives on a small asteroid, B-612, where he daily cleans both extinct and active volcanoes and must diligently practice basic husbandry to forestall the growth of baobabs that would destroy his little world. He loves watching the sunset, especially when he is sad. One day he watched it set forty-four times. And one day a seed blows from an unknown locale and begins to sprout. The little prince watches vigilantly, lest it carry a new strain of the dangerous baobab. But a bud of a flower appears instead. Eventually, a beautiful coquettish rose blooms, born at the same moment as the sunrise. The little prince is unrestrained in his admiration of her loveliness. He tends to her needs faithfully, watering her, putting her under glass during the night and shielding her with a screen. He tolerates, too, her conviction that her four thorns are adequate to defend her against tigers. When she boasts that she is a unique flower, he believes. But her vanity torments him until he begins to doubt her. In his words, "I was too young to know how to love her..."

So he escapes his little world, latching on to take advantage of the migration of a flight of wild birds. On his pilgrimage, he meets many interesting and perplexing characters. Eventually he lands on earth in the Desert of Sahara where he meets a snake. The snake communicates his power to solve the ultimate riddle of Life, and promises to relieve the disease of homesickness should it grow in the little prince's soul.

Then the prince happens upon a rose garden. Five thousand common variety roses face him, exact replicas of his unique flower, his beloved rose. Bordering on despair, the little prince lies down in the grass and weeps.

Then the fox appears. They greet one another. The little prince asks the fox to play with him. The fox replies he cannot because he is not tamed. The prince asks what "tame" means, but the fox jumps ahead with his question, "What are you looking for?" The little prince answers "men."

But since he never drops a question he has asked until he gets an answer, he repeats it. He gets it, and when he tells the fox that he is really looking for friends, the fox explains that one only makes a friend by observing rites or rituals requisite for taming. He says,

'To me, you are still nothing more than a little boy who is just like a hundred thousand other little boys. And I have no need of you. And you, on your part, have no need of me. To you, I am nothing more than a fox like a hundred thousand other foxes. But if you tame me, then we shall need each other. To me, you will be unique in the world. To you, I shall be unique in the world....'

'I am beginning to understand', said the little prince. 'There is a flower...I think that she has tamed me'.

Then the fox asks the little prince to tame him. He draws the parallel between the golden color of the wheat, the prince's golden blonde hair and the very sun striking his life with wonder.

The little prince says he would except that he has find friends and learn to understand many things.

'One only understands the things one tames... Men have no more time to understand anything. They buy things all ready made at the shops. But there are no shops anywhere where one can buy friendship, and so men have no friends anymore.
If you want a friend, tame me...'

The little prince tames the fox. When the inevitable "moment" of separation comes, the fox say, "I shall cry." Troubled, the little prince says he never wished to create harm, and expresses amazement that some good might come from the weeping. "It has done me good', said the fox, 'because of the color of the wheat fields." And he sends the prince to revisit the rose garden so that he might see that his rose is truly 'unique in the world'.

The little prince goes, and grasps the difference between the common garden variety rose and his rose: 'my rose'. And then he returns to say 'goodbye' and to learn the fox's secret.

'And now here is my secret, a very simple secret: It is only
with the heart that one can see rightly; what is essential
is invisible to the eye... It is the time you have wasted for
your rose that makes your rose so important... Men have
forgotten this truth... But you must not forget it. You
become responsible, forever, for what you have tamed. You
are responsible for your rose'.[32]

*The little prince repeats each of the fox's sayings, so that he would
not forget. Yes, repeats so that he would always remember.*

*"I'm not too young to know how to love you," I said to Rima, when
she closed the book. I must have sounded serious. She replied, "And we both
are willing to run the risk of weeping." She was serious too. We hugged, a
bit tighter than usual, smiled at one another and then off we moseyed to
the Dairy Queen.*

Out of left field, my mother decided one morning over breakfast and
after I had eaten my third sausage biscuit to comment upon my chunky
physiognomy. She referred to my teenage version of a "spare tire" as
my 'baby fat'." Most likely, she wanted to soothe my sensitive anger
without even hearing from my mouth that I was distraught. You must
remember, however, that I wore the label of a "sensitive child." My most
recent behavioral therapist might have given her a plan to extinguish
my "negative emotions" or at least to contain them. And don't forget
that I didn't talk much in those days. Mom was forced to sharpen her
mother's anticipation on my silence. In response to her comfort-less
words, I wrote in my diary, "There is no excuse for 'terminal ugliness',
no matter how small you are, how heavy, or how... lonely."

I started to sprout. For weeks on end, my mother enjoyed
chirping that I was "stretching out." When she used that phrase the
first time, I lost my usual sangfroid demeanor and nearly panicked!
Had she been foolish enough to peek at my Diary? Or since it was
washday, I feared she had just spotted a few stray stains on my sheets.
However, mom wasn't born yesterday. I got some of my intelligence
from her side of the family. She didn't even have to use her intuition to
know about my secret solo flights. She just never knew the launching
times.

Rima noticed that I was growing too. One day, we happened to be standing in front of a full-length mirror in a department store. I had gone shopping with her to help pick out a dress for an upcoming wedding

"You've done gone and caught up with me, Glowworm," she said, "We're the same size."

Her spontaneous ejaculation about my physique, said with obvious pleasure, instantly made me shy. I blushed, and she noticed it. Maybe it was the wedding talk or because now I was looking at her through different eyes, but I had to pole vault over the embarrassing conversation with a quick quip: "Maybe I'm filling out, but unlike all of your sweaters mine still do not come equipped with conical shaped bumps." She absorbed my feeble attempt at humor and chose to refrain from commenting upon my blush. Nevertheless, I saw a shadow ease across her face. She knew that I knew that she knew that the atmosphere was changing between us. My intuition grasped -- well, I am my mother's son -- that she had no more idea than I about how we were going to handle the new forecast of higher relative humidity and oncoming heat.

The day was 6 August of our second summer together. In the Roman Christian calendar, it is the feast of the Transfiguration. In Georgia, these are the dog days of summer. Rima and I were sitting on some moss in our woods chewing on white birch limbs. I loved watching her peel the exterior to expose the green underneath. I loved, too, watching her munch. She broke the silence.

"Scientists have discovered that Indians chewed tree bark for a purpose, Glowy, fer toothpaste and medicine. It's got vitamin C. That's what prevents scurvy."

I had read that and just commented, "Maybe logical thinking isn't so bad after all."

"Heaven's to Betsy," she squealed. "Logic's got nothin' to do with it. I figure some groovy lady just decided to use her imagination and found a way to interview dead Indians. That's the only way any scientist was going to find out about old-fashioned toothpaste and all the natural remedies of the forest."

"You got a point," I said, "President Jefferson instructed Lewis and Clark to observe the Indians on their Northwest expedition. He thought that white men needed to learn from the red man's 'smarts'. Scientists never had to synthesize, in the first place, destructive chemicals like aspirin."

Rima was just giggling, apparently still thinking about dead-interviewees. She was definitely not thinking about logic, science, or history. "Can't you just picture a dead Indian opening one eye and seeing TV cameras? Imagine him being told, 'We can only do two 'takes' so you'd better get it right the first time!" Then she slapped her tight, howling and infecting me with her laughter.

"There's something else we can do with birch," I interjected, when we both had stopped laughing. "If we peel the bark off larger branches, then we kin make stick-horses. They would be white. We could pretend they were golden Palominos."

As she often did so naturally, she rebounded off my words. "A boss-A idea. Then we could ride our horses to Kentucky. I bet our Palominos would luv to graze on the blue grass of Kentucky!" She paused for a second. "But when we got home, they'd have to chew on some birch bark so as to clean the blue stains off their teeth." She started giggling again.

"The blue grass of Kentucky isn't really colored blue, Rima," I said. "It's just a figure of speech."

"Mercy, Glowy, figures of speech are very important," she exclaimed. "Besides we wouldn't have to explain colors to our horses. We'd just let them chew to their hearts' content. And you and I could pretend for 'em."

I agreed with that. And I felt stupid for introducing "reality" into the "real."

"I got another good idea," she said. "Let's cut our stick horses tomorrow. Today, let's fly!"

I knew that I was in for another surprise. However, I don't think either of us could have anticipated what the Mystery had in store for the both of us.

"Com'on! It's been a coon's age since I bendy-bowed!" Let me show you how."

She approached a young white birch tree. With quiet dignity and reverence she said, "Hey Woody, you be strong and flexible. Kin we play with you? Spe-cif-i-cally, can we bendy-bow on you?" She turned to me, cupped her hands to cover her face, and whispered, "He's just a teenage tree and very sensitive. So I don't want to shinny up 'im without askin."

Satisfied that she got an affirmative answer, she started to climb.

We were both wearing shorts. Rima planted the bottom of her Reeboks against the bark and turned out her legs so as not to scratch them. "Gimme a boost." She requested. Awkwardly, I placed my hands on her rear and pushed, feeling her firm warm flesh resist. Her blithe body started to ascend the tree. Looking at her from this unprecedented angle, I stared at her tiny bottom moving away from me, skyward. My eyes riveted on the crack between her bums. The sight took my breath away. Me, who could always find words to describe whatever was happening -- even if I never spoke them -- could not name what I was gawking at. Her appearance was absolutely ethereal. Yet her two round-mounds, the flanks that I had just touched, were solid proof that she was of this earth. Can something be incredibly innocent in the very moment that it awakens one to what is beyond innocence and in some significant sense puts it to an end? As I gazed at the vision of her inching carefully up the tree, I got an erection. It was the first time my sexuality had stirred in Rima's presence. Heretofore, my hard-ons had been reserved for late night secret solo flights. Now, I had a complete one in broad daylight and smack dab in the middle of her bendy-bowing. I felt warm in a way that I knew I would never be cold again.

I looked up from my predicament and focused upon Rima's two tiny hands that were circled around the white neck of the tree... holding on for dear life!

When she reached the top, gracefully she let her body free-fall into open space. The young white birch, as if purposefully pliant, bent and eased her slowly to the ground. She released Woody as she landed. He sprung back into a straight position and quivered a little looking very proud. To me, the total picture looked holy.

"Mission accomplished," she said, "Now it's your turn. Com' on, try it! That was fun, wasn't it, Woody?"

Then she noticed my face and exclaimed, "You're glowing! What happened?"

I just stared at her, dazed.

"You must 'av liked it", she said, "Or you wouldn't be glowing! So come on! Do it! Woody's ready for another launch, ain't 'cha, Woody?" She was bubbling with spunk.

At first, I stuttered. "Wa-watching you soar like a bird pu-put the glow into the Glowworm, that's for sure." Then I started to motor-mouth. "Now we can really be the Wood Sprite and the Glowworm. You were on a magic carpet flying through the air! Or a female Tarzan, yeah, Sheena the Jungle Queen flitting from tree to tree! You were a wood-nymph, Rima, the bird-girl from *Green Mansions*...."[33]

I babbled, as if to return to play. While my mouth was in fourth gear, my erection lingered. I didn't know where to locate it within our relationship. Rima didn't associate to my word salad. She just fell quiet, looked me straight in the eyes, and appealed to the depth between us: "Risk it," she said. It be me you talking to, only me."

Looking down, I sucked in hard, shuffled my feet, and let the truth trickle, "I got a hard on watching you shinny up the tree. It was your ass. You've got a perfect ass. I could see the crack between your cheeks because of your shorts. I couldn't take my eyes off your butt. The whole thing was perfect. You huggin' the tree and turning out your knees so that they wouldn't get scrapped. Then you flew. You looked like an angel with a beautiful cracked ass. I done got me a boner."

Then I ran out of breath.

"Oh! She said, "Is that all? Then she giggled. "Av course, you ain't never seen my butt that way!" Then she squealed, "A beautiful cracked ass! That's so funny." And she slapped her thighs, joyfully.

She made it sound so natural and so ordinary that I felt rock bottom fine inside. Effortlessly, she cradled my detached moment of arousal and laid it down precisely where it belonged: squarely in the middle of everyday life... smack dab at the node of our growing history together. From that day forward, sexuality has always fit for me into something bigger than even the biggest conceptual box.

Then the extraordinary situation became truly extraordinary. She approached me, put her arms around me, and drew my lips to hers. It was exquisitely gentle. "This is long overdue," she said, and we kissed again. We munched. At least, I munched on her lips. It seemed like she munched on mine, too. Then we stopped as naturally as we had begun.

"It was a feast," I said. "I've been to a banquet."

"Sure as shootin'," she said, sounding like a pixie. "But now you've got to fly to Heaven too. Start shinning up the tree. I want to stare at your cracked butt!" And she giggled: "But w-a-i-t a bit. Wait until you soften. You be plump loco to climb a tree in your condition! It'd hurt ya' like the Dickens."

As soon as she named it, we both chuckled then everything shrunk and settled into its place. For someone who is a perennial klutz, you wouldn't believe the adroitness with which I shinnied up that tree!

When I dropped back to earth after my debut of swinging in the birches, she greeted me with another kiss, this time more softly, so softly that any softer would have felt like a dream. "We'll always remember today, she said. Looking at each other across a clearing wide enough for seeing clearly, neither of us had to voice the living question that hovered between us: "Where in the world did the two kids just go?"

Then Rima pivoted deliberately and fetched a rock.

"Com'on! We're gonna carve our initials into Woody so he'll always remember us." We walked up to the tree. Rima coaxed, "That's OK if we carve on you, isn't it Woody?" After a pause and looking satisfied that we had permission, she handed me the sharp rock saying, "Here, you carve mine first and then I'll carve yours."

We cut our memory into Woody's heart. I swear the trickle of sap from the birch looked red, as if we had performed a ritual transforming us into blood brother and sister.

Incidentally, Sir, Woody has grown into a splendid mature tree, straight and tall. Today he looks extremely dignified. The marks etch him still, adding to his simple beauty.

That night I wrote her a note:

> *Thanks for the lesson in ascending, Rima. Once upon a time twenty-seven months ago, the length of three human pregnancies,*

you transformed me into a person who could shine. Today you
transfigured my sexual body. I will never be dark and dull again.
The light will last for always.
Love,
Glowworm

When I gave her my note the next day, she handed me a piece of paper,
the only letter she ever wrote me.

Tonight I leave for Miami to celebrate me-maw's sixtieth
birthday. I appreciate that you are my true blue friend, Glowy.
And I'm glad that my cracked-bottom made you rise. Mostly, I'm
tickled pink we finally swung through the birches. We've been
bendy-bowing since we met, for 862 straight days. We be bendy-
bowing all the time. That's what our tenderness is, the thing in
our lives that bends a thousand ways but never, ever breaks.
Love Always,
Rima

I don't know what sense you're making of my meandering story, Sir. But
I warn you! Bite your lip before you reduce "Glowworm" to a sexual
symbol. Rima and I would indict you a boring grownup. It wasn't
lust between us. Between us was a young and tender love. Tenderness
between us is what it was.

Suddenly, she was gone. Her jet vanished into the Bermuda Triangle.
Until today, the case of her missing plane -- like her coming into my
life -- remains an unsolved mystery.

We have collided with the Millennium, have we not? Recently, the
Heritage Foundation of the State of Georgia designated the woods
where we used to play a "historic site." Don't worry! There won't ever
be any stray "straight lines" or random "square boxes" popping up in
wonderland. At least on that patch of earth, dreams and daydreams will
be preserved into perpetuity. The wrecking ball tore down half a block
of our little town, including the Dairy Queen, our personal cathedral
containing the Breezes and Blizzards that kept feeding the hairs on my

chubby tummy. To replace it, they built a "world class" parking lot. Laugh if you want to about so-called progress. Or in nostalgia, weep.

In this century, I have learned to talk like the man on the six o'clock news. I'm still a voracious reader. I laugh whenever I finish the latest new wave book trying to explain to me... in another way... the Mystery.

Whenever I hear the word "miracle," I want to ball my eyes out.

Countless times I've been told, "It was so sudden. If only you knew the whole truth." The unexpressed "attached file" to those words is that... then... maybe... I could grieve... normally... Mercy, Lord, mercy! Is it a sin for the heart to feel too much? Is it not absurd to imagine there is something in life so pure that it can ease the longing of lost love? Can you think of anything more ridiculous?

Put yourself in my shoes. Wouldn't you prefer to have etched permanently on your brain the picture of initials carved on a white birch tree? Wouldn't you rather fancy spending the rest of your life chasing the scent of honeysuckle, the sound of the wind through Georgia Pines, and the echo of... forever? Wouldn't you prefer the presence, for always, of one true blue friend? You would rejoice, would you not, knowing that you have available whenever you want them... fresh tears?

My critics have been severe. They've labeled my analyses of the modes and manner of technology as "hick ideas" that creep and crawl like roaches out of the Boondocks. My idiosyncratic Biblical hermeneutics has earned me a new nickname, "Hillbilly Theologian." I laughed when I read that, glad that my Glowworm Days have never come to public light! I am acquainted with what it is like to be a leper and the scum of the earth. To me a "hillbilly roach" is more beautiful than... a cipher.

I roared when a Polish social scientist, obviously in love with his native picturesque language, tagged me a "busted ass-hole" who -- and I quote his anal poetry verbatim -- "just blows his ideas out of his rectum." I grinned, too, wondering why from my "stepfather-arse" to a book reviewer repeatedly anal poetry entertains me. I cried picturing Rima shinning up Woody in her skin-tight cotton shorts.

My personal writing style irritates minds clinging to pragmatism positivism dualism reductionism. Ah, yes, you can hear Rima giggle, can't you, "Doctor. Glowworm, you know more –i-s-m words than Mister Webster hisself!"

Tender passion is the mainspring of my thinking.

The phrase "true blue" originates in a sixteenth century proverb now obsolete which reads, "true blue will never stain." The proverb refers to a blue dye that was fast and never ran; and refers to blue tread made in Coventry in the middle ages, prized for holding its color. Thus the phrase means extremely loyal, unwavering… faithfulness.

Now it is time to say "Good-bye."

Rima and I were soulmates. While developing common ground and a common language, we also carved out a *Weltanschauung*. Descartes found the point of connection between the split-off body and soul in the pineal gland of the brain. We discovered, near the top of a young white birch tree, the point of convergence between Heaven and Earth.

Analysis of the Chum Relationship

My chum is someone I can be myself with, my "kindred spirit." With him, I can "let my hair down" or "let it all hang out." Everything feels so natural and easy with my pal. We are easily "in synch" and get on the "same wavelength." We keep no secrets from each other. Rather, we can't wait to talk about things, to "compare note" and to share everything. Not unusually, you finish the sentence your friend began, or say, "He took the words right out of my mouth."

"Ain't it good to have a friend; people can be so cold," sing Carole King and James Taylor.[34] "Just call out my name and you know wherever I am I'll come running, to see you again." Simon and Garfunkel croon a ballad for the ages, "bridge over trouble waters."[35] With our buddy, we experience many of our "firsts": sneaking down by the creek to smoke our first cigarette or swig a beer; the first time we take a furtive peek at *Playboy* or *Playgirl*. Together we engage in all sorts of "wild" things, the kind of craziness that "keeps us from going insane" and allows us to brag, "If you think I'm crazy now then you should have seem me when I was a kid." Specifically, my chum and I go "boy crazy" or "girl crazy" together. We have "crushes" on teachers, coaches, celebrities, sports heroes, stars and starlets of the day: on Johnny Ray, Greta Garbo, Frank Sinatra, Pele, Elvis, Mickey Mantle, Marilyn Monroe, Elizabeth Taylor, the Beatles, Michael Jordon, Michael Jackson, Madonna, Brad Pitt, Jennifer Lopez, Beyonce...

"You are what I am," strums Gordon Lightfoot[36] in a modern paraphrase of the classic line from Horace's third ode: "animae dimidium mea," "you are half of my very soul."[37] The chum's openness is second only to the supreme innocence of the young child in terms of spontaneity, honesty, enthusiasm and sincerity.

The parable depicts a concrete and specific version of the chum relationship. However, it also reveals its essential structure of what all might experience. I make the same claim about the other narratives in this book. Organizationally, I choose a double-barreled approach. In addition to the natural surge of the parable, I also express key concepts analytically. The narrative and analytic cross-fertilize each other thereby offering the reader the most comprehensive picture of first friendship.

My research request, "Please describe your first best friend," solicited many responses not woven into the parable.[38] In point of fact, they did not mesh with the "storyline" or fit the specific context and dynamics of the bond between Rima and Glowy. So the following analysis includes both the parable and the descriptive data.[39]

The issue of age

To start, first we backtrack. The time between six to twelve years is the designated "gang age." Freud names it "latency,"[40] Erik Erikson "the age of industry,"[41] and Harry Stack Sullivan the "juvenile era."[42] Sullivan says it is "the actual time for becoming social." A new need emerges for peers or "compeers," playmates like oneself. The youngster outgrows interacting with the "imaginary playmates" of childhood. A long discussion of the dynamics and structures of the juvenile era would take us too far a-field from our theme. The relevant point is that a new type of interest emerges during this period of heightened socialization. Into one's consciousness a need erupts, not just for playmates but for closeness with one particular person. Sullivan calls it "the need for interpersonal intimacy." Popular or unpopular, having friends galore or all alone, each of us craves a special friend.

Time of occurrence

Developmentally, therefore, the chum relationship is a pre-puberty happening. Sullivan dates its first time occurrence chronologically between eight and one-half and 10 years. He melds his interpersonal understanding with general developmental findings and normative data. However, the relationship can and does happen earlier. Above and beyond numerical age, the psychological disposition of the growing youngster is more significant. In a theoretical discussion that follows the psychological analyses of the relationship, I return to the issue of time.

Fluidity of occurrence

As soon as we make dated-time relative and understand the chum as a psychological achievement not just an automatic happening, it is evident that it might happen earlier chronologically but also much later. Sullivan cautions us, "If it happens at all." And he gives us to see that many people never reach the level of psychological preadolescence. They never learn to love. They stay wrapped up in themselves. "What kind of fool am I, who never fell in love?" is the songwriter's self accusation. There are persons who never become emotionally convinced or who only pay lip service to the lyrics that go "people who need people are the luckiest people in the world." Sullivan also insists that often psychotherapy "works," not for the formal reasons that the therapist documents, but more truly because the therapist becomes the first best friend the client has even experienced.

A chumship, therefore, is not an inevitable or determined occurrence and not the outcome of the false Darwinian idea of an evolutionary unfolding of the human organism. We are not programmed to make a friend by genes, chromosomes, DNA or RNA. Making a friend is a personal achievement. Preadolescence is a psychological event, a developmental happening. There is no recipe for it in some cookbook and no self-help, how-to-do it manual with all the tricks, hints or short-cuts. It requires taking a leap.

A cardinal idea of this book is that love relationships are not pre-programmed. I will return to it in subsequent chapters. On the other hand, after we co-create our first friendship we gain the knack or flair and develop the courage to risk making another. Afterwards, likely we will make friends repeatedly.

The sense of the miracle

Why does Sullivan adjudge this preadolescent event a miracle? It is the moment that satisfaction of my chum's physical and security needs assume an importance as equally important as my own. He means in matters such as freedom from harm and the needs for esteem, security, happiness, comfort, and success. A peer becomes as important to me as me. "Nothing remotely like this has ever appeared before." It happens for the first time. It is the first budding of love. It is the prototype of mature love. Thus, it is "the most health inducing" event that can happen to an individual.

Remember the astonishing experience of feeling hurt when you friend was hurt? Perhaps a parent, teacher, coach, or another peer inflicted injustice upon him. Remember feeling like a failure when your friend failed even though your might have come out a winner? Or feeling joy at the happiness forthcoming to your pal even if you were going through hard times yourself? If you had an article of clothing, a tee-shirt or a sweater, which you friend did "dig" so much, was it not a bigger kick to let her wear it or to give it to her as a gift even though the garment was also your own personal favorite? Equally splendidly, and often easy to arrange, was that you each bought the same item to wear. At mid-century, wearing MAD tee-shirts together was the prototypical example. Insofar as the two are equally in the relationship, chums don't play games in the sense of phoniness; they put on no acts in the sense of mini-dramatic psychological performances. The total bond overrides such nonsense. Slowly, good friends learn each other's moods, learn how to interpret them, and know what one should or should not do to influence them. They keep nothing back in reserve or nothing furtive for fear that it might shock, scandalize or disappoint. If you have ever been able to "get off" on another rather than just yourself, then you've had a preadolescent chum experience.

The matter of gender

Sullivan accents the homophilic possibility. One's first chum is apt to be a peer of the same gender. Same-gender composition is common within the school, sports teams, other social groups such as scouts, and the juvenile gang itself. Sullivan's point is that falling in love with the same gendered person precedes, facilitates, and indeed prepares for falling in love with the other gendered person. Of course, we know now that biographically it happened for Sullivan that way. Therefore, we can slacken his taut line about "same gender" to say that it is possible to happen otherwise. The first best friend can equally be a heterosexual other.

An appeal to languages other than English helps communicate faithfully Sullivan's core thought. The Greek word for child is *teknon* a neuter noun; so are the German word *kinder* and the Scandinavian word *barn*. The wisdom of these languages captures the pre-puberty child as functionally neutral and aptly considered gender-wise neuter. The gender of the person is not the crucial variable. The essence of the phenomenon, or the miracle of the miracle, is that a new meaning erupts into my life: the "I" gives way to the "we." It is no longer "just me," good old "#1." Whenever... as soon as... if ever... I reach this level of development I am capable of a new type of "collaboration" with another human being of whatever gender. So it is not the gender of the person but the person of the person that matters most. In Martin Buber's[43] classically beautiful depiction, I-Thou supplants I-It as a way of relating to the other. In a brand new way, sensitivity to the other begins with the chum relationship. It is the inchoate experience of empathy.

Closeness unencumbered with sexuality

The relationship between closeness and sexuality is always subtly pervasive. Sullivan states adamantly that the love between chums is unburdened by or "unencumbered" with the "problems" that sexuality introduces into the life of the puberty age youngster. In a beautifully poignant statement he says,

> *I trust that you will finally and forever grasp that interpersonal intimacy can really consist of a great many things without genital contact; that intimacy means... closeness, without specifying that which is close other than the persons. Intimacy is the type of situation involving two people which permits validation of all components of personal worth.*[44]

Interpersonal validation

Closeness and personal worth constitute the kernel. My chum affirms and validates me for more than the finite reasons that I am the fastest runner on the block, the prettiest girl in grade seven, or the strongest boy in the neighborhood. She does not validate me for being the "brain" of the class who shares my homework; he does not prefer me because of my big boobs or because I am the only girl in the neighborhood with a swimming pool. Possessions and appearances take second place to whom and how I am. In the language of Gabriel Marcel,[45] my friend validates me and cherishes me not for my "having" or "doing," but for my "being." In "True blue," Glowy experiences the gift of Rima as an "epiphany" or manifestation. Sullivan remarks that we all reach preadolescence in some way "warped" by experiences with our loving but imperfect families. The chum relationship provides a splendid corrective experience because it undoes the warping. It introduces me to the experience of being treated tenderly. It's a tremendously humanizing experience.

Precision about the word 'love'

Is it not redundant to say that this kind of relationship is always beneficial if ever and whenever it happens? By living it, I leave behind the last vestiges of childhood, my life among the giants, and enter the domain of tenderness. Sullivan is precise in speaking about love, convinced that it is one of those terribly misunderstood four letter words. He adds precision and refinement. As children living at the dependent level of existence, our love for our parents commingles with need, security, and with survival itself. This original parental bond grounds our loving capacity. But it is not yet love in the strict psychological sense. Consider it this way. Our parents love us. Well, they have to love us, don't they? We didn't ask to be brought into this world! It is their duty, their responsibility to care for us. We, on our part, owe them love mixed up with obedience, duty, and respect. So the dependency-dependability dimension shadows the parent-child bond no matter how much it grows and develops, even if to the point that parent and child become friends. Here and now nevertheless, this other human being from outside the family who does not have to love me, lo and behold, does love me. Without the miracle of the chumship, therefore, we would not know love unalloyed with need and duty. A necessary ingredient of mature or intimate love is that I experience myself as a person in my own right and experience the other as a person in her own right. Antoine De Saint-Exupery writes, "True love begins when nothing is looked for in return." The chum exemplifies such graceful, even unconditional, love.

Cognitive reversibility and emotional empathy

Jean Piaget's[46] views on cognitive development shed light on the chum relationship. At the age eight to twelve, he demonstrates that the growing younger reaches the level of "concrete operational thinking." Cardinal to this new conceptual ability is the capacity to reverse. That is, one now can see something from another's standpoint and not just one's own. If you and I are placed in polar opposite positions with a model of a mountain placed between us, I can now understand that if I am looking at the face of a deer you are looking at the tail. Pertinent to the chum relationship, twinborn with cognitive reversibility is emotional reciprocity. I can feel the feelings of the other. If I score high marks and you score low, I feel your sadness even though I experience personal satisfaction. If you win the race and I finish last, I am happy for you even though I feel miserable over my own failure. Rational dualistic thinking artificially rips asunder these two human powers. The two are one. As soon as we are capable of building a friendship, simultaneously we cognitively reverse and show emotional reciprocity. Both-and.

No reduction to sex

In the same vein, Sullivan beautifully accents closeness as preeminently personal in order to detach his thoughts from "pan sexism."

Consciously and deliberately, he wants to counter the tendency of a debased psychoanalysis to reduce all relationships to their libidinal basis. Instead, he privileges the interpersonal and the socio-cultural. At another juncture of this book, I will give a fuller picture of Freud's views on his own terms.

Common ground and common language

As part and parcel of building a common ground between them, the chums develop a common language that is a secret or special language so arcane to the grownups that it leaves them in the dark about the messages exchanged. Youth growing up in the 1950s communicated in "pig" Latin. And although chums did not invent the "inside joke," they surely coin more than their share of them. Nowadays, the explosion of information technology and the machinations in cyberspace provides the youngsters with tools, a vocabulary, and emoticons that keep 99 % of the grownups on the sidelines. Likewise, the chums invent special phrases or concoct subtle gestures that economically and in an instant express an elaborate meaning or evoke an entire situation. All it takes is a word or a gesture to make the friends break out in hollowing laughter. The outsider, the grownup in particular, can only inquire weakly: "What's so funny?" "What did I say?" "Tell me!"

Psychological Reflections

Both natural beneficial and painful consequences result from making a best friend. To these psychological issues I now turn.

The beneficial consequences of a preadolescent love relationship

Permanent presence

The more intense the preadolescent relationship, the more it explodes or liquidates the fearful fantasy of "being different." I do not mean different in the limited sense of not belonging or of being ostracized. I mean that once a chumship forms, I am no longer and nevermore will be a strangely disconnected alien. The Glowworm, after bonding with Rima, no longer fells like a cipher.

Taming and being tamed means that I have surely contacted another like me and have touched and been touched by a kindred spirit. I have reached another and am reachable by that other. I have chosen someone with my hearthead and not only with my cognitive register or my practical sense. My life is enriched by a presence that does not depend upon objective, measurable space and time but transcends them.

Presence-absence

An unsurpassable phenomenological reflection elaborates this meaning. Jean-Paul Sartre[47] has clarified the structure of absence. What is it? Absence is not nothing. Absence is a mode of presence. I walk into the cafe looking for my friend. Where is Pierre? He is not here. He is elsewhere. In Algiers is where he is, by rumor. His absence is a haunting presence. I am more present to him as gone and perhaps unreachable than I am to the physical surroundings. Thus I scarcely hear the music playing in the cafe, or smell the smoke, or catch the laughter, or see the colorful clothes.

Likewise, I experience being present to one who is physically present but absent in meaning "I miss you most when you're here but still gone." I see the "far away look" in the other's eyes. "I don't see me in your eyes anymore." A vacant look: here she is, but she is gone.

My first best friend, therefore, bequeaths to my life an abiding, enduring, and often permanent presence. She provides invaluable support while I am having problems with my peer group. If I am a victim of harassment, ostracism, bullying, mobbing, her presence helps me to cope. I'm never alone. Amazing changes come with the revolution of puberty and adolescence. My chum sustains me while I endure the "growing pains." Her knowing eyes bolsters me whenever I feel betrayed as my body starts growing like a weed, sprouting hairs, pimples, breasts, and appendages. My friend isn't fooled by appearances, but knows, accepts, and understands the essential me. He doesn't expect me to act "in character." Her soft smile orients me during those times when, under the siege of my own impulses, drives, emotions, and ideas, I cannot even recognize myself! In spite of the passage of chronological time, my friend and I will always be able to pick up the relationship at the personal level and communicate at the level of core emotions. My chum is an enduring reference point. "Old friends" is a phrase of deep song, supremely beautiful.

Ebb and flow

This stellar gain balances the more usual and unfortunate occurrence in our highly mobile "future shock" postmodern world of information technology and cyberspace. Nowadays, friends are disposable. Friendship has become a matter of convenience. In cyberspace, by the click of a mouse, we end in an eye-blink what is really an ersatz friendship. With a poignant plea, Rima says, "We're more than just... of use to one another... ain't we?"

Likewise, the structure of our modern-postmodern world typically spatially separates the chums early. One goes off to university; the other marries young and bears a child. For the time being, they stop sharing areas of essential relevance. Perhaps after many yesterdays, eventually they have a reunion. It takes only a few minutes of catching up on what has transpired during the interval. Remarkably soon, the two are right back on the same wavelength, communicating as if all the yesterdays were just... yesterday!

Self-distortions

In a second beneficial spin-off of the intimacy, I borrow the eyes of my friend to look at myself. His view as often as not challenges and even jars me; but it also creates wholesome advantages. With a new double vision, I am able to alter distortions about myself. I cannot see myself from the outside. A discrepancy exists between my experience and my behavior. My experience of my pain, for example, is more available to me than to you. Sensitizing you to it is the best I can do. My behavior, however, is more visible to you than to me. You see my comportment better than I do. You are an existential mirror. Because of our love-bond, I see what otherwise I might never see about myself or maybe what I do not wish to recognize and acknowledge. Call it feedback; call it constructive criticism. It allows me the opportunity to make necessary changes in my comportment.

Parental prophecies

I am able to break the stranglehold of parental prophecies for me. My parents have expectations for me and anticipations about what I am to do with my life or of how I am supposed to "turn out." If I do not become consciously aware of them, and see equally vividly alternatives, I run the risk of turning unconscious parental wishes and hopes into self-fulfilling prophecies. Thus the feedback of my chum and his eyes on me helps me to make a gigantic step outside of the symbiotic circle of my original family.

George Herbert Mead[48] proposes the notion of the "looking glass self." He calls the social self a series of "reflected appraisals." Evaluations of my parents and family members readily ossify into powerful influences upon how I see myself. My friend tells me, "There's more to you that that" or "You're otherwise..." They prompt me to reach for the more and stretch for the otherwise. Maybe even "shoot for the moon."

Stated somewhat differently, the chum relationship puts a dent in the "natural attitude," the taken-for-granted view that things are the way they are. Chums raise questions, scour possibilities, and adopt a critical standpoint. Within my family, I inculcate a certain world-view and accept their image of me. Who do I look like? Who do I take after? How am I in comparison with brothers or sisters? Are my brother and I really different as night and day? Various markers along my developmental trail etch these views. Indeed, I count upon them to orient me. In turn, they sustain me and serve me well. Now in a mini-revolution, my chum and I spin our own personal myths about "who we are," where we fit in, and how we stack up. In a spirit of collaboration, we co-define each other. We spend hours developing our own world-view, including conclusions about all that matters. In fact, preadolescence partners become "first philosophers" who develop a *Weltanschauung* that becomes "ours," i.e., this is the-way-the-world-is by our mutual consensus. We chisel out basic attitudes, values, morals, and an orientation to living that rival the fundamental viewpoints we absorbed by osmosis in the process of growing up in our families. The preadolescent chums figure out their own views and formulate their own conclusions about age-appropriate matters: the dynamics of boy-girl relationships, sexuality, war and peace, their respective family system, teachers, other peers, and religious beliefs. It is a preliminary understanding of the "ways of the world." It's the beginning of implicitly and without awareness asking Husserl's[49] questions about roots, origins and beginnings, Kant's[50] questions about conditions which make something possible, and Heidegger's[51] questions about responsible shepherding of Being.

Putting a dent in the natural attitude is a major contribution that the preadolescent era makes to the youngster's life. The natural attitude is the taken-for-granted viewpoint that things are the way they are or that things are already always constituted. "You can't fight city hall" is merely one expression in favor of this prejudice. Never to question this so-called "realistic" view is to be saddled with what Nietzsche calls the "herd mentality." Swallowing it hook, line and sinker means that one wanders through life like a sheep. But the chums teach each other to question critically and to cross-examine particularly the most sacred of the established order's sacred cows. It is too much to say that most chums become what Paul Ricoeur named Marx, Nietzsche and Freud: "prophets of suspicion." But it is safe to say that the germs of revolutionary thought are planted early by two friends who refuse to swallow totally normative views and directives. Albert Camus writes that there must be on the planet at least one rebel otherwise the human race would decay into extinction.[52] We must applaud and champion the rebellious spirit that chums engender in each other.

We weave collaboratively these major life-viewpoints. In doing so, we give tremendous power to our chum in matters of advice and consent. In kind, we assume a weighty responsibility. We have named it, and it is so. Our mutual consensus creates a reading of the meaning of the world in all its complexity. This consensus is powerful. Our conclusions persist into adulthood. In moments when we need counsel, struggle with a grave decision, or face a crisis, we appeal to conclusions carved out between my chum and I while standing in line to buy an ice cream cone during our school lunch hour. They remain standards unless, or until, another powerful existential event or epiphany challenges them. Typically, either a new love relationship or ideas that we meet in books, songs, from a university professor, etc., persuade us to re-think and revise.

Fixing flaws

The chum relationship also remedies certain personality deficiencies. Sullivan counters the deterministic tendency that plagues western psychology. The dynamism of the chumship opens the personality for alteration and shaping in significant ways. Sullivan singles out the "show off" youngster, accustomed always to be performing on center stage; the ostracized, socially isolated lonely child; the disparaging child who builds self up by whittling down the other; and the malevolent child with "the burnt child reaction." The reaction results from the infliction of a large dose of anxiety in those moments when one needs tenderness. Sullivan puts these words in the unfortunate child's mouth, "Once upon the time the world was a good place; then along came people."

Within Sullivan's vision, nothing is determined; development is open to ongoing transformation. The chumship mitigates self-defeating or viciously inappropriate way of interacting with others. Preadolescence is one of the prime times for both undoing and re-directing a warped pattern of relating. One is also vulnerable to new and unprecedented hurt. Nobody is permanently lost or permanently saved.

The painful consequences

Parental jealousy

All other things being equal, parents typically are at least mildly jealous, a little bit hurt, and even somewhat resentful when they see their little boy or girl making this definite preference for another outside the primary family. It is never easy to let go, to end, to part with a person with whom we have a bond. I repeat: we lack genes, chromosomes,

DNA, or RNA that might program us to let go or grieve a love-bond. Letting go is will-inspired and sometimes an act of courage. At best, it is a mild ouch and a slight tug at the heart strings to watch your child grow up to be on his own. It happens that a parent or other family members express misgivings about my new friend. They want to know all about her and her family. Or worse, the parents might see the chum as a rival for whom they must compete for affection. In this anxious-possessive attitude, the parents actually "put down" or disparage my chum. They drill me about him or harp at me with words like, "He's not your type"; "Why don't you play with 'so-and-so'?" If the lad or lass happens to be of a different race, color, social class or religious creed, the vocabulary is more intense and more denigrating: "Stick to your own kind." Pick any time during modernity until today -- or until tomorrow -- and some group constitutes the ready-to-hand target for prejudice and the downright racial hatred that decays into ethnic cleansing. Most times, prevalent social-political conditions define the "outsider." Georg Simmel writes that the "in-group" for reasons of cohesion always needs the "out-group."[53] So always there exists the stereotypic outsider, the stranger, or outlaw. Historically, a Gypsy, Jew, Black, or Communist has worn the label and carried the burden. Nowadays, the outlaw is the so-called "terrorist" and most apt a brown-skinned Arab, Muslim, or Hindu. Western prejudice is so deeply ingrained that few can articulate the ethnic differences between peoples of the Mid-East. Alan Jackson[54] wrote a Grammy award winning song after 9-11 with the telling lines: "I'm just a singer of simple songs / I'm not a real political man / I watch CNN but I don't think I can tell you the difference in Iraq and Iran." The myopia of ignorant prejudice is destructive at both the personal and the geopolitical levels. An upsurge of parental racial hatred toward my chum cuts deep wounds. It carves a rift that is difficult to bridge.

Bracket the rhetoric of politicians or preachers

A family might have its "preferred" outlaw, the proverbial "Hatfields and McCoys." Something as simple (and yet as complex) as a Northern and Southern Italian relationship suffices to sound the words, "She's not your kind." Germane to the chumship, two youngsters become caught up either in cultural feuds, social prejudice, or family tradition. As soon as the words surface, a problem begins to sprout. My decision-of-the-heart is under siege. Narrow-mindedness, bigotry, ignorance, or political maneuvering is sabotaging my beautiful love. If the family does not slacken its prejudicial viewpoint, if the emotional attitudes do not become balanced, and if the matter does not clarify relatively quickly, then the non-acceptance by parents of the chum becomes a source of long standing bitterness. In a later chapter, I discuss the outlaw relationship, an even more intense manifestation of this dynamic.

Some parents become upset or "uptight" out of a different type of ignorance. Witnessing an enthusiastic love-bond, they panic at the possibility that their child and her friend are performing sexual acts together. They fear the chum is leading their darling child astray and down the garden path or straight to hell! If the chums are of the same gender, then parental homophobia might surface. "Where did we go wrong?" is the alienating insinuation and the insulting judgment. Whether the youngsters are heterosexual or homosexual in orientation, the disdainful words are difficult to retract and as difficult to forgive.

Peer intolerance of the intimate connection

If the bond forms within the eight-twelve year period, the rest of the "gang" probably has not reached preadolescence. The close relationship threatens the others; they don't understand it; it is beyond their ken. They label it "homo" in order to have some way to comprehend it. Although this ignorance makes sense, it is unconscionable and reprehensible especially when it manifests itself as the violence of ostracism or actually in giving the chums a physically punishing "lesson."[55]

Chum jealousy

Our young loves are apt to be possessive. In love for the first time, we tend to lay claim to the beloved totally. We make the person our whole life and reason for living -- what *The Prophet* names "filling one's emptiness." Anything or anyone that takes my beloved away from me even briefly is perceived as a threat to our special connection. The poignant and painful side of taming and being tamed is that we also have to let go and to set free. The hard lesson to be learned is that no one relationship is perfect, complete, or all-embracing.

Differences in the timing of puberty

The magic of the special preadolescent love-bond runs its natural course. It must grow and change, although not necessarily fade away. Still, the psychobiological revolution of puberty comes. It disrupts the preadolescent loving peace. Chances are the chums will not reach puberty simultaneously. It is fortunate if the timing for the twosome is even close. Sometimes, a great gap of years occurs. At this tender time of life, a brief chronological spread measures immense in terms of "lived time." With puberty, of course, one's interests shift. It is painful for the preadolescent who lags behind to watch her love-partner develop sooner and start developing breasts or branch out into the concerns of teenagers, i.e., romantic, sensual, or sexual interests in the other gender. It is painful, too, for the preadolescent who accelerates to find self shifting and thus leaving his chum behind in the lag and in the lurch. It is heart-rending for both. It is the end of an era.

Sexual distortion of the closeness

The timing of developmental progression is rarely synchronized. If one chum should experience the lust dynamism first, it is not unexpected that she might bring to her partner the newborn power of the sexual drive. Not surprisingly, the other partner might not be ready and might find the introduction to lust confounding and confusing. A premature initiation to sexuality leaves in its wake a scrambled mess about what is sexual, personal, and spiritual. A premature introduction blurs the sense of intimacy. If the sexual components dominate, confusion reigns, making later choices about sexuality difficult. Radley Metzger's[56] classic film, *Therese and Isabelle*, based upon a novel by Violette Leduc and starring Anna Gael and Essy Persson in the lead roles, depicts this structural dynamic in a powerfully poignant way.

Loneliness

Sullivan's articulates a provocative notion. Loneliness in the strict sense is only possible if one has experienced the need for interpersonal closeness and especially if she has had a taste of it. So loneliness only occurs during preadolescence and afterwards. This idea requires elaboration.

Anyone can feel alone, either a child who has not reached preadolescence or a chronological adult who has never achieved the capacity for intimacy. Or one of us might feel the sting of being "dropped," "dumped," or "rejected" by a former friend. But in Sullivan's vocabulary, loneliness is not the failure to be in a relationship. For such left-out-ness, other more suitable names are feeling abandoned, overlooked, deserted, or ignored. Anyone is vulnerable to the anxious, panicky feeling of being alone. We can all feel needy for someone. But we are only raw for the experience of loneliness if we have tamed and been tamed. Within the miracle of preadolescence, the capacity for intimacy and the susceptibility to loneliness happen simultaneously. It is a figure-ground structure. We can't have one without the other.

In support of Sullivan's insight, I affirm that much of our frantic searching for someone to fill our void, emptiness or aloneness interferes with establishing intimacy. Our fear of being alone is a defense against loneliness: "At least I have somebody"; "At least there was always a boy hanging around"; "It's not love, but it's not bad."

Nowadays, the plethora of possibilities of Information Technology buttresses this defense in an unprecedented way. Meeting someone Online is a snap. Look at almost anyone alone on the streets, at the bus stop, sitting in a restaurant. Her fingers are busy or her eyes are glued to an SMS message. Being alone is under my control; I can end this contact at the flick of a mouse or delete the message. Loneliness, however, means that I have let the other get close enough to hurt me on her terms or for his reasons -- which I may never know. I repeat that our fear of being alone is a defense against loneliness.

Footnote about loneliness

If one does not experience fairly early the need for intimacy and fairly early get a taste of it, he will lack the "feel" for it and lack the knack, skill, or flair for entering into and establishing an intimate relationship. In Sullivan's apt sentence, "There are many situations in which lonely people literally lack any experience with the things that they encounter."[57] It is one of life's frequent tragedies that one will overlook an orchid while searching for a rose; or ignore a diamond while trifling with cheap glass. Loneliness breeds loneliness.

Theoretical Reflections

Two faces of time

From the start, it is important to understand the viewpoint on time that permeates this entire work. St. Augustine so wisely says, with a touch of frustration, that we all know exactly what time is until we have to explain it! Mainstream developmental psychology takes time for granted as linear. Time is objective; it can be measured. Theoreticians break it up nicely and neatly into stages and phases that punctuate the line which spans from our birth to our death. The Greek word for time so conceived is *chronos*, i.e., clock time, calendar time, the sand slithering through the hourglass. But the Greeks have another word, *kairos*, that signifies lived or personal time, the time of subjectivity. *Kairos* means the "right time", the "ripe time" or that which occurs in the "fullness of time." The distinction is so obvious, who can gainsay it? From the perspective of this book, mainstream developmental psychology is deficient insofar as it ignores lived time in favor of measured duration. To attain the most sophisticated understanding of change and development, researchers and practitioners need to respond to the challenge to integrate both faces of time. My intention is to juggle continually this complex, subtle and pervasive relationship between objective time and personal experience of age. It is important for all the relationships treated in this book.

Clinical hebephrenia

Now, here comes a mini-tour into psychopathology. It throws into sharp relief the extreme consequence of the failure to reach psychological preadolescence. Based upon extensive and intensive therapeutic experience at Chestnut Lodge, Sullivan has remarkable insights into schizophrenia. He insists that the phenomenon must be understood first and foremost as a human process, and not in terms of the medical mythology that reduces it to genetic faults or flaws in the brain or central nervous system. So it is that he sheds light on the theme of friendship by describing and reflecting upon the style of schizophrenia known as hebeprhrenia. The word comes from the Greek referring to the goddess of youth. Hebephrenia is the most regressive form of the schizophrenic styles.

The mid-teen period, age sixteen is the statistical average, is the target age for the first schizophrenic break. Catatonia is the term that describes the psychotic break: the excitement, hyperactivity, and restlessness of manifesting extreme struggle with "going crazy"; the catastrophic war between God and the Devil. The individual battles openly in frenzy and in panic with all the basic polarities of existence: to be or not to be; truth-error, good-evil, sex-spirit and innocence-evil. It is a "moment" of despair-ing that is characterized by hallucinations and uncontrolled behavior. Our current powerful psychiatric drugs muffle quickly the berserk episode of such psychotic breaks.

The catatonic, in dire agony, still holds on to a sliver of the possibility of intimacy. Indeed, the catatonic break precisely is often the response to a broken intimate connection. It is the extreme form of lovesickness or most drastic response to lost love. It is the experience of the broken heart. The "moment" is suicidal.

The frenzy abates either as a result of drugs, or naturally because of exhaustion, or the "excitement" phase turns into its opposites, the "stupor" in which the individual "freezes." Eventually the dis-ease will take another shape. One face it might eventually wear is paranoia.

Paranoia is, at minimum, the penultimate expression of distrust and suspicion. It is a "solution" of the heaven-hell crisis of the psychotic break. It gives the individual options and more psychological avenues to maneuver. The individual concocts a happy delusional explanation that answers his troubles and woes. He becomes convinced it's "they" who cause his conflicts, the very ones he always suspected in the first place and the ones he will suspect ever on. Thus, the paranoid schizophrenic splits the world into the absolute "good" that he loves and the absolute "evil" that he hates. Never will the twain meet. The paranoid, a tragic victim of the broken heart, finds a zone of psychic safety by keeping at bay the treacherous others, the sinners or terrorists who are out to hurt and deceive him. He must remain vigilant and cover his flanks. The enemy always lurks. He must keep polished his perfect hate for her or them, the children of Satan. He must consort only with "saints," uncorrupted like him. The thread that wards off total despair is the secret hope that love is still innocent and pure somewhere, even if not in this world. Even in moments of lucidity, the countenance of the paranoid glints with suspicion. A gleam of hope in the eye is rare and fleeting. The balance is perilous.

The point of this mini-tour is that the hebephrenic has never experienced preadolescence. The person who concocts a paranoid identity after the psychotic break has lived life's love-hate drama. Now, he clutches to a tenuous explanation of the havoc it wreaks and the pain it creates. The hebephrenic outcome must be understood on the basis of developmental considerations. Hebephrenic "dilapidation" signifies that the individual has never experienced the interpersonal intimacy of the chum. His very physiognomy attests to the lack. At age twenty, twenty five or thirty five, the individual looks like a child. He or she, for example, exudes no sensuality or sexuality. So the grown woman, facially and figure-wise "good looking", by her manner and talk evokes no sex appeal or sensual attractiveness. She is like a child, or like a doll.

Sullivan tells us dilapidation occurs because the individual experienced the break before ever becoming embroiled in a preadolescent love relationship. She may have experienced the need for love, romance, erotic contact; she may have indulged in fantasy. But "it" never took place. It was all imaginary. Maybe he had a massive crush on some unattainable starlet or a teacher or librarian who scarcely knew he existed. After the psychotic break happens, there is no concrete tie and no actual memories of a loving other to prevent the downhill slide into psychic deterioration. The individual, therefore, gives a vivid picture of the power of the chumship by showing us what its absence wrecks. Of course, the implications for psychotherapy are awesome. The therapeutic task is to spark intimacy for the first time. R. D. Laing,[58] who understands schizophrenia in terms of its root meaning, 'broken heart', says that "The broken heart will mend, if we have the heart to mend it." Implicitly our ordinary chums are heart-doctors!

CHAPTER 2

Adolescent First Love

Who can't remember falling in love for the first time? Or remember the newness of experiencing a "two-in-one-being" and the conviction of "it's you and me against the world?" Everything felt fresh, breezy, light, and wonderful. This initial attachment with the heterosexual other, when we were first graced with a soulmate, is our "first love."

Whenever the experience of the love happens -- if it happens -- it opens us to the One, the Good, the True, the Beautiful, the Magic, and the Tragic. First love is splashed with absolutes: perfect, together forever, never part, always one. Idealism and innocence mark the relationship. Typically, my partner is also someone consistent with my roots and someone easy to bring home to mom and dad. Sexual expression happens within first love, but it is incidental and not essential to the love-bond. The parties are authentic debutantes that "come out" in specifically manly and womanly ways.

Who's First?

"The ailments of love are different from any other."[59] Rumi

I don't know why my boyfriend is acting jealous! I told him all about my Big Love, every detail. Well, almost. Who can tell it all to anybody? One's first love is so sacred, or more than sacred, that always you must keep back something and hold some secret in reserve. So I shared… almost everything.

With good reason, too! I wanted it out in the open from the very beginning. I wanted to come squeaky clean before it ever had a chance to get dirty. Let there be no ghosts hovering was my idea when I decided to tell him, and no jack-in-the-box surprises popping out unexpectedly or at the most inopportune time. I was a bit selfish, too, because I didn't want to "kill" what looked promising with my new boyfriend. I wanted to get started on the right foot. Doesn't every Norwegian know that exposure to daylight is the way to kill a Troll?

"What did you tell him?" you ask. Good question. He needed to hear about the astonishing beauty of it, the wild happiness in it, and the thrill of it all. Søren Kierkegaard writes: "The first love is the true love, and one only loves once." I don't know if I believe that. But I felt that either the Universe appointed me to meet my first love or that God Herself sent him to me. It was perfect.

At its peak, I wrote my first ever poem with the key line, "We are God's chosen ones picked at perfect prime." By then, our communication was so awesome that he and I must have exchanged a thousand words. But in response to my poem, he wrote only one simple sentence, "I'll love you for always or forever, whichever come last." Until today, nothing has ever touched me more. That one-liner describes in a nutshell the essence of our relationship and our complete mutual trust. As corny as it sounds, we assumed our future and then took keen aim at eternity!

Does that sound naïve to you? Actually, it was pretty ordinary. Everything about our relationship was consistent with our roots. He and I grew up in the same town and our families held similar values. My parents, especially my father, were tickled pink that I picked someone just like them. His parents welcomed me as the daughter that they never had. Everybody just took it for granted that someday we'd get married.

I had no clue about what I wanted to do with my life before we were 'Us'. Loving him gave me direction and actually oriented both our lives. Our future took concrete shape. We planned to attend university first and then get married and have three kids. We discussed possibilities about everything, like the careers we would have and the dream house we might build someday. We were talking about the rest of our lives! It was exhilarating and peaceful at the same time.

God, I was "coming out" all the time! Since we shared one "first" after another after another, I was a perpetual debutante. We awakened each other to the One, the Good, the True, the Beautiful, the Magic, and the Tragic. We were supremely idealistic, obsessed with poetry, philosophy, and depth psychology. We were convinced that love could save the whole world!

Political causes also engrossed us. We were furious with our government's polices about war, immigration, refugees, and civil rights. Diagnosing capitalism as a disease, we championed the causes of the poor, oppressed, and the disenfranchised and of widows and orphans. "Are not love and peace more important than power and money?" I said. He replied, "John Lennon was right. 'All we need is love'."

When the dual magic of romantic lust struck us, our sexual expression was intense but innocent. We'd just lie together all night naked, holding each other, relishing the wonder of our bodies. Our embrace was so tender that it actually hurt sometimes when we broke it or even when we stopped touching each other's skin. One time when we only had a few minutes together, he said, or I said -- or we took the words out of the other's mouth -- that ending our caress was "an amputation." There is no better word.

In fact, it took forever before we had sex. And the first time was as natural and spontaneous as rain in the fjords. Believe it or not, we were listening to Beethoven's sixth symphony at the time. The part of the music that pictures the calm after the storm captures how it happened with us. We drifted with completeness and feelings of deep satisfaction because we had waited until the right time to have our first time; waited until we were ready or until the life in us ripened for the warm glow.

Sex was never the biggest part of our relationship. Intercourse itself was incidental to our greater bond. Kissing was a bigger part, and hugging too. Like I indicated before, we were touching each other all the time. We couldn't get enough contact. I remember one day when we on my bed and he was reading me a passage from Boris Pasternak's[60] *Doctor Zhivago*. The doctor was telling Laura -- you know from "Laura's theme" -- that they had been taught how to kiss in heaven and had dropped down to earth to see if they had learned their lessons well. That's how it was between him and me. We used all those words lovers all over the world utter: "I want to eat you up"; "You touched me on the outside and I felt it on the inside"; "You leave me breathless!" Geez, there were so many phrases like that that I could probably spend an entire hour remembering them and telling you. Pretty romantic, eh? I often wonder if we were just too star-struck or walking around all the time with rainbows in our eyes. But you know, even if our heads were stuck in the clouds, I still think that if I'm with a guy and I don't feel the excitement of wanting to eat him up then what's the point of being together? Wouldn't that be ultimate boredom? I don't want to resign myself to being with a guy just to have a man around! Doesn't everybody crave a tender passion?

Most people don't understand me when I say that sex wasn't the pivot of our bond. I get either quizzical looks or a straightforward question, "How could it have been such an amazing love if sex was merely irrelevant?" Do you know what I think? The whole world has watched too much American Soaps, Sitcoms and too many Hollywood movies. People get hung-up on "sexual batting averages": how-many-times-with-whom-in-what-positions. My love said to me one day, "Screw this quantitative technology of distance." I replied, "Touch me."

Our emotional connection mattered most. I felt feelings that I never experienced before, unprecedented emotions I used to think were the privileged fare for heroes and heroines and not for little old me. But the tenderness, oh, my! It was excruciatingly tender. Just the way he would look at me with adoration in his eyes. And the way he would touch me like I was worth more than silver and gold. The gentle way he would speak to me with such -- well, I almost said 'respect' but that doesn't capture it. There were moments when his tone of voice was reverent. In these special moments back then, I used to tremble. I'm trembling now even as I tell you because it's all coming back to me. Aren't "awe" and "adoration" words that should be reserved for the Divinity? But I suppose that is part of the Mystery. We were discovering the divine in each other, bringing it out, relishing it, and sharing it with others.

As a human being, I have never been any better than I was in those eighteen months. I'm a fuller person now, more mature, down to earth and more realistic in worldly terms. Like the song says it, I've seen life from both sides. I'm more dependable and reliable, too. I used to be a delicate butterfly, easily crushed. Everybody told me that I wore my heart on my sleeve and hung out on the limb, vulnerable to being smashed to smithereens. My hope-splashed idealism and trust-infested optimism were brittle. It wasn't that I had sharp edges, but I was a tad touchy. Once after he and I had a major argument during which we both said things we both wished we'd swallowed, he quoted lines of an Art Garfunkel song: "I bruise you; you bruise me; we both bruise so easily."[61]

The emotional connection between us could never be compressed to sex. "If everything can be reduced to a sexual meaning," I said, "then what does sexuality mean?" "Yeah," he responded, "What's the big deal about sex? We're making love all the time."

We were also continually doing alchemy and changing each other from children into lovers and from lovers into grownups. At the end, we discovered that the magic and the tragic were twins or flip sides of the same coin. Our feet really touched the earth then. At least, mine did. For me it was an airplane crash. I wanted to cash in my frequent flyer points with Scandinavian Airlines because I knew that we weren't going to be 'flying united' anymore.

After our breakup, I cried my eyes out. In my diary, I wrote that our love was so great it would never happen again in my life, ever. Doesn't that sound tragic? I also emailed him Duras'[62] words: "Nothing else will happen in my life except this love for you." How's this for a tragic line! "The pain of having lost you is unrelieved, incurable." I wrote that sentence while I was still carrying the torch for him... a year and one-half later.

Honest to God, I was in grief for about two years. What a journey! Mostly he and I had listened to Rock music together. We got into the intensely emotional stuff of an old American singer from the '60s, Roy Orbison. While carrying the torch, I played over and over and over his repertoire of heart-rending ballads and cried and balled and wept each time. Every time I thought my tears were depleted, just thirty seconds of Orbison crooning lines like "You won't be seeing rainbows anymore"[63] had me sobbing again. At last, I was forced to conclude that, no matter how much you cried, there are always more tears. At the same time, I read a novel by Spanidou[64]: "Only the first love tears the heart... the rest come and go and the sooner one knows that, the better." It was time to get on with my life.

It's ironical. Actually it's embarrassing to mention. I told you that with us sex took a back seat to tenderness. But during my deepest darkest grief, I indulged in masturbation. The only thing that could, uh, push me over the brink was fantasizing scenes between him and me. And this was taking place after I started to date other guys. So it was definitely time to move forward.

Finally, I hit upon a metaphor to end it. I dug out his letter with the wonderful sentence, you know, the one that said, "I'll love you for always or forever, whichever comes last." I took a bunch of different colored magic markers and drew X's and O's all over his precious one-line! The sheet looked like a rainbow that had been scrambled by some half-crazed Troll. Then underneath it I wrote, "Which part of forever didn't you understand?" I scratched my signature, stuffed it into an envelope, and mailed it to him. My grief-work, long overdue, was finished.

Why did I have to unload all of this on my new boyfriend? Weren't such disclosures too heavy to dump on a young man all at once? More good questions! Meeting me basically through the lenses of my first love relationship might have sowed seeds of jealousy right from the start. It was by no means the best calling card or the preferred way to introduce myself.

Back then, I said to my best girlfriend, "Let's see if he can handle it! If he can't, I might as well know it now, right?" At the time, it seemed logical. Shouldn't he know from the start that he wasn't the "first?" And that not in any way would he ever be my first? It even seemed wise. You can't re-cycle virginity. I couldn't even claim that I was any longer a psychological virgin. But it's possible that an overkill set-up a boomerang.

When I look back, I think I had an additional agenda too. I kept emphasizing that the contexts for my "firsts" were not cheap or merely impulsive. Maybe I was trying to keep the beauty and the innocence alive to prevent profaning my love. If you think that unconsciously I was keeping alive hopes for a second chance, the following piece of behavior-without-awareness supports your interpretation.

I was ending my mourning during spring semester. For my philosophy course, I wrote an essay on the concept of repetition. I argued, with Kierkegaard as my support, that repeating is not regressive but positive and potentially creative. What, pray tell, do you think I was really writing about? Anyway, probably my words at the time sounded like chants to my boyfriend: First love is dream-laden and heavenly, infinite and mostly mystical. It is idealistic, innocent, and absolutely pure. It is pure gold!

I had another equally loud refrain about my long bouts of "rebounding." I made it plain as the nose on my new boyfriend's face that I had suffered while loving! What I told you before about the tragic is only the half of it. The other half was my long bout of longing, of homesickness, of an ache to return back home. See, when I was in my first love's arms and our chests were touching, it was home. I never had any doubt about it. Thus I spared no adjective in spelling out my old nostalgia: empty, aching, yearning, hollow, half.

My best girlfriend at the time invited me to her psychology course. The professor introduced us to the ancient Persian poet, Rumi, arguably the world's greatest love poet. The professor said that the amazing Sufi has written more eloquently about longing for a lost love than anyone else ever. That pricked my interest! So I bought an English translation of Rumi.

Reading his poetic-mystical gems was like drinking water for my soul. I tried to share it with my boyfriend. Instead of being impressed, he got irritated with me. "I don't like the stuff," he said, "It's too sentimental." So I just kept Rumi to myself and read him so often that I memorized a lot. Funny, I still remember some today:

> *Listen to the story told by the reed,*
> *of being separated.*
> *Since I was cut from the reedbed,*
> *I have made this crying sound.*
> *Anyone apart from someone he loves*
> *understands what I say.*
>
> *Anyone pulled from a source*
> *longs to go back.*[65]

I've forgotten the rest of it. But I do remember lines from another Rumi poem:

> *How does a part of the world leave the world?*
> *How can wetness leave water?*
>
> *Don't try to put out a fire*
> *by throwing on more fire!*
> *Don't wash a wound with blood!*[66]

Probably, this brutal honesty did set up an unreachable standard for my new boyfriend. I guess he construed my first love partner as a permanent rival, a formidable force to be reckoned with, or someone with whom he was always competing. Someone he could never live up to. Could that be the source of his jealousy?

One time when I was raving on and on that I had compared every new guy to my first love and had found each one lacking, he yelled, "I don't want to hear about it anymore!"

I asked him, stunned, "Why not?"

He said, "You were just chasing rainbows and seeking a Paradise Lost. Christ, grow up already!"

It felt like a slap on my face, a gunshot to my living heart. I yelled back, "So what? "Why should it upset you?"

He replied, "How in the hell can I hold a candle to your old flame? You say I'm in first place in your heart, but it feels like I'm playing second fiddle."

I started to defend myself. The next thing you know we're into a big argument. I remember him screaming.

"You don't talk about 'it' like you talk about anything else. You always refer to it as if it were some kind of being in its own right!" Then he screeched something about 'enshrining' it.

The more I tried to defend myself, the angrier he got. We both were shouting nasty things. I accused him of immaturity and stupidity, of preferring to muffle it, of wanting to deny it, or to pretend that it never happened. I spit out words about his "dumb male ego" worrying about who had the bigger "dick" and wondering if he were the better man in bed. Most of it is a blur. I can't remember the sequence or the flow. But it felt ugly. I remember kind of collapsing to the floor because my knees were shaking and rubbery-weak. I couldn't say anything anymore. I sat there, wiping my snots, with the image of a Big Triangle forming right in front of my eyes. He got quiet too.

Finally, I stammered, "With the best of intentions, or so I thought, I hoped that telling you the whole story would shoo away the ghost. Instead, I installed a spook into the heart of our relationship. I'm sorry!" By now, I was boohooing again. I mean I'm sobbing like there is no tomorrow.

He came close and whispered, "You're right. That's what you did. Think about it!" Then he wrapped his arms around me and hugged me tight, you know, a good hard, almost-crack-your-ribs type of bear hug. "I love you," I said. "I love you back," he responded. My chest was heaving. He was crying too. We didn't talk about my first love anymore after that.

Until now!

I thought about that argument, however, a lot. In fairness to myself, I was trying hard to let him know that I had gotten over my pain. By the time I met him, I was beyond it. Scarcely! Only barely did I make it through. But I had healed. Wasn't it an asset that I'd finished my Big Love? Now, I was more ready for love with my feet on the ground. My first love happened. It was everything. It ended. It lingered. Finally, I was over it. The footprints on my memories were fading. They would never be gone, completely, right? "Why fool myself?" I said to myself, repeatedly. "Why fool him?"

In fairness to my boyfriend, my first love would still slither between us in intimate moments. Not every single time, but once in awhile my old flame would flash at my moment of climax. I excused it because of my habit of conjuring up him while masturbating after the break up. I wasn't letting it count. But after this particular argument, I admitted to myself its significance. I had personal work still to do.

The great playwright, Ibsen, says that to write is to sit in judgment on oneself. So I took a page from Norway's master and, deliberately eschewing the word processor, took pen in hand. Ibsen was right. Writing put a mirror to my face. It showed the sorrow in my soul. It was searing. Often while writing it felt like I was juggling razor blades. My dried blood is still sprinkled generously on most sheets of my text. But I discovered that sorrow springs the trap on distorted memories. That's probably why I can easily remember all that I am telling you today.

I wrote that the end of first love is sad in a beautiful way, and that it leaves a gentle melancholy. I wrote that I was never going to hate what I once love before; that I was always going to miss dreaming my dreams with him; that I learned lessons which diamonds and gold can't buy: a heart can be broken and still survive, and that the hollow cut wide and deep in the heart creates more room for love inside. I was on a verbal roll. But those conclusions came only after I put it squarely to myself: "Hey, human, who do you think you are? You thought that your perfect love would never end. You believed that he would be true. When the future exploded in your face, you couldn't handle the intruder in your love-nest. You couldn't cope with the lies and cheating that besmirched the blessedness of your love." I stared into the Void and faced death as real and personal and as mine. The "moment" put me in second place absolutely, not second relative to anything or anyone else but absolutely second.

Clearly, my story is common. I'm not the first woman kicked out of the Garden of Eden holding a love-cocoon destroyed by deceit. Finally, I forgave him. I began to tolerate better my flawed and imperfect way of loving. It hit me! Mature love is not perfect but mixed with life's ambiguities. My lover who is amazing, kind, loving, generous, and honest is also irritating, frustrating, selfish and, under certain circumstances, a liar, a coward, and even unbearably cruel. I could actually accept that my new boyfriend loved me even though I could never be worthy of love.

I though I had erased all my old love's footprints and that my present and future were steeled against his disruption. Hadn't I moved on? "Once you've loved somebody, you always will," I told my sister "If it was 'right' for its time so why not just find a place for it in my heart?"

Every now and then I hear a certain song, especially one of Orbison's, and it all comes back. I'm entitled to a bit of nostalgia, aren't I, and to some sentimentality and tinges of regret? You know, "if only... if only not." But it's resolved. Listen to me! I've accepted that it's over. It feels settled. I've resolved it as well as any flesh-and-blood woman can get it done. The proof is that things between my boyfriend and me have been going well. Our sex-life's gotten better. We're even talking about having a baby.

So what's the problem now? Why did I make this appointment to see you?

Guess who's back in town?

Yep. He phoned me at work. He wants to see me.

What was the impact of his call? You know what 'they' say about getting your heart stuck in your throat? 'They' do say that don't they? Well, there was his voice on the telephone after all these years. I couldn't get any words out because my heart was... well, because in the moment one big heart was all that I was. He was saying, in some language, "Hei, or Hallo! Are you still there? Don't hang up!" How do you say anything while Yesterday is passing your way again? How speak while whirling and caught in a Time Machine... with the years rapidly turning back... with emotions flooding you. I finally said, "I'm really busy right now. Give me you phone number, I'll call you back as soon as I can." He just said, "Promise?" One word; only one, said in a certain way, with a certain tone, in a certain pitch. His voice invaded all of me. If the human heart has a throat, then his one word seized my heart's throat or filled up the heart in my throat or spoke to every single part of me -- what am I saying? I don't know! Me, who always gets easily in touch with her feelings; me, who should have a job labeling feelings, I didn't know what I was feeling! I was dizzy. Obviously, I turned white as a sheet. One of my colleagues joked, "What's wrong? You look like you've just seen a ghost or talked with one!" I blushed profusely. She just looked at me quizzically but had the reserve to excuse her self and make an unnecessary visit to the toilet. But our little exchange snapped me back to reality. The first thing that came to mind, or came out of my heart, was a question: "Does one return always to one's first love?" And weird as it sounds, I remembered a line from a West African adage: "A fire that once had blazed, after being quenched, easily kindles again."

You know how it is when you are caught with your pants down? There is no place to hide. Something like that happened. Because I knew beyond a shadow of a doubt that I always had this question in the back of my mind and it was exactly the one that my new boyfriend had in the back of his: "What am I going to do if "he" ever comes back?"

Who's first?

Analysis of First Love

Two adolescents meet, ready to risk flowing out to each other, ripe to love in a brand new way. Time stops. In a wondering state of freshness, two heretofore egocentric worlds tangle, mesh, and stretch to include each other. Within a radiant dance, a newborn couple rises to newness. Each partner, beckoned beyond self, now draws from down deep. Together, they shine towards the world. Time begins afresh. This is an advent. The two are awakened. Everything is new now, inchoate, fresh and phosphorescent. Their lives, rapt in one another, are galvanized by the wonder of the debut. "We're together alone," they say, "we two against the world." A new egoisme a deux has emerged. It is no mere mundane relationship, their first love, but rather a blessed, mystical union. Ask them, and they will tell you, "Nobody ever has loved as we do... nobody!"

Their nascent love forms an existential platform that sustains their respective pasts and also supports a bridge arching towards an anticipated future. In pristine innocence and amazement, they seek no guarantees beyond their love-cocoon. They are enchanted with each other, enthralled and in thrill. They suffer not at all the disease of doubt. Has not the universe granted them a mystic charm? Seeds will sprout, bud, and ripen because they are watering the ground with magical dewdrops. With a golden wand, they are fashioning a cornerstone upon which to build the rest of their lives. Only they hear and heed the herald who announces softly that everything is possible. "You sigh and the song begins. You speak and I hear violins. It's magic... dreams run to dreams in continuous flight."[67] Like existential alchemists, they introduce each other to the plethora of life's "firsts" and to the awe-full dimension of desire for sensual tenderness. They grasp not with fierce pawing, but reach with hesitant caresses while seeking the haunting absence of the miracle yet to come.

They also appropriate all that is the world's common property without qualms and spontaneously, as if it is their due. Without a touch of arrogance, they crow, "Our song, our poet, our movie, our moon!" Each stakes a claim to the beloved fully, too, and feels reciprocated totally. To the belief in their "us-ness"[68] fiercely they adhere. With little experience to shield them from reality-shocks, however, their trenchant and steadfast grip is mostly a half-blind groping. F. Scott Fitzgerald laces the rapture of first love and its apparent "forever" with ominous hints of its volatility:

> *They were full of brave illusions about each other,*
> *tremendous illusions, so that the communion of self*
> *with self seemed to be on a plane where no other human*
> *relations mattered. They both seemed to have arrived there with*
> *an extraordinary innocence as though a series of pure accidents*
> *had driven them together, so many accidents that at last they*
> *were forced to conclude that they were made for each other. They*
> *had arrived with clean hands, or so it seemed, after no traffic*
> *with the merely curious and clandestine.*[69]

The structural characteristics of first love

My request to participant-subjects is, "Please describe your 'first' or 'big' romantic love."[70] The following categories, showcasing the defining characteristics of first love, are culled from the descriptions which they gave and from the parable.

Absolutes

The relationship is splashed with the sense of being absolute and eternal. "There's nothing I wouldn't do for you." "I love everything about you." "We'll never part." "I can't get enough of you." "Nothing else matters as much as you do." "I'll never love again, I love only you." The boy's poem in "Who's first?" says it beautifully: "I'll love you for always or forever, whichever comes last." With searing truth, Marguerite Duras in *The North China lover* captures the life-lasting force of her first love: "A love... so great that it never happens ever again in life, ever... Nothing else will happen in my life except this love for you."[71]

Uniqueness

First love partners are convinced their bond is not only special but original and unique. "This kind of love has only happened to us." Popular music insists, "They say for every boy and girl there's just one love in this whole world, and I know I've found mine."[72] Or "Only once in a lifetime is par, to find someone rare as you are ...there's one in a million like you."[73] "Their love was great...extraordinary.....the moments when passion visited...like a breath of eternity were moments of revelation, of continually new discoveries about themselves and life."[74] The Latin term, *sui generis*, "one of a kind," captures the experience.

Nietzsche met Lou Andreas-Salome in 1882. She was the only woman whose combination of eroticism and spiritually ever captivated and captured his sensitive soul. In St. Peter's at the Vatican at the first meeting he said: "From what stars have we fallen to meet here?"[75]

Perfection

The relationship is also without taint, flawless and perfect, pure and blessed. It's a generous affaire of the heart. It's heaven on earth. It's divine. It's ecstasy. "You are my one and only, my true love!" "My mystical lover, you are my Angel sent from up above." "Together we're one, divided we're through." Marguerite Duras writes that her first love had "fallen from the hands of God."[76] In Sabina Spielrein's correspondence with Sigmund Freud, she wrote on 12 June 1909 about Carl Jung's importance to her, about his "profoundly sensitive soul" and of her transcendent love for him. She told Professor Freud, with the pristine innocence that hallmarks first love, that she told Jung, "first love has no desires."[77] In contrast to the imperfection and ambiguity of mature adult love, first time love is as close to perfection as possible.

Togetherness

"We are merely wires -- and the circuit is on... I cannot draw a line dividing you and me."[78] The dominant word is "ours." Everything filters through this newborn togetherness. Any event, concert, movie, game in which the world at large partakes is special because it's "ours": "The song we fell in love to and the movie which told our life." "We did everything together. It seemed like we were the only ones in the world living. Everyone else seemed outside." One feels like half of a whole without the other. If parents or peers should see one party alone, they ask, "Where's your other half?" The couple creates a love-cocoon within which their most important self-validating needs-desires are gratified and satisfied. The cocoon is a haven. It protects the fledgling and delicate relationship from external, disturbing, or intrusive influences. From one angle, nourishment from within strengthens the relationship. But from another slant, the togetherness so veers toward exclusiveness that it unwittingly sows seeds of potential over-dependence and possessiveness. "Wanting only you is my life now," he said and meant it. No surprise, a precipitous or poorly handled ending ushers in an inherently homicidal-suicidal stance.

Idealism

Unmixed with the ambiguities of adulthood and unalloyed by the practical work-a-day world, the love emerges as an oasis wherein the youngsters can postpone facing the stark indifference of the world. First love is dream laden and devoted with a sharp accent on openness, wonder, and possibility. Two images of rampant idealism include the perfect spot of Camelot and Don Quixote's "impossible dream." Happening on the innocent side of life, the love-bond is full of respect and sacrifice. Idealism modulates the partners' sexuality. Sexual expression, but not necessarily sexual performance, takes place. Even if genital behavior does transpire, it is incidental not essential, as the woman in "Who's first?" takes pains to clarify. The relationship qua relationship is central. "I had her on a pedestal and respected her too much to soil or defile." "An absence of flirtation marked our relationship. Our unspoken intention was to share and communicate with a whole person, not only with a sexual other." "We never profaned our love. Even our physical touches felt sacred." "They'll ruin us if we let them. If they think we go to bed together, let them even though we don't; it's their filthy minds and decayed lives, not ours… We did go to bed together once. We played music of the *Doors* all night and lay in bed half-naked, kind of feeling around at each other, too awed to do anything more. It was exquisite."

Communication

Communication is cardinal. Interaction is not turning out the lights and getting physical. The partners share everything. They cannot wait to communicate. The speaking eyes blend with and yield to the spoken word. The two always have something to say to each other, especially words about feelings, thoughts, and plans.

During modernity, it was the telephone call that concretely symbolized the need for continuing contact. Parents would express amazement that as soon as their darling child would enter the house after having spent several hours with her boyfriend, immediately she had to make one more phone call to utter a new insight which flashed in the interval between the goodnight kiss and the present moment. Nowadays, the mobile or cell phone, with its capacity for SMS is a zillion dollar industry supported in large part by youth who pour their allowance, meager or large, into their phones. They must stay constantly "in touch."

In the same way as preadolescent chums, the first love partners cultivate a common ground and carve out a common language. They do more than just interact; they commune. The original and nascent acts of undressing each other's mind occur in love letters, in poetry, in words which trustingly trickle off the lips: risk-talk. Each learns the pristine lessons of what it means to be vulnerable to the other-gendered person.

Emotional connection

The communication that flows and unveils is heartfelt. It is not sufficient to say that the partners experience core emotions. Their relationship is the veritable crucible in which the birth of unprecedented emotions occurs. "With her, I came to explore my new depths. She called up feelings I needed to explore from places that I hadn't visited before." One begins to enjoy and suffer through emotions that she had only read about in novels or witnessed on the Silver Screen. Hitherto unknown or unexpressed feelings emerge: of possessiveness and jealousy; of deep thrill and tenderness; of responsibility which makes you cry; of pain in loving; of astonishingly discovering that pain can be lived with, gotten over with in time, and that it softens us, makes us kinder and more sympathetic. Not unlike the chums, the first-love partners unlock the doors for each other to the beautiful experiences of empathy, generosity and reciprocity.

Reciprocal involvement

Reciprocity is incipient and rudimentary in one's tender years. Nevertheless, the first love partners live the give-and-take which is so vital to loving. The accent is not merely on the "togetherness," but upon the ebb and flow of the hyphenated I-Thou. In the speaking-listening dialectic, not only are two separate worlds revealed, but "our world" is created. "He lived always with her image before him. Without her, he was his old self. That old self wasn't him anymore. He was now the one who was in love with her and shared as much with her as possible. From her and with her, he learned how to share a life."

Pervasive presence of the beloved

For the first love partner, the beloved is everywhere. "I am never alone. My love is with me at every moment whether or not physically present." "He is with me in spirit even if he isn't at my side." Like unto the chum relationship, the reality of the relationship does not depend upon manifest expression. It transcends actual or sentient presence. The absence of the other is a form of presence.

Orientation to the future

A sharp appetite for the future develops. The partners begin to imagine, plan for, and at times actually build a common future. In meeting the other's family and seeing the other's place within that family, each comes to understand a history which is separate and unique from one's own. It lays the foundation both for understanding better the other as other and for planning a possible future. Motherhood and fatherhood emerge as concrete possibilities and not just general abstract notions. The partners share dreams and fantasies about the home they would build, the family they would raise, the careers they would pursue, and the ways in which they might deepen their bond. They are at the first stage of understanding the gravity and the beauty of adult commitment.

Consistency with one's roots

The first special someone with whom we envision our future is apt to be a person compatible with our roots and consistent with our family background in terms of central values, basic attitudes and orientation to life. Often, that will include being of the same race, color or creed. Most likely, your mom and dad welcomed your partner into their home, approved your relationship, and even blessed your future plans. Not infrequently, a special bond develops between the individual and the parents of his or her counterpart. A fondness grows between them such that they greet each other with the endearing terms, "mom" or "dad", "son" or "daughter."

The upbuilding results of first love

Coming out

Voiced or unspoken, certain questions haunt us as long as we feel unseasoned and unsure about our ability to love. "Into what kind of man am I growing?" "Will I be capable of truly loving another? Or will I only selfishly care that another might love me?" The answers can only be discovered within an intense and protracted relationship. The tremendous advantage of dwelling within the orbit of first love is that the experience calls me out of myself. The relationship is the nestling ground within which blossoms the emergent style of my unique manhood or womanhood. "Until him, I felt in soft focus waiting for someone to come along to sharpen the image and to draw me out. Suddenly, I found myself evolving into a woman." "Before we met, I felt lonely and not as big as the other guys. I remember riding my bicycle over and over around the block, strangely tangled up inside and languishing in the doldrums. Then she softly but forcefully said, 'Come to me.' By responding, I found my vitality." "My father had the habit of telling me that I was still green and wet behind the ears. But she called me by name and I ceased being raw." The first love couple comprises an authentic psycho-spiritual debutant or debutante.

Informing presence

My first love not only calls me out but also informs me and shapes my nascent sense of self. A movement occurs from nebulous confusion to a sense of direction: "She set standards which challenged me. Or rather, life itself through our relationship tested my strength and courage. I struggled. Then I began to believe in myself." "Suddenly, I didn't feel like a backward, shy, plump tomboy anymore. It was the first time that I had been singled out as desirable. I discovered my own beauty and value." "I doubted that I was an attractive person. No one except my parents had ever told me so. Incredibly, I had won this beauty by being gentle, understanding, and caring." Ultimately, the first love that catalyzes my life becomes a foundational referent, influentially powerful and long lasting.

Orienting presence

The relationship orients me spatially and temporally and grants a sense of structure that replaces feeling rudderless and bewildered: "Before I met him, my life felt like many mismatched pieces of a jigsaw puzzle strewn over the floor. Nothing seemed to fit together properly. I was frustrated, befuddled, and mostly lonely. He somehow put into focus a horizon of possibilities, expectations, anticipations, and promises." "During physical education, I would walk on my hands around the gym. That's how topsy-turvy my world seemed then. Somehow, my world stabilized by the way she would press back when kissing me goodnight. For the first time, I could see a pattern to life." The French word *sens*, which means both "meaning" and "direction," splendidly expresses first love as an orienting or alchemizing presence.

The painful side of first love

Within the ambit of first love, we grow psycho-spiritually by dealing with pain. Hard but valuable lessons learned about relating include the need to give up infantile illusions about boundless love and the realization that everything is not under your control or on your own terms. If the neophyte love is to grow into a solidly steadfast bond strong enough to support a long-term future, then this painful shift from a self-centered to another-centered orientation must occur and persist.

The experience of loss within married first love

More than a few first love couples do marry. For them the painful crisis happens at various points. It looms whenever the magical beginning wears toward the imperfect edge of everyday life. Either or both have to face aloneness or find their own bearings. Take the situation in which a young couple has to square their idealistic vision with a cold, hard fact of a still-born son. Or suppose they have to deal with the loss of innocence in the shape of an extra-marital affair, drug addiction, or a suicide attempt. The couple with the resiliency to face the pain of disillusionment, disappointment, and disenchantment can deepen their bond and parlay its special quality into a greater intimacy. Pain, however, that is not endured plagues the relationship with bitterness, cynicism, cruelty, indifference, or despair. A popular alternative is divorce.

The loss at the breakup of the first love relationship

For those relationships which do not lead to marriage, a break-up occurs. Marguerite Duras sets the tone for all endings of the relationship when she refers to "the wild happiness of first love and the unrelieved, incurable pain of having lost it."[79] The more truly reciprocal the relationship, the more it is a mutual loss and a genuine death experience for both parties. It requires "grief-work" through the same dynamic-structural issues which Freud clarifies about mourning and melancholia in the face of any death.[80] If the relationship is one of balanced reciprocal desire, then it is as painfully grief-laden for the one who must end the relationship as for the one who feels rejected, in common parlance "dropped" or "burned." For the one who could not foresee the ending, the break-up comes as a cruel, precipitous shock leaving in its wake a gaping hole and a myriad of unanswered questions: "Why did she all of a sudden stop loving me?" "What did I do that was so wrong?" "Did I abuse the privilege of loving him?" The one who lives seemingly endlessly with rehearsed words of parting carries the painful burden of knowing he will hurt that precious other, the one whom he had tamed and who has tamed him. Pained, the instigator says about ending "it": "What kind of a person am I? How can I hurt him?" "What is wrong with my capacity to love? Why can't I deliver my promise of everlasting?" "Am I making a terrible mistake?"

The breakup of unbalanced first loves

The ending is no little thing. It must be taken seriously by involved adults. This is not teenage, "puppy," or "calf" love. This is the youngster's first broken heart. It is devastating. The demise of an unbalanced relationship particularly crushes the weaker, more needy, or over-dependent partner. Instead of the dynamics of grief-work, desperate reactions follow: the "slump" of lost interest in school work, extracurricular activities, family relations, and peer interactions. More serious outcomes are common: depression, physical illness, anorexia nervosa, suicide attempts and schizoid episodes.

Postponement of the grief labor

First love cannot remain evergreen forever. It is never easy to suffer the loss of a love that cradles so many hopes, promises, images, ideals, and dreams. How cope? Here are typical ways of evading the hurt and pain by putting off the grief.

Parrying the loss

One way to postpone the grief work is to ward off admitting that the relationship has changed: spoiled by the dimming of its vital spark; eroded by jealousy or possessive smothering; choked in the rarified atmosphere of dwelling on a pedestal. Some refuse to see the changes, whereas others delay the act of separation: "I'll put it off until tomorrow." "Someday I'll end this. I've got lots of time. I live one day at a time."

Someday I'll leave her, but I'm not ready yet." The parrying often is rooted in special significances known to the person alone. Suppose the young girl has "lost" her virginity to her first love partner. She might feel that she "has" to marry him even though the relationship has gone stale. Her counterpart, knowing that he "took" her virginity, might feel that he cannot discard her as "spoiled goods." Or maybe tucked within one of the conflicts between desire and duty, the couple had muddled through an abortion. The line is always fine, permeable and thin between the evasion of a genuine existential death of the "real thing" and the eschewal of a narcissistic wound at the conclusion of a magnificent obsession.

External circumstances also contribute to procrastinating about the ending. Of foremost importance is family involvement. The pressure is strong to stay in the relationship so that you do not have to lessen the many binding ties between both families. "I worked in a convenience store," one young woman reports. "Everyday his mother would stop for some small item. I always called her 'Mom' as she passed a moment while bagging her milk. How would I address her now?"

Carrying the torch

Remaining "hung up" on one's "old-flame" after an actual parting also avoids the grief work. Carrying the torch seeks a duplication of the first love in any subsequent relationship, attempting to recapture its magic. While carrying it, one compares constantly new partners with that special someone. The act, therefore, exemplifies Jean-Paul Sartre's "good faith-bad faith dialectic."[81] One accepts the ending in fact, but leaves its meaning obscure and unresolved.

The most prevalent condition which makes it possible to carry the torch is when the love appears pure and good until the end. Stunned by an unsuspected loss, we are left saddled to good memories with nothing to fault or regret except the ending itself. A touch of pleading poetry says, "If you can't undo the wrong, undo the right!" Until we personally assume responsibility for the undoing, we keep seeking the duplicate. Sometimes, the search takes the form of finding someone with whom we can work out our process about the issue so that we might finally finish our first love. At other times, we keep chasing a paradise lost and setting ourselves up for repeated disappointment, in the process treating new partners unfairly for not being true echoes or traces. Still again, we may carry the torch into a marriage haunted by questions. If we do not know what we would do if our old love returned and wanted us back, then our doubts orchestrate feelings of jealousy. Our new love or spouse feels the futility of trying to compete with a live ghost. 'Who's First?' depicts graphically and thoroughly this drama.

When Death pays a visit

The most touching stories about the impossibility of tarnishing the love are those of young people who, at the high noon of their first love, suffer the loss of their partner to physical death. The other is absent in body but remembered as perfect. It is easy to carry the torch; it is difficult to resist the temptation to enshrine one's lost love.

In Alexander Solzhenitsyn's classic, *Cancer ward*, Vera is just a schoolgirl when her soldier boy is slaughtered on the battlefield. "He was dead but his star burned, it kept burning... But its light was wasted."[82] She devotes her life to medicine. "Fancy remembering a dead man instead of looking for someone who was alive!"[83] She went about

> *like someone in a permanent gas mask... There was a great*
> *satisfaction in remaining faithful; perhaps it is the greatest*
> *satisfaction of all. Even if no one knows about your faithfulness,*
> *even if no one values it... He... remained a young boy with*
> *unclouded, vulnerable eyes.*[84]

Fancy?! Ah, easy to fancy...

Anais Nin describes love's chord as a weave of death and myth that resists breaking, "...the corpse of our human love is illuminated and kept alive by our first illusion, and one is uneasy at burying it, doubting its death. Will it rise again and remain a part of our life forever."[85] She understands the act of writing, specifically the "alchemy of fiction," as the necessary "act of embalming" that will restore meaning.[86] Adrienne Rich also wants to restore whatever is lost, forgotten, or unexplored. Because the existential event that prompts her act of reclamation was her husband's suicide, fittingly she writes a poem entitled "Diving into the wreck."[87]

> *I came to explore the wreck*
> *The words are purposes*
> *The words are maps*
> *I came to see the damage that was done*
> *and the treasures that prevail*
> *the thing I came for:*
> *the wreck and not the story of the wreck*
> *the thing itself and not the myth*[88]

Age has no special privilege or burden. Who can fathom the mystery of the death of love? Or understand those who are so in love with love-and-death that they prefer to die when they lose it?[89]

On the rebound

Not all first loves end still looking "solid gold." To get our bearings after being manipulated deceived, exploited, or betrayed, we rebound. The three styles of rebounding are: withdrawal; playing the tyrant; and playing the victim. While we rebound in either way, rarely are we fully conscious of what we are doing or its impact on the other. It is an exercise in self-deception which is always simultaneously deception of the other (Sartre's good faith-bad faith dialectic again). We know what we are doing, but we do not let ourselves be cognizant of why or what it means.

Withdrawal

An ending that tears into our trust provokes reserve. The cliché applies: "Once burnt, twice shy." "After you, when someone smiles at me I'll wonder what's the price. After you, I'll be suspicious of anyone that's nice." The end of a destructive first love is a "natural" time in life to be paranoid: careful not to become too vulnerable; cautious not to commit too soon.

Playing the tyrant

In bitterness and with vindictive revenge, we act out on our new partner the same "games" played on us. Steeled against another pain, we trifle, tease, or punish the new other for our old hurts. "What did I do to deserve that?" my new partner complains. "Who are you really interacting with? It's not me, that's for sure?"

Remaining victim

By seeking someone who will hurt us in an old familiar way, our rebound repeats a pattern. We find someone who feeds us the same lines so that we can fall again; someone who toys with us like a puppet on a string so that we can play the fool once more; someone who cooperates in making love another bridge to burn.

Psychological Reflections

What calls out first love? Nobody would sensibly claim that it is biologically determined or socially constructed. How do we account for it? Is it just a fluke, a sheer accident? It is ordained by some divine power, as individuals with a strong religious belief might argue? Throughout this book, I attempt to understand phenomena not explain them. The most fruitful question about first love is to pinpoint the prime time of readiness for it to occur. That "moment" I call the "ontological revolution."

The ontological revolution[90]

First love and the ontological revolution are dialectically related. Dialectical means there is no cause-effect relationship between the two occurrences, but still the two are mutually implicated and influence each other. Under the power of first love, the individual is open or ready for this particular revolution. If one is going through the revolution (writing poetry or songs, keep a diary as a vehicle of self-expression, or committing herself to causes), she is ripe to fall in love in a particular way and primed for the carnival of affections and the kaleidoscope of images with which first love teams.

What precisely do I mean by this ontological phrase? Adolescence is a four-fold radical revolution in human life. Radical means at the roots; a revolution turns 180 degrees. Mainstream social science focuses on and elaborates only three phase of the total change: 1) the bio-physical revolution, in which the growth spurt leading to puberty is salient; 2) the psychological revolution which focuses upon the crisis of identity; and 3) the social-cultural revolution, the "coming of age' within a peculiar historical period and specific culture (which may or may not grant ceremonial recognition of adult status with the successful negotiation of ceremonial puberty rites). However, from an existential standpoint there is another phase of the revolution. Adolescence is not just the emergence of blossoming pubic hairs or the addition a few inches of bust line; not just shedding one's childhood identity or assuming a new social role. It is also a change in existence. Adolescence is a total change in one's being.[91] The growing youngster ascends beyond the dependent level of the child, beyond the technical-functional level of the juvenile to the specifically personal level of existence. She becomes a self in the strictest sense of the term, cognizant of her psychic reality as the source of dreams, desires, fantasies, intuitions, and feelings. She is also aware of being a unique individual. Henceforth, this personal self will feel both "apart of" but also "a-part from" one's family of origin. Twinborn with the awakening of the personal self is a sense of primordial wonder and a multidimensional openness to the world at large. It is a three-dimensional experience with the movement running and expanding vertically, horizontally, and in depth. One has the abiding sense that there is "more" to life. Vision and insight erupt to evoke a poignant awareness of the One, the Good, the True, the Beautiful, the Magic, and the Tragic. At this level, the youngster gains the intuition of the possibilities of peace on earth and of brotherhood-sisterhood of humankind. He becomes preoccupied with such self-introspective acts as keeping a private diary or writing poetry. Intellectual wonder and emotional empathy blend such that I take the other inside of me and feel for him. Geopolitical matters of justice and horror grip the soul of the individual, realities such as the widening gap between the rich and the poor, the swirling cycles of revenge, genocide, and the hypocritical language of "market economy," "extraordinary extradition," "friendly fire" and "collateral damage."

The correlate of this shifting orientation is cognitive development. Just as the chum relationship and the development of pre-operational thing are twinborn, so too are first love and the developmental of formal operational thought.[92] The youngster is now capable of the highest levels of abstraction of logical thought, of espousing the most sophisticated concepts of justice, and of embracing the most mature forms of love. Too far, and too high, and too deep are not enough. Of course, these highest levels of possibility are not always concretely actualized and often not sustained. Many of us sell ourselves short on one or another count. Or we sell out to collectivized norms or the expectations of some individual or the "Club" we aspire to belong to. Nevertheless, a possibility, once posited, can be realized in an eye-blink. To repeat, nobody is permanently lost or permanently saved.

Until the ontological revolution, the growing youngster is subsumed within the network of three distinct, overlapping rings: family, peer group, and adult authorities (teachers, coaches. clergy, scout masters, ballet instructors, soccer coaches, etc.). In Kierkegaard's vocabulary, the human person is a "synthesis of psyche and body sustained by spirit."[93] Before this ontological "moment," both the spirit and sexuality are present first as "dreaming" (infant and child) and then as "seeking" (juvenile). Now, both spirituality and sexuality are present or "posited" in fullness as "desiring." The adolescent, aware of his unique selfhood, ceases to be a "satellite" to the threefold network of relationships. The ontological revolution is the point in life of turning away from infantile dependence and collective fusion, beyond juvenile, preadolescent and puberty-age skillful independence, and thence unto full selfhood on the way to mature dependence in intimacy.

It comes as no surprise that the romanticized and sensually awakened adolescent is flooded with optimism and idealism. The adolescent now craves something to believe in. Erik Erikson[94] names this new experiential demand "fidelity." The need to be faithful or loyal grips the nascent self. At this ontological level, the young person manifests a keen sense of loyalty to a cause outside of self, especially to one presented as transcendent.

In terms of the theme of relationships, these ideas provoke views about love that run counter to the mainstream. What are the most significant drives concerning love? The confluence of the need for

strongly or often enough: there is nothing inevitable about the eruption into life of existential happenings or relational events. Our genes or chromosomes are not programmed to evoke them. They are not necessary, not automatic, not caused. But they are not accidental either. There is a rhyme and reason to their emergence. We can comprehend what factors made the individual ripe even raw by examining the context within which they are embedded.

As a phenomenon possibly appearing first in the mid-teen years, first love warrants serious study. Like the chum relationship, it is consistent with our roots and yet it rivals in force and meaning the influence upon us of our primary childhood identification-figures. Just as in the case of our basic childhood anchors, we do not outgrow or change with the simple passage of chronological time values-attitudes nurtured within first love's cradle. They are essential to the man or woman we have become. The relationship, therefore, is not simply a memory to dredge up nostalgically, chuckle about lightly, and then dismiss preemptively. The parable, "Who's first?" attests to its tenacious and lingering hold. Neither does sheer calendar time ease memories of either unprecedented wonder or pain. Without those memories, we would become suddenly empty. The song nominated to express the theme of the extraordinarily persistent nostalgia about first love is "Not fade away."

The color of first love

In describing their first love, participant-subjects randomly mention its color. Over the years, I have put the question to groups in which the relationship had been the theme: "If we do 'word-play', what shade would you use to color first love?" Individuals would respond. I would ask the reason for the appropriateness of the shade. First love is white because it is innocent and pure; it is green because it is new and fresh; pink because it is alive and vibrant; yellow because it is bright and cheerful; blue because it is like the sky and includes a touch of melancholy; lavender because it is sad in a beautiful way; grey to characterize grief at its end. One afternoon, as the rest of the group was slicing the rainbow into its happiest shades, one guy said: "My first love was black!" And then he told the tale of her deception and of his agony. And the color of your first love is...?

The investigation's experiential touchstone

The "moment" is etched on my consciousness. The girl was nineteen. She had now spent three years in a psychiatric hospital in the Greater Pittsburgh area. I was her third psychologist. When she was sixteen years old, she fell in love for the first time. He was everything; he was her life. Without a word, he left her. He sailed back to Spain, his home, and never made contact again. It broke her heart. She went into a slump. Her mother, who I interpret as always wanting an excuse for it, trucked her to a psychiatrist. Gretchen wasn't going to school, or eating, or talking with anyone. Even though she was not pregnant, momma insisted she was. Momma had gotten pregnant with Gretchen when she was sixteen years old; the father abandoned them both. I have a sneaky suspicion, never confirmed, that the same thing happened with grandma-ma, the matriarch who held the purse strings and all the power in this family of these three females. R.D. Laing's "knots"[101] laced and bound their lives in all ways imaginable.

At her first visit, Gretchen said the doctor asked: "What's wrong with you, my dear girl?" He had confirmed that there was no pregnancy and no virginity either. She answered: "I have a broken heart. My boyfriend left me." Gretchen said that he said, "Oh, it must be something more serious than that!" Gretchen said she said to her self, "My God, what's wrong with me? I thought I knew what's wrong with me. I thought my heart was sick. What's wrong with me?" Within a few weeks, 'they' admitted her to a psychiatric hospital with a schizophrenic break.

It matters not whether the physician actually said those dense words, and it is doubtful that the medical profession will even admit that love gone bad can trigger a major psychic disturbance. What matters is to take young love seriously. When you are sixteen and in love, nothing can possibly be more serious than your relationship. Whatever other personal roots I had to tap in order to understand first love, this experience was my immediate spur. Not only would I never make light of it when a person had a story to tell, I would labor to learn the whole story. You have just read as much of it as I have gathered.

CHAPTER 3

The Outlaw Relationship[102]

"Guess who's coming to dinner?" Do opposites attract? Do we only want what we can't have? Do we prefer love on the sly? These questions cease being hackneyed as soon as one meets the forbidden one, one's "tall dark stranger" or "outlaw chick." Lo and behold, this "hunk" or "beauty" is the very one your parents always warned you to stay away from. Still, you experience a "sudden rush of a threat out of nowhere." Something strange is happening, very strange!

The Outlaw is the significant stranger who brings a world totally different from yours, one at odds with your roots. She or he also presents powerfully sexual possibilities and challenges. The combinations are endless: black-white, Chinese-American, Serbian-Croatian, Japanese-Canadian, Muslim-Hindu, Sunni-Shiite, and Arab-Jew; or older woman-younger man, younger woman-older man, catholic priest-parishioner, or one or both parties are already married, or living together, or in a committed relationship.

If first love is white, green, yellow, or pink, then color the outlaw scarlet, purple or crimson. Sexuality and spirituality ram into each other; promise and danger jostle. You cope with a person so different from you and yet seemingly always known. Some say, "You are playing with fire." You feel you were hit by lightening. The confrontation makes you question all you have taken for granted about yourself and your background. The relationship challenges the meaning of who you are; the inevitable clarification of values shows the difference between what you preach and what you will practice. Being with her is sometimes "heaven" and sometimes "hell." When the differences begin to grate, and grate deeply, the ending can be bitter and destructive. Self-definition happens, however, constituting a major milestone while we spiral towards adulthood and reach towards maturity. I will never be the same after meeting my outlaw.

Let Enter the Stranger

"Beware of the tall, dark stranger, if he comes riding into your town. A tall, dark stranger is danger. So don't let no stranger come around."[103] Buck Owens

Do opposites attract each other? Is there such a thing as a "sudden rush of a threat out of nowhere"? Is it true that "ladies love outlaws?" Is forbidden fruit the sweetest? I used to think such questions about love were ridiculous until I met the man I hungered for and hankered after, black and forbidden.

It was wild. It was totally crazy! It was pure unadulterated madness. Only a collision of two worlds could have created it. I couldn't believe what was happening to me. I don't know how many times I said under my breath, "Girl, you are 'beside' yourself!" It did not seem possible that it was I who was living through this relationship. Yet in most ways, I seemed more me than ever, either before or since.

While under his sway, I wasn't acting "in character." Both my mother and my chum kept preaching at me, "You're not being yourself!" "Stay away from him." "He's not your kind." "You've gone too far head-over-heels! "You are playing with fire, and you're gonna get burned." Time after time, my mom kept repeating -- as if she hadn't said it in the first place -- "You've got it 'bad' honey, and that's no good!" But I wasn't listening. Even though by then I had felt the danger crawling, nevertheless the more they criticized him and warned me and pleaded with me, the more stoically I defended him. Maybe they should have "let it be" to let the fire burn itself out.

He's African and older. On top of those two "handicaps," he's divorced with two pre-teenage daughters living back in his village of birth in Ghana. I never really grasped the depths of my family's prejudice until I said, "Guess who's coming to dinner?" Well, I didn't actually say that! The whole situation for me was unnerving enough. Even though our relationship lasted slightly more than two years, I had the presence of mind never to bring him home for a meal. That tells a lot all by itself. I knew he wouldn't be welcome, truly welcome. So why put him through a charade of politeness? Why put them through it either?

While growing up, at some level I must have absorbed by osmosis their racist views. Otherwise why was I attracted to him in the first place? I've had to look real hard at the possibility that I might have been rebelling unconsciously against my upbringing. Of course, that idea sucks. I'd like to believe that it more real than that. Ever since this happened, I've been wondering "How does a passionate bond start?" "Who attracts whom?" "On what is attraction based?" Sometimes, I think that the attraction is just there. Who can explain it? You meet a person and both feel the spark. Body chemistry or animal magnetism, the heat of a touch, and the light in the eyes! You feel the lure involuntarily without thinking about it. Before you can reflect upon it, you're already hooked. That's the way it happened to me. When our eyes locked the first time, his gaze penetrated me and I shuddered. Then I blushed. A magic floated in the air. A totally unfamiliar sexual atmosphere enveloped me.

Do you see why I'm calling him my outlaw? He was different. I had never met anyone like him. He scrambled all my ideas about the male species. Oh, I can tell from the look on your face what you must be thinking: "How ordinary! All lovers think they are unique." But listen. He was larger than life to me. And he was untamed. That's the weird part. He was incredibly off-the-wall and unpredictable, and yet I felt I knew him and that I had always known him and that I couldn't remember when I didn't know him. He was my familiar stranger. Our bond seemed too good to be true. And you know what 'they' say, "If it seems too good, it probably isn't!"

Did I say he was my forbidden one? It was more. He was my ultimate temptation. My life went topsy-turvy after he got into my system. The way he saw the world amazed me, flabbergasted me, shocked me, and scandalized me. I run out of words trying to describe it. He was outside of my normal frame of reference, outside of my law of living. He just saw society 180 degrees differently from the way I had been taught about it. But while we were "getting it on" together, I borrowed his sight, even though his lenses changed my perception of everything imaginable, everything from heaven to hell. Quite frankly, at the time I didn't know which was which. Sometimes, I felt that I was dreaming of heaven but living in hell. Because the deep pleasure we shared was... well, it was always... precarious. Stark fear came creeping into the most blissful moments. But I was "mad" about him, you know, swept away mad. I was angry with him too, complaining constantly, "Why does it feel between us all the time that we are on the edge?" I still don't know what I really meant by that. But it was so extremely intense between us that we seemed always to be straddling the borderline. Sometimes, I felt ever so close to going insane. Like everything was going to bottom-out at any moment. But God, it was never humdrum or boring and most of the time I loved it. Crazy eh!

Until today, I still don't see the world the way my family and friends do. But I don't say much about it. I just get this ache inside. Sometimes, when some story breaks on the news and I hear my family discussing it, I just...well...I bite my tongue. No point in repeating a useless senseless argument about matters like racism, the politics of oil, or dropping bombs on some already troubled country. I can't even talk about the banality of mass popular culture without an argument ensuing. Uh...and, well, sometimes I see a new film, or hear an old song, and a tear comes to my eye. Certain close people, like my husband and older sister, understand where the emotion is coming from. But they don't say anything either. As the saying goes, we just "let sleeping dogs lie."

God, even saying that reminds me of him. In reaction to my "bad habit" of using everyday common phrases instead of expressing my own ideas, after awhile he started to go ballistic whenever I would mouth one of those old clichés, the ones that my mom uses all the time to cover any and all situations. Like, "Absence makes the heart grow fonder" or "Out of sight, out of mind." Right, mom, simple! Just depends upon the context. Or upon who is absent.

You ask why I did it, yield to the pull of unfamiliar ways and then keep doing it. Lyrics from an old Waylon Jennings song nail it perfectly: "The devil made me do it the first time; the second time I did it on my own."[104] I used to call him my "dark wizard" my "devil-man" or "my demon in disguise." I still think of him that way. As far as taking responsibility for it, God knows I did take the handle into my own hands. I swallowed everything, hook, line and sinker and swallowed often. There is no denying that.

After our second kiss, it took on a life of its own. I got sucked into a whirlpool or vortex that tossed me helplessly spinning out of control. It was so physical. I mean it was intensely sexual, sexual in ways beyond my wildest dreams. Until him, I had always wondered what the big deal was about sex. With him, I couldn't imagine there was anything grander. The lines of an old song kept cascading in my noggin, as if they were written specifically for me: "I want to know where love is; I want you to show me."

Every time we kissed, I thought to myself "These lips are strange, and they will be always. So why do they feel so familiar?" Talk about kissing! That's how it started. I met him at a social gathering at my church. Go ahead laugh, if you think it's funny. But things like this do happen, you know. Anyway, he asked me to go outside with him. I forget now the pretext. I already mentioned experiencing a threat rushing at me pell-mell from out of the blue. As soon as we got outside the door of the hall, he touched my shoulder. To my own shock, I spun to face him. The first kiss was shy. The second was the sort that innocent me could never possibly have imagined. After we opened our eyes and stared at one another, it was all over for me. Everything was different and always would be. From a kiss like that there is no going back. If you've never experienced it, I don't know how else to communicate it. It was lethal. It transformed my life.

But it wasn't just his kiss. The way he looked at me was just as voraciously tender as the way he used his lips and his hands. I never could believe that he only had two lips. And there is no way you are ever going to convince me that he had only two hands. Whenever we were lying naked and touching each other, it felt like it must be an octopus caressing me. I loved it, craved it; couldn't get enough of it; never experienced anything like it since; don't ever expect to either.

What else can I say? Without a relationship like this, how was I going to ripen? He noticed very quickly that I was incredibly innocent, "green as grass" as the saying goes. The first time that he called himself my personal "Ripe Banana-Man," I blushed profusely. But I sure wasn't going to learn to enjoy my sexuality by reading the Bible or by attending philosophy lectures. No. We mingled flesh, his seasoned and mine raw. I learned to inhabit my body. Did I ever!

Honestly, it was as much spiritual as sexual. With him, I was forced to throw away all the boxes that separate the body from the soul. His eyes, voice, and touch were more than simply physical. Especially his eyes! Especially his touch! Or what was especially special? To me, even the hairs on his arm were more than just hairs. I lived for the taste of his lips, for the smell of him, and for everything.

Once, I said to him while we were kissing, "You take my breath away." He answered, "No. I'm giving you breath. Catch it first. Then just breathe." See what I mean? Every time I was expecting pure lust, he gave me something more. The really strange part is that I knew that I was giving him more than he ever got from a female, too. I wasn't sure exactly what I gave him that was rare, but it mattered to me and mattered fiercely.

My best girlfriend eventually appreciated our extraordinary drama, although at first she had been terrified for me. And then she wrote me a Haiku:

> *She is innocent*
> *Her eyes are full of wonder*
> *Soon, she will not see.*[105]

Can't you see that I gained greatly from my dizzy spin in the vortex? While dealing with the desperation of it, I stopped soaking in others' expectations of me. My outlaw ordeal plucked me off the "barbed-wire fence"[106] of my adolescence, steered me in a new direction, and then twisted my world upside down. Only slowly, did it begin to turn back again. From the very start, I was disturbed by the trouble he signaled. But I was so pregnant with the rich promise he offered that I spent a lot of time worrying about getting pregnant. Sounds silly, but it's true. The dangers that I could never exactly put my fingers on loomed always. I was afraid that I was losing everything: my family, friends, values and morals. I was afraid that I was losing myself.

He was out of line with everything I stood for. I know, I know, I sound repetitious. Be patient with me. Because honest, there were split seconds when he looked to me totally unfamiliar, alien almost, as though he had come from another planet. In most ways, he did. Still, he got into my bloodstream so thoroughly that, as I said before, I couldn't remember the time when I didn't know him. The phrases that 'they' use to describe such things sure do fit. Like getting "on the same wavelength" or being "kindred spirits." I must be sounding more and more banal. Pretty soon you probably think I'm going to break out into some sweet sentimental song: "Some enchanted evening," or, "Once in a daydream I stood on a hill, and a stranger came close and touched me."[107]

Sometimes, I wondered if he was just some figment of my imagination. I might just as well come out and say it. I used to pinch myself to see if "it" was real and to feel if I were still real. Or still alive in the way I used to be alive. I had become alive in a different way. I was befuddled too. Was he just someone I had conjured up to fill needs that I didn't even know I had until he came? Like satisfying my sexual desires, spiritual longings, emotional needs, and intellectual yearnings? Was he just my ultimate outrageous fantasy or my invention of a man with whom I could act out my most extreme protests? Was he my confederate helping me to conduct my own private revolution? While he and I were exploding at one another, I did all that and more. I repudiated what I didn't disavow and rejected what I didn't deny. And ain't that a mouthful?

When I first laid eyes on him, I wasn't looking for anybody. Consciously, I was in a self-imposed "time-out" from guys. At the time, I needed a moratorium. After my first boyfriend broke my heart, I was suspicious of any male who smiled at me. That's a horse of a different color, that is, the tale of pain and glory of my first "Big" love! Remind me to tell you it someday.

Anyway, lots of guys flirted with me back then because I wasn't that bad looking. But instead of catching smiles, all I saw flashing were sharp pearly white shark's teeth! I swear to God! Instantly, I'd visualize the picture on the video box of the movie *Jaws*, that old Hollywood flick that I walked out of because it spooked me so badly.

Where was I? I think I was… Ok. Before, I started talking about whether or not there is a rhyme and reason to passionate attraction. Or do only fools seek reasons for its mystery? Like I said, I wasn't looking for him. I remember emailing him a Merle Haggard lyric to that effect, "I wish I'd never turned around to look at you a second time, because I really had my life all together until your eyes met mine."[108] And I quoted him from a Bowie song, from when ole David was getting rich the first time, "In these days of grand illusions, you walked into my life out of my dreams. I don't need another change; still you forced your way into my scheme of things."[109] I copied a line from a John Steinbeck novel, "You've tumbled a world for me, and I don't know what I can build in my old world's place."[110]

He emailed back presuming to "explain" my experience by saying we had met at the "right time" and that I had been "ripe" for him. "Love does not climb when people climb," he said. Something about these words pushed my irritation button. The smug, all-knowing asshole! His unmitigated gall enraged me. Maybe it was because he was typically extolling the virtues of chaos theory, and now here he was trying to structure my perplexity within a tidy framework. I responded, "Thanks for those pearls of wisdom. Was that Mr. Ripe Banana-Man talking, or Mr. Ultimate Anarchy! I'm surprised you didn't tell me it was destiny, or karma, or vow that we were lovers in a past life, or promise to meet me in the next one! Now what? Are you going to loan me your magic flying carpet so that I might pay a visit to the Fortune Teller of Love in Accra?" I was on a sarcastic roll! I added, "Precisely! I was 'ripe' for you! Oh, I was yearning for just one look at your black belly button and a glance into your outrageous laser eyes! So I got up that Sunday morning and looked into the mirror saying, 'Today I'm gonna meet my Outlaw'!" I punctuated the email with a smiley face and hit the Reply Button. As soon as my missive was gone, however, I doubted that it was funny.

He didn't find it amusing. He wrote back calling it merely a "piece of bitchy cynicism" unworthy of me. He added that the "bit of wisdom about love" comes from the Tsonga-Shangana People. If I got his words straight, the thought about love and people not climbing simultaneously means that love does not always happen at the best of times, or when it seems most probable, or even when one seeks it desperately. But my understanding might be flawed because his juxtaposition of the words "a mere piece," "worthy," and "bitch" made my anger incredibly anxious.

Once when we were discussing the mystery of our attraction, I teased him with collective words of wisdom: "Wouldn't 'they' say that what we call our 'perfect love' is 'too-good-to-be true'?"

Quicker than a cheetah, he snapped at me. "Do you know who 'they' are?

"I flinched and answered a bit perplexed. "What are you talking about?"

"The 'they'," he repeated. "Do you know them?"

"It's just a figure of speech" I said in a weary tone, or an exasperated one.

"Is it?" he asked, in a mocking voice. "Martin Heidegger writes" -- and now there was a smirk on his face -- "that the 'who' of the 'they' is nobody, and therefore nobody has to take responsibility for anything."[111]

That bit of condescension boiled my blood! "Oh, Heidegger," I said. "Do you mean the philosopher who accepted the post of Rector during the Third Reich?" I could taste the venom that was starting to secrete. "Are you referring to the same colossally brilliant 'thinker' who betrayed his Jewish mentor and friend? The same Heidegger who had an affair with his young Jewish student and replaced her with another Jewess? Who didn't betray any black teachers or gypsy friends only because he didn't have any! Has Mr. Black-Power-Banana-Man swallowed the fruit of white supremacy and racial cleansing? What the hell exactly is the 'Final Solution'?" Never before had my speech been so relentless. When I paused to catch my breath, he shot back,

"Heidegger wasn't a Nazi! He just pretended that he...."

And then, we had one of our oft-repeated intellectual fencing matches, the ones in which while my spleen filtered hot-bubbling blood he wore a comfortable smile with his lip bending to a sneer. As usual, we ended up in bed after our conceptual duel. Typically, our lovemaking was most intense then because the ooze from the both of us was rage-tainted. In those bodily collisions, it always felt like we were screwing our brains out.

After this particular "Das Man" session, for the first time ever I had the last word. "If Heidegger hadn't been so arrogant," I whispered, "He wouldn't have aspired to being Philosopher King."

"I take the point," he said, "I take heed, yes. Pardon me, please, for sounding so pompous. Yes, forgive me."

I put my hand on his hand and caressed it.

"Thank you," he said. We embraced. Soft-eyed, he asked, "Shall we do "it" again?" With no hesitation, I grabbed the part of his "point" that never had patronized me and put it into my mouth. He did not only concede; he surrendered.

Eventually, I had to make gut-wrenching choices and decisions about everything. My life had become suspended. Now, it needed to flow. Everything was interrelated, and so it couldn't be piecemeal. I couldn't pick and choose, as if I was selecting my favorite veggies in the supermarket. But I was totally perplexed about which was what, courage or cowardice.

Not surprisingly, the coward in me came out first. I tried to do it the easy way. Maybe if I closed my eyes or blinked, he'd simply vanish. I tried to wash him out of my hair. I tried to delete him like a computer file. No go! He was still there. The flick of my mouse did not make him disappear. In fact, flicking the mouse just served to prove that he was no daydream. No sense trying to be subtle about the impact he had on me; and no sense being crude. He was a real, carnal, spiritual presence in my life. He was not going to fade out like last night's dream. Whenever I played mind-games to protect myself, he eluded every idea, escaped every image, and resisted every stereotype. When I projected some "shit" onto him from my unconscious -- and some from my collective unconscious -- he wiped the stuff away with a few sharp words spliced with some four-lettered Anglo-Saxon, uh, poetry.

I kept making my trips to heaven and to hell and enjoying and hating them simultaneously. "Sweet misery" is what I called it. When I talked to the therapist I saw after our break-up, she named it "the dialectics of tenderness and hatred." But she had a weird orientation in psychology. Nietzsche or Hegel was her hero. But whether you're a Freudian or not, I guess my sweet misery satisfies the criterion for hard core ambivalence, does it not? I was torn. I didn't know where my various comings were going.

Then my whole world changed in the proverbial New York minute. You think I exaggerate? Listen. He was at my place using my computer and went out to buy food. He was going to cook me a traditional meal that night. I sat down to email my father. On my system, I stumbled across a missive that he had just sent and neglected to delete. It was a love letter to "Mona" back in Accra.

There are no accidents in life. Maybe he wanted me to find it. I don't think I was looking for it. But who knows? Perhaps my uneasiness gave me an inkling, like when you feel the chill of an early autumn. Just then, there was no particular reason for writing my dad. I was just going to tell him that I loved him and missed him. Anyway, I'm digressing. My conscience and I wrestled; and like 'they' say, I won the battle but lost the war.

In an incredibly poetic tone, the missive described his "carnival of dreams" about her gorgeous face and agile mind, dreams of the night before! I died on the spot. A hammer hit me on the head. A knife pierced through my living heart. Nausea, coming like relentless waves, seeped into every pore of me. He had never come close to saying anything that endearing to me. And worse, we had slept together in my bed during his unconscious visit to her in dreamland.

Do you know what it is like to feel like an absolute fool? Like you just broke out in leprosy? The revelation of his parallel lives crucified me. He had been stringing me along, double-dealing, and lying to me throughout our relationship. I figured he had been lying even when he told me the truth. "It's not supposed to be that way," I kept repeating, as if I wanted to undo both the wrong and the right. Or to find out how he was able to do the wrong so right that was it me who was feeling like the scum of the earth.

Mona was an older woman, for crying out loud, his university philosophy professor. It's crazy, isn't it, the thoughts that flash when you are in a totally terribly unfamiliar predicament, when you have no pre-wired circuits to process what's coming in? I pictured the two of them lying in bed, naked, reading *Being and time* with his fingers slowly caressing her Delta of Venus while she is expounding the texts about care, resolve, or taking responsibility! That's so dumb isn't it, just warped? On my other mental track, I wondered if that was the source of my aversion to Professor Heidegger. Still, the scene haunted me for months especially my imagined ending of it when she puts down the book deliberately and gently looks at him and takes... the cover off. I couldn't obliterate that image even though it killed me, daily, especially at night when I was trying to fall asleep.

Anyway, he came back with the chicken and started to cook. To borrow the picturesque language of my favorite Aunt, I couldn't have said "shit" if I had a mouthful! I pretended to read while he prepared the food. While it simmered, I saw him sneak into Eudora to erase his sickening "poetry." At table, his incessant talk about "hot and spicy" was not even a thin veneer for the "dessert" that he was expecting later. But before the "goodies" might be served, I vomited. Undoubtedly, he didn't suspect heartsickness. But the stinking spew was a lead-pipe excuse to skip the foreplay, avoid the rumble, and miss the aftershocks.

For three months afterwards, I was in a daze, heartbroken. Who can describe it? My anxiety was sky high. I couldn't focus on anything. I lost all orientation. Like a slow train, the days trickled by. You might say I started to sleepwalk though everyday life but was wide-awake every night, except for the odd hour of fitful sleep and dreadful dreams like one of a bloody axe that was hacking the line of the Equator into slices, thin as razor-blades.

When I told my best friend the tale of deceit, she sent me a cartoon. In the picture, a man is sitting in his physician's office with a knife stuck into his back, listening to his doctor's diagnosis, "Thank God, the test results indicate that it's not life-threatening but just a strained and misguided metaphor." I roared with laughter, touched that she cared enough to be involved thoroughly in my pain. With that belly laugh, the pornographic black and white movie ended its protracted engagement.

This tale, I know, is meandering all over the place. Its time sequences are scrambled. I'm sorry. There is no linear sequence to this. Nobody lives life in a straight line. There are no straight lines in nature. How did we ever come to believe that our soul-life should be explained by chemical equations? Or could be subsumed under a ding-dong bell-shaped curve? Christ, no correlation coefficient is ever going to explain the way just one perfidious letter hijacked two years of my life.

God, now I'm sounding like the stereotypic abstract philosophy student. But you see, by now I doubted everything that had taken place between us. I knew that I would never again trust a single solitary word that would pass his lips. Until today, I refer to email as the "arch-soul-thief" of cyberspace. I know. I should be grateful I found out when I did. He was never going to tell me the unvarnished truth. So yes, now I'm glad I discovered it. Back then, my anxiety did abate a lot because I was forced to face the truth. The loss, which I guess was always looming in our relationship, had taken place. I wasn't plagued with worry or mystified about what was going on, hoping against hope while he refused to confirm my feelings or intuitions. So blessed to know, it is; so devastating. Well, today I can joke about it: "Where the hell is cyberspace, anyway?"

Where was I? Oh, yes. Before I lost it completely, my mind I mean, I phoned my dad. He and my mom had separated when I was a kid, and he lives an ocean away from me. But we are close friends. Earlier when I was getting nothing but flack from my prejudiced family and narrow-minded friends, I told him about my outlaw. We had one of those rare marker event conversations between father and daughter, a pivotal meeting of our spirits. It was a talk to which we have returned on several occasions over the years, as the years have arisen to meet us.

Dad had an unusual way of looking at it. He said that my outlaw was Lucifer who brought me both "angelic light" and the "fires of hell." Only my choice would determine the direction, either illumination or destruction. He trusted in me, he said, with a holy trust and promised that my deepest integrity would cradle whatever mistakes I might make. That part about his sacred trust really touched me. Right there over long distance, I cried for the first time since my blessed outlaw troubles had begun! I needed that. Then dad encouraged me to follow my own path, warning me that the road that seemed easy, sure, and safe in the eyes of others would be my sure road to psychological death.

So when I phoned him this time about Mona and the dream-festival, he understood that I was on the verge of collapse. He shared with me some of the local cowboy wisdom from the southwestern United States. "Down in Oklahoma, folks are apt to say, 'She just had her first rodeo. It's the first time she's been 'throwed'. Her bottom be sore for a spell, but it's a necessary hurt. It'll grow her up, that pain!'" Knowing dad, he probably made that up. Instead of preaching advice, he let me use my own heart and head to figure out what was most important to me. His indirect way did the trick. It jarred me out of my doldrums.

My outlaw hadn't set foot into my apartment for two weeks. He had been reading for his philosophy exams. "Who's Mona? I blurted out almost as soon as he sat down and opened his mouth. Shall I tell you that he turned a pale shade of white? Naw! He squirmed and looked like he was about to shit his pants! I could see that he didn't want to lose me.

"She's just a friend," he said weakly, but struggling to get composed and straining to gain control. Then he muttered a threadbare alibi: "She and I, uh, we share the same philosophic vision."

"Bullshit" I replied. "Level with me! Aren't I enough for you? Aren't you and I worth more?"

"This is not about being worthy," he said. "It's a different kind of relationship."

"Tell me about it," I mocked. "Surely we both can't have incredibly agile minds! Has it all been just white lies and other putrid fiction between us?"

He didn't enjoy being caught with his pants down, not this way. And he sure as shit wasn't gonna let himself shit himself! So what did he do? He retreated. I witnessed his eyes slowing rolling inward, going away from me, leaving the shared field between us, leaving me alone, and starting to exercise incredible power over me precisely by being gone.

Suddenly, he started singing in his own beautiful dialect a traditional tune or a church hymn, I could not distinguish. "Please don't sing now," I requested, annoyed. "Not now. We need to talk about this. Can't we talk?" But he closed his eyes with head tilted back and with his body swaying slowly to his own music, dancing. "Stop it," I insisted. "Please listen to me." I called him by name, appealing to him while feeling vulnerable. The music kept coming out of his mouth, only louder. His body looked self-possessed, with the music wrapped around him insulating him from me and shutting me out. "Don't do this! Don't exclude me! Is this how you respond when your daughters call to you?" Now, I was almost shouting. I started to shiver with cold while standing there in my warm apartment with my sweater on, hopelessly raw, shaking and trapped in a bizarre dance with emptiness as my frozen partner. Still, he kept singing, transported now, almost chanting, gone from me, seeming lost within his own movements. "I don't deserve this," I protested, my voice weaker now and almost pleading. "I am here. Please, let me back in. Don't act like I'm not here!" I reached across what felt like an infinite distance to touch his face, gently. He jerked away from my caress, violently, as if my hand had invaded the private space of his dance and had violated his private ritual. He continued singing and alternately whistling. "Don't ignore me! Please." I was coaxing him now, and holding, as if it were broken, my left hand that his cruel gesture had rejected. And I kept trying to speak his name across the great divide between us even as I wept and choked and shivered while kneeling down in dejection, still staring fixedly at his self-absorbed dance and sobbing, for a long time sobbing, and weeping sore.

Just as suddenly, he stopped. The silence roared like thunder. The stillness goosed me. Still sitting back on my legs, I straightened up, wiping my eyes and blowing my nose. With deliberate steps, he came to me picked me up in one swift motion as if I were a rag doll and kissed me non-stop while he carried me to the bedroom. Even as I relished the deliciousness of being carried away, a question vibrated through my red hot flesh, "What on earth are you doing?" Once we were in bed and tugging at each other's clothing, the passion between us was more intense than usual. It was as if we were both trying to cross some elusive border, as if between us there was only a hunger, an insatiable hunger. He made love to me that night as if there would be no tomorrow. I loved him back that night as if the world was ending.

When we were finally still, side-by-side and silent, soaking wet and spent, there was no afterglow. The smell of him was strong and I could still taste him. Loud at my ears was his breathing, as if he were still singing. I could catch the rhythm of his breathing just as surely as if my hand were upon his diaphragm, or inside it. Deep inside of me, wherever is the bone marrow of my soul, I knew that this time was the last time. And I knew why. At last, my anxieties subsided.

How did it happen? What tipped the scales? Who has any words for a "moment" like this? My warm flesh was still in recoil. My whole being felt like it had been blistered. Yet finally, I put my finger on the lack in our relationship. Everything fit between us. But the vital part was missing, the most important piece. How did I know, definitively? How can I convey to you the insight that had gripped all of me? Don't make the mistake of thinking that the decisive factor was my jealousy over Mona. Or even that I reeled in the face of his treachery. It was more basic than that.

With my outlaw, you see, I felt free to explore everything in heaven and on earth and in hell, too. He encouraged me to violate taboos and to tear down icons. And he never clung to me. He always gave me the freedom to go my own way. Yet, he could not give me the freedom to stay. My life needed more than anything else a staying power. I knew it then beyond a shadow of a doubt. Saying I knew it does not even come close to describing it. Because I was touching and being touched by something rock bottom. He had shut me out by conducting a "song-fest" to avoid discussing the "dream-fest." And when he withdrew into his musical hideaway precisely at the second when the truth of our bond was wavering, then I had an image of myself searching frantically to find the key to a dank and dingy jail-cell! Wasn't that the core of my anxiety? After his astonishing withdrawal and our desperate sex-session, I clearly understood that I craved, not prison but the freedom to stay. It appeared a lifeline as vital as blood and as necessary as breath. Unless I could feel at home, then what did it mean the hankering to join our bodies? Anyone can have sex. Without feeling homeward bound, what good was the fertility of our mental digging? I needed more than a spiritual counterfoil, someone with whom I could test my strength and courage. Without the freedom to stay, I would never be "at home." I would be evermore homesick. Always, I would be longing for home.

Our relationship lasted exactly twenty-four months and thirteen days. Excuse me, while I double-talk. Only fragility had infested this "fragile bond." How else can I say it? We had been preoccupied only with planting sticks of dynamite in a garden of roses. We had not begun even to look for a homeland for our hearts. So we would never be constant companions. Not on this earth. We would never grow old together. Not in this lifetime. We would always be outlaws to each other. Never would we share everyday life together. In that regard, only outlaws. Thus, I could not make the "leap" to him. It was that simple. It was as simple as that.

On a windy afternoon the next day, I stood on a hill in Pittsburgh overlooking the three rivers. On the solid earth I spread wide my feet. My passionate chaos needed balance. If he were listening to this, oh, man, he would really accuse me of being trite! But that's how it started to turn. I needed grounding and needed heading in only one direction. I gazed for the longest time at the Allegheny and the Monongahela blending to form the Ohio River. That is what started happening to me. The submerged roots of my raising began to surface. I could feel the future coming at me, hard driving, like the rain-pelts that had started to fall.

It's funny. Time stood still. In an anxious eye-blink, I had the urge to jump into the water and just drown all my fears in suicide. Instead, I resolved to finish it with him. I think that was the scariest moment of my life. It could have gone either way. Strange, my outlaw had brought me to that edge of crisis, and yet our fiercely tender sharing helped me to resolve it. I choose life, my life and my future. Without him, would I ever have had the courage?

Who can assess such a thing?
With a well-executed jump, I stopped the singing.

He understood. He was wise enough to understand that I had to leave him. He was unselfish enough to let me go, too. Of course, he left brands on me. In the heat of our sexuality, often he would mark my neck and breasts with hickeys. With deeper marks and indelible stains, he also branded my psyche because he wouldn't let me forget or erase all our shared conclusions about what was most important in life. At the end, he let me know that he knew that I knew that he knew that I was different. I don't know any other way to say it. I was not just civilized, socialized, homogenized, and tame. I was not just like everyone else. I could stand out too. He had tamed me, but he had tamed me... wild. I would always have that far away look in my eye. I'd always be restless, like a candy cotton cloud. I'd never truly fit in. Don't get me wrong. He didn't scar me. He didn't jinx me or curse me. There was no malicious hurt and no attempt to undermine me or to keep me off balance with mental-tricks. In the final phase, when people are in the death throes of saying "good-bye" to something this intense, it is so easy to push each other's buttons and to inflict deep bruises. It's even easy, out of spite or revenge, to go for the juggler. He did none of that. We didn't do it to each other. We didn't even re-write history or invent it.

He gave me massive love-bites, but I bit back! Perhaps that is why he did not suck the blood out of me and why we didn't drain each other dry. The blood-circulation was a co-circulation, one of respect. We had been in it together. We were leaving together. It was the only healthy way to go apart.

The ending saddled me with memories, some searing and some slow burning. I was left with a truly ripe sexual body. Oh, man, I had to be really careful during the ensuing months in that regard. Let me put it this way. About the marks and the stains I alluded to, well, he tattooed the entire world. We shared a thousand songs, half as many books, two rainbows that appeared at the same time, a few constellations in the sky that never change, and one ever-changing moon. And that ain't the half of it. There is almost nothing that couldn't remind me of him. They still do. But I smile now in gratitude and hold it close. Then I take a walk. Or ride my bicycle. Sometimes, I dance.

The rainbow...ah, that reminds me. My first therapist asked me, "With what shade would you paint the picture of your outlaw relationship?" It was by no means any color in the rainbow! My relationship was crimson, scarlet and deep purple. Blood red! How else does one nuance ongoing jostling with chaos done on the edge of destruction? I can't explain it. I don't understand it. But I loved it and I hated it!

Ultimately, I think I met my perfect...stranger in that part of my psychic landscape where creation and destruction divide. I chose the Light. If I had not chosen to get out when I did, get while the getting was good, I think it would have turned very dark. I didn't jump, despairingly, into the muddy waters of the Monongahela River. Today, "the green, green spring is waiting for the sun to shine." Stars still sparkle radiantly in their constellations; and you wouldn't believe how many gorgeous sunsets regularly assault my eager eyes. For the whole world, I would not have missed this awesome episode full of agony and grace.

Why do I bring it up now? Why tell you about it after all the water has streamed under the bridge? He broke the silence. By post today, I received a large envelope from Ghana with two small ones inside that gave directions about the order for reading them. The first note said,

"You know as well as anybody that sometimes the songwriters phrase it perfectly. These words speak my heart's truth. And you know what 'they' say, "If the shoe fits, then wear it.""

A grin started small at my mouth and then spread wide. I read the lyrics:

I broke your heart, I made you cry
Didn't raise a hand to wipe the tears from your eyes;
I guess I had your leaving coming to me. I guess I had your
leaving coming. To tell the truth, I told you lies, Can't say I
blame you for telling me 'Good-bye' I guess I had your leaving
coming for so long. I finally got what I deserved. I guess it serves
me right, being left behind. I guess I had your leaving coming.[112]

The second message was short and sweet... and earth shaking... "Chances are I'll never see you eye-to-eye again. This letter could be my last one. You need to understand that my heart is overflowing with endless regret. You need to know that you were the best thing in my life that I recall. I have never stopped yearning for you. We are still worth whatever it would take. Let me come to you."

With characteristic lack of guile, he included his email address.

"I'll be dammed, here comes your ghost again," I started to hum as soon as I recognized his handwriting. While reading the enclosures, I sang ironically, if it is possible to sing with irony, "You and me, Lord knows, we had it all." And I carefully drew a picture of a Black Rose that I knew I would send him. "Do you believe me now," I kept singing softly, "I told you time and time again." After reading one time his citing of familiar Vern Gosdin lyrics and three times his words, I put down the texts next to my drawing and I closed my tired eyes. My first association was, "Everything is interwoven." In my second image -- and don't you dare laugh -- Martin Heidegger returned without uniform speaking as if reading poetry: "The dreadful has already happened."

I suppose you want to know what I am going to do.

Don't 'they' say, "a thousand years is like a day?" I remember forgetting him each day and each day a thousand times. Last week, I gave up smoking. Doing that was rough. This one is easy.

Analysis of the Outlaw Relationship

Collision course

Two worlds collide. In the aftershock, time stands still. This man and this woman are ripe for each other, but raw. They are involved. Their relationship is outlaw. Everything in their lives is up for grabs. A pause is necessary; a rebound follows it. Two people must pick up the pieces now and rebuild their respective shattered worlds. For better or for worse, this has changed their lives. The drastic turning triggers a life-death crisis.

From the get-go, it is important to clarify the texture and flavor of this collision. This is not simply a woman and a man meeting, experiencing a strong sexual pull, yielding to it, and then entering each others' lives. It is more serious than that. This man and woman embody for each other drastic differences, radical differences. The matter is not only whether she is "too good looking to be interested in me," or "He's too fat to turn me on"... or too ugly, too short, bald, too tall, the wrong hair color, no ass, the wrong shape of the nose, a flat chest, the wrong occupation, beady eyes. At stake is something deeper and more profound than sexual attraction, the need to be approved, be desired, or the opportunity to exercise personal power. The two simply live physically or metaphorically on opposite sides of the tracks. They inhabit different life-worlds.

"Strangers when we meet"

Outlaws are strangers to each other. They don't belong to the ordinary context in which each dwells. They are outsiders to one another from the start. Their differing life-patterns are at odds with their respective roots. These differences concern weighty issues: ethnicity, age, color, religious creed, political convictions. Their worlds collide in terms of values, basic attitudes, or matters of faith. "World" in this context is not just a place, a spatial locale. World is a system of meanings central to who I am. The magnetic pull of the outlaws towards each other and its consequences runs deep. He is the "wrong" man and she is the "forbidden" woman precisely because their meaning-matrices clash.

They are not strangers in the sense that they have just met. This is not the hackneyed situation of meeting "Mr. Right" at the "wrong" time. One's world has not toppled merely because last night you "heard the "right" words trickle off the lips of the "wrong" woman. They are strangers because they never were supposed to have met in the first place... much less be lying side by side... naked... and stroking.

It bears repeating. By background, family of origin, ethnicity, social class, or religious persuasion, each is the other's designated alien. Maybe even each other's devil. In the Indian caste system, there is no word adequate to describe how extremely taboo it is for a members of the lowest caste dalait, named the "untouchables" by Gandhi, to relate intimately with someone considered higher in the social hierarchy. Under Apartheid in South Africa, it was a felony for a black and a white to perform sexual acts with each other. Especially in the southern states of the USA, the same racist laws existed and were repealed only a pathetically few years before 1990 when South Africa's newborn multiracial democracy, the Rainbow Nation, erased them from the books. Nowadays, it is tantamount to a death sentence in Iraq for a Shiite and Sunni couple to be romantically involved or even married

Chances are both outlaws have taken inside the eyes of parents, priests, rabbis, the Prophet or Buddha. They judge themselves by the vision of social authority-figures. They monitor their comportment by what H. S. Sullivan calls the "forbidding gestures"[113] of their original caretakers. Each has heeded the voices of the socializing agents that raised them. Whenever they hear the voice of their own conscience, it echoes the words of the "father" and the "father's father." They feel guilty whenever they violate that voice or whenever their actions defy the accusatory, condemning eyes of those who have loved them and socialized them. So the tension about the outlaw relationship has nothing to do with interests in books and music, with artistic tastes, or with preference for the rules of scientific experimentation. It has nothing to do with superficial categories listed on someone's profile on some dating service somewhere in cyberspace. It has almost nothing to do with simplistic sexual moral codes tucked within the conservative question, "Do we have sex before marriage?" or the liberal one, "Do we sleep together on our first date?" The sexual temptation, indiscretion, or "sin" matters not in itself; but the outlaws' actions are maximally important because sexuality is part of life's larger matrix. Sexuality is always bigger than itself.

Whatever social agents forbid out of whatever fear, ignites desire and excites lust. Not surprisingly, duty and desire huddle together with only a thin and permeable line separating them. In part, that helps make "forbidden fruit" the sweetest.

A familiar stranger

Polarities typify the outlaw bond. This stranger who clashes with my roots and who injects new music into the corridor of my life also seems incredibly familiar. Almost from the first, you felt a sharp affinity for him. Put simply, the seeming mind-boggling and emotion-stirring paradox is that my outlaw is my familiar stranger. "We move together to the different drummer." "We're kindred spirits." "I have been looking for you all my life." The sense of mutual affinity and the possibility of sharing common ground are dazzling. You feel like you know him, have always known him, and can't remember when you didn't know him. To explain the familiar strangeness to one another, the partners give what the mainstream calls parapsychological, new wave, or metaphysical views: "We are destiny's children." "Fate brought us together." "We must have been lovers in a past life." "We were once 'star-crossed' lovers, now reunited."

The outlaw is not a "one night stand." She is not your "overnight sensation" in Singapore. He is not your "fling" on your wild week tour to Dakar. An outlaw is not an affair that will fade in a month or two and not an interlude that will burn itself out. You are embroiled in this one. The collision creates a revolution. Coping with new structures and new dynamics will take a protracted period of time. This one is going to cost you dearly.

Outlaw is not about whether or not one will take off one's clothes, or perform anal sex, or shoot for the moon. Outlaw is world-tumbling. It's live-changing. It is potentially life-wrecking. Hosts of men or women might enter my life to attract me, seduce me, get into my pants, manipulate the hell out of me, or prompt me to squander my money, or tug at my heartstrings. Only my outlaw can devastate me…destroy me.

Under certain circumstances, outlaws must sneak around and court secrecy or whisper on the phone and send cryptic email or SMS messages. The social class difference between them might be huge. One exists in dire poverty; the other is surrounded by filthy wealth. On lives in the mansion on the hill; the other has "done time" behind bars and lives on "the wrong side of the tracks." Maybe simply but complicatedly, one or both are married. So they met in "out of the way places at the dark end of back streets where friendly shadows cover them." Then and there, they explode at each other "in some room above the street under the covers where they don't belong." Sparks fly.

Here comes a tale about an upper-class lady and an ex-convict.[114] She was born with the proverbial "silver spoon." Her day time routine includes hob knobbing with so-called "blue bloods." He hails from "the poor side of town" where he "hangs out" and "cruises" the streets. They meet at a bar in his neighborhood. He's on parole, "at large" again after serving seven years for armed robbery. So he's back "in circulation." And she has crossed the invisible, elusive borderline to find something she doesn't get at home. Sitting in the friendly shadows at a corner table nursing a Jim Beam, he sees her out of the corner of his eye. She sashays over, "comes on" to him and wraps him around her little finger. He remembers making "wine promises." He laughs when telling me that she drove them to the hotel in her classic silver Thunderbird and that she unlocked the door.

It lasted eleven months. When it came unglued and she called it quits, he told me that his "prime turned over." He started back on "the road of no return," weeping and cursing, trying not to go straight downhill and straight back to hell.

Then one night, she was standing there in front of him. "I didn't know if it was real or a dream," he tells me. But she was wearing the same black dress as the first night with the same slit showing a thin strip of sheer white silk and a dark silhouette. "If the words fit, use them," he said, and he sang to me the lyrics:

> *Don't you think you should have called, to tell me you were coming down? Oh, you look so out of place on this troubled side of town. It's a place where losers go, when they know there's nothing left. After losing you, I just lost the will to live. Do you believe me now? I told you time and time again; my heart-and-soul is in your hands. Do you believe me now?*[115]

He said she said, "You're pussywhupped." He added, "With disgust in her spittle, Miss High Society walked out on me and was gone for good." His voice broke on the next lyrics and kept repeating itself... ."Do you believe me now do you believe me now do you believe me now...."

Life-world definition

Operational definitions, if ever they have any use beyond satisfying somebody's experimental design or half-baked theory, surely are useless in regard to revealing the sense of the outlaw. I capture the gist of the phenomenon as both an experience and a metaphor in this paragraph:

> *By an Outlaw Relationship I mean an encounter with a significant stranger who comes from a context different from*

my habitual, everyday situation and who represents a realm of meaning outside of my law of living. My Outlaw's overpowering sexual-spiritual presence shakes the roots of my existence, tumbles my taken for granted world and invites me to transgress my ordinary ground. In the confrontation with my Outlaw, I am forced to confront radically myself and to make choices which reveal genuine preferences and actual priorities. Under the provocation of this life-death crisis, I eventually make decisions for which I must own responsibility and which irrevocably will shape the face of my future.[116]

That's a mouthful by any standards. It needs to be spelled out, elucidated, and unpacked. In an analytical sense, what are the specific detailed characteristics of this phenomenon? An outlaw relationship happens at three interlocking but distinguishable levels: the Involuntary, the Voluntary and the Intertwined.

The involuntary level

Encountering one's outlaw suddenly and surprisingly sweeps one off his feet. Her physiognomy evokes intense bodily responses, heartfelt responses,[117] and gut-reactions. These are pre-personal or involuntary. They bubble forth without my will having anything to do with them. They sizzle even against my volition. In the first blush of the encounter, we turn away in order to catch our breath, regain composure, or ponder what is happening to us. Some of us blush profusely.

Common phrases which describe this "moment" include: "She knocked me off my feet." "He blows my mind." "She blitzed me, ah hell no, she blindsided me." The powerful sexual-personal presence of the other carries me away before choice or before decision. You feel drawn like the proverbial mouth to the flame. Carrying me away marks the outlaw relationship. "A fool can get lost in a dream. Desire always covers the wrong." One has no will power. One wonders if he will ever have a will again. Because why?

Polarities dominate one's life now, that's why. Whereas once upon a time -- a minute ago -- your life manifested clarity, coherence, and cohesion, now everything is topsy-turvy and near shambles. You, who are so typically cool, calm, and composed, have discombobulated. Another has invaded your life-space and occupies it. She mesmerizes you with her bodily style; he overwhelms you with his physical presence. You feel hooked and tethered. If there is an exit from this, there surely is no neon lighted arrow pointing the way out.

Other typical descriptions of the experience include being "turned on by the electricity buzzing in the air," "dazzled by vibrations," and "shook up by the body chemistry" between the other and you. What's happening seems primitive, almost uncivilized. And it is. It feels quasi-mystical, spiritual. And it is. How come?

Touch

You touch. Nothing is more basic. Touch touches everything. Our skin is the basic medium of access to the world. Diane Ackerman writes that touch is as "essential as sunlight...and the key organ of sexual attraction."[118] Skin is a fragile two-layered membrane, so frail and so porous. With touch, the outlaw worms himself into your scheme of things. "She's gotten into my bloodstream," you are apt to tell your chum. The experience feels so fluid, intense, and pervasive you say, "It's more serious than if she seeped in under my skin. This is a matter of blood." Nothing reaches to the bottom of my soul more profoundly than touch.

Touch is a double bladed sword. When I say, "You touched me," do I mean you touched me on the outside or on the inside or both? The ambiguity is un-resolvable. If I failed to touch you on the inside, perhaps on the outside I should have refrained. In the truest sense, touch is both physical and nonphysical contact. It is no wonder I can never give away all my touches. Touch is infinite. With its raw and ambiguous power, touch is indispensable to an outlaw experience.

Her touch is warm. Her touch feels very warm. You want to whisper, "If this gets any hotter, you will scald my skin." Say it eventually you do. And then she answers, "Sure. And next I am going to blister your soul." Polarities: ultra-material and amazingly spiritual.

The eyes: sheen and speech

"He stared at me, and I looked back. Our eyes locked. I got lost in his. I think he got lost in mine too." Eyes talk. Emmanuel Levinas pens arguably the loveliest lines in western philosophical literature: "The eyes do not shine, they speak."[119] A female outlaw writes:

> *I was conscious that he was looking at me and it made something in the bottom of my stomach turn over. His soft eyes seemed to have a lot of depth to them. You could see understanding in them but also some sort of mystery. Those eyes seemed to have some kind of a hold on me that kept getting stronger.*

D. H. Lawrence, in his hauntingly beautiful *The Virgin and the Gipsy*, describes the gipsy's impact upon Yvette:

> *...the feeling that she had been looked upon, not from the outside, but from the inside, from her secret female self. She was dressing herself up and looking her most dazzling, just to counteract the effect that the gipsy had had on her, when he had looked at her, and seen none of her pretty face and her pretty ways, but just the dark, tremulous potent secret of her virginity.[120]*

The kiss

The gaze and touch coalesce in the kiss. Nothing is more intimate than kissing. It is more expressive and intimate than sexual intercourse.[121] The kiss of the outlaw shocks me. It is beyond what I had known or could have imagined, as the female in "Let enter the stranger" expresses it. Isn't a kiss just a kiss? There is a finite range of ways to do it, right? Aren't all kisses basically the same? Of course not! It is myopic to reduce the kiss to the contact of mouth, lips and tongue, and to the exchange of saliva. The kiss is human expression. A kiss is how it is experienced and what it means to the individual. For example, Zora Neal Hurston in *Their eyes were watching God*, describes Johnny Taylor's kiss as "lacerating" Jamie.[122]

Kissing my outlaw, especially for the first time, unmistakably drives it home to me that these are new lips and that these lips are strange. Some examples should suit: Take the white European gazing into the dark eyes of this yellow skinned woman he has just kissed. Stunned, he notices she is crying: Outlaw; Or a dark-haired Iranian woman looking into the blue eyes of this German man, who has just licked and nibbled her breasts, waits with bated breath and trembling: what might he do next? Outlaw. Or this woman from Ghana, sitting with legs uncrossed, has just danced to the music of Hi-Lite. This man from Japan gently kissed her finger tips and now hesitantly is caressing her jet black thigh with his feather-light fingers touching his outlaw as if she were gold.

Smell

Smell shares with touch and the eyes the power to lure. Smell is elemental. It roots in the "vital psycho-physiological matrix, the precursory foundations of human life."[123] When we were infants, at least six months before we could possibly represent our primary love "objects," we possessed remarkable radar to identify by smell our mother, her breasts, our father, or grandfather. The registers of smell and taste are our basic sensing-emotional "equipment," the tools with which we navigate our non-speaking, in-fant world.

The assumption of the upright posture minimizes the proximal senses of smell, hearing, and taste. Distance modalities take ascendance. We use sight now to scan the horizon. We look off, far off. Our hands, no longer necessarily support locomotion, are free to discriminate, make tools, and even build us a spaceship to fly us to Venus. But we never lose completely the original radar.

We smell our outlaw. Bracket for a minute her perfume or his after shave lotion. Her natural smell, the scent of her flesh, is an incredible aphrodisiac. It identifies her and hooks me to her. In "True Blue," Rima mentions that friends smell each other. Glowy replies immediately, "You smell like honeysuckle." And she responds, "You must really like me if I smell that pretty."

I smell her. The scent of a woman is a powerful lure that defies reason. "I'd give all I'd own for just a minute there."[124] If and when the outlaw relationship ends, the lingering smell of him will haunt you. One whiff of scent, like one bar of music, has the emotive and memorial power to bring back an entire episode.

Forbidden pleasure

None of this should happen. It is not allowed. This is outside the rules. I should stop it now before this goes too far. Get out while the getting is good. Stop touching this black skin that I never was supposed to touch in the first place, this touch that I wish would never end. Turn away from these Chinese lips that I wish I could devour. Look away from this pool of blue eyes that I want to drown in. The forbidden sense of the outlaw encounter, flaunting all norms and linked to all one's history, is poignant and painful.

Polarities dominate. The draw towards blatant, crude, or coarse sexuality plays tug of war with a sense of mystery, wizardry, hypnotism, voodoo, and elemental spirituality. Classic lines of the American standard go: "Bewitched, bothered, and bewildered."

Promise and danger

Promise jostles with danger. You are sucked into an over-powering relationship, in it over your head and afraid you are in it over your heart. Peril creeps. Threat crawls. They lurk. You can't shake the ill-ease. Yet simultaneously, you sense acutely a promise. Anticipation rushes.

We kiss the strange lips that invite us; the future bites back. We straddle two worlds. Now what? Straddling means separation. We leave behind the familiar and reach towards the unknown. All the lines are blurring. It is exciting, intoxicating, and terrifying. "Who will I become now?' we ask. The future advances with its teeth into us, not only as something soon to come, as an absent and remote possibility, but concretely moist. We are already living into and appropriating its threat. Yet simultaneously, we feel a vital pulse, and a jolt, and the fire of life. With a moment's hesitation, I can lose it all. About that there is clarity; what remains unclear is what would be loss or what gain. In fear and trembling, I project myself into my new future with all I can muster and with all that I am. Promise courts danger. Danger menaces expectation.

The voluntary level

Soon or later, I must choose. The straddling must end. Lest I fall flat on my face, I must climb down from the fence or jump. Voluntarily, I project self forward into my future; I find out for sure what I stand for and what I truly put into practice as opposed to what I merely preach. I separate "mouthing" abstract ideas from actually living my own preferences. My outlaw encounter, therefore, challenges me and provokes a confrontation with my limits. In the "moment," will-power and my conscious self enter into the drama. De-cision literally means "to cut." A common theme of existential phenomenological thinkers is that we who are free nonetheless are condemned to choose. Few express any better than Robert Frost the humble, ordinary way choosing comes to pass:

The Road Not Taken

Two roads diverged in a yellow wood,
And sorry I could not travel both
And be one traveler, long I stood
And looked down one as far as I could
To where it bent in the undergrowth

Then took the other, as just as fair,
And having perhaps the better claim,
Because it was grassy and wanted wear;
Though as for that, the passing there
Had worn them really about the same,

And both that morning equally lay
In leaves no step had trodden black.
Oh, I kept the first for another day!
Yet knowing how way leads on to way,
I doubted if I should ever come back.

I shall be telling this with a sigh
Somewhere ages and ages hence:
Two roads diverged in a yellow wood, and I --

I took the one less traveled by,
And that has made all the difference.[125]

The outlaw stirs radical self-confrontation that leads to an all-encompassing value clarification and the disclosure of actual priorities. Notice that Robert Frost does not imply that the choice necessarily ennobles us. Your outlaw may indeed tempt you into becoming a revolutionary! Or less radically, she was born and raised in one of the former Soviet bloc countries. Hailing from Russia, Romania, Serbia or the Czech Republic, she was not educated in democratic-capitalism. She does not see political ideology the way your western county has socialized you. She sees "market economy" for what it is -- greedy capitalism. Borrowing her sight, you are "forced" to cross-examine all you have been taught and taken for granted about you country's agenda to impose "free trade" on the whole globe at any and all costs. For example, opposing interpretations of the invasion of Iraq in 2003, and the bombing of Lebanon in the summer of 2006, ended not a few friendships and love relationships. War and invasion are outlaws! As soon as some grave matter like the politics of oil surfaces within a serious ongoing dialogue between lovers, rose-colored glasses shatter. Consciousness is dangerous.

Discussions about a jihad or the war on terror also drag conversationalists to a fork in the road.[126] What or who most menaces the globe? Is it not unconscionable that the gap between the rich and the poor keeps widening? In the face of the Holocaust, Rwanda, the Balkans and Darfur, what does it mean that the United Nations cannot come up with a legal definition of genocide? In his careless lecture, did Pope Benedict betray Catholic bigotry and racism? The belle of the ball in Baptist Texas is cocksure about the evils of abortion, homosexual marriages, and stem cell research. Her outlaw comes from ultra-liberal Amsterdam. They have come to loggerheads over euthanasia. They have come to the crossroads. They are coming to the borderline. Change hurts.

The possibility is concrete to borrow the other's sight to see ethical, religious, and geopolitical issues differently: Should the USA sign the Kyoto pact? Shouldn't the international community thwart nuclear aspirations of Iran and North Korea? Hamas is Palestine's feely elected democratic government. How can the west in conscience stop aid, punishing the average citizen in the West Bank for making a free choice? Is that not hypocritical?

Sex: not the answer

"Let Enter" demonstrates that a "good roll in the hay" does not resolve these thorny, complex, and controversial matters. The ultra-conservative Muslim from Saudi Arabia you just made love with asks you to turn off the "Reality TV" show as a sick and evil program, the last thing that should be allowed to proliferate in her country. Capitalism clashes with Muslim culture. You see her point, don't you? You're not an infidel, are you? Aren't you just a nice Irish kid from Boston? What do you say in response? Do you defend the American Dream? And what will you do when she calls your American Dream a nightmare and tells you your country has decayed? With relish, will you plant a kiss on that maverick freckle near her nipple that you had just licked for almost five minutes... just five minutes ago? Will you then immediately phone your father, a politician of some rank, and tell him that the only authentic solution for the quagmire in Iraq is for the USA and England to withdraw imminently? It comes with outlaw territory, such deep clashes of world-views. Not surprisingly, over such global political matters outlaw partners come to their wits end. Push comes to shove. One feels backed against the wall. Either you accept your outlaw's "deconstruction" of secure and safe structures -- thereby risking alienating family members or friends -- or else you reject his slaughter of your sacred cows and risk losing him.

Home! What is home? Home we take for granted. "Home is where when you have to go there they have to take you in," Robert Frost tells us, "something you somehow haven't to deserve."[127] Another way to describe the life-death crisis is that in making a choice I may lose home. And for a minute there -- or for a lifetime -- I am not sure where truly my home is.

Problematic sexuality

Sexuality cannot solve the problems, indubitably. Truth be told, sexuality might be the problem! The meaning of sexuality is at the heart of the outlaw bond as equally as over-arching values and beliefs. Sooner or later, its place within my psychological economy and over-all philosophy of life or religious credo must be resolved. Sexual acts that are simply natural and wonderful to one partner are "sins" and legal felonies to the other. With the outlaw, therefore, one wages war with temptation and sometimes temptation wins the fight. "The devil made me do it the first time; the second time I did it on my own."

The permutations and combinations of sticky sexual situations are endless. Is one partner laboring under the "burden of virginity"[128] when they meet, i.e., cherishing it yet simultaneously feeling inexperienced and naïve because of it? Or one partner may still be "psychologically virginal."[129] One or both parties may be either married or in a committed relationship. The sexual experience with him exceeds anything you ever imagined or hoped for. But as soon as you put your clothes back on, the daily life predicament you face is convoluted. You've never had to handle a tangled rope of lies before. This is not as simple as turning off your vibrator. How will you strike a balance between what you body craves and the rest of your commitments and responsibilities?

Once we take our clothes off for the first time, it is easy to disrobe again. But it is never so easy to undress one's mind, soul or spirit. Thus, an individual might have many and varied sexual experiences, but still hold in reserve her greater self. Now, with your outlaw you are ready to release. Letting go makes you more vulnerable than ever. I am not talking about orgasm. The issue here is not climax, but surrender. Your outlaw holds the powerful promise of taking you one step beyond. You feel it. "I've never been this far before." Advance, however, ultimately demands surrender. If one truly does face the sexual challenge that the outlaw poses and goes the whole nine yards, the encounter transforms the meaning of your masculinity or femininity. You will be more seasoned and wiser although not necessarily proud of yourself or ennobled.

The above discussion expresses the passionate intensity of an outlaw encounter. You are not toying with the boy next door; you are playing with fire. Participating in an outlaw relationship means that at some level you are ready to test the height, depth and breadth of your sexuality. However, sexual intercourse might not necessarily happen. Surely, outlaws indulge in most forms of sexual behavior ranging from innocent touches, to passionate kisses, to petting to climax and to intercourse. Probably, most outlaws do make "sexual love." But whether or not the relationship involves sexual intercourse is not the defining matter.

Expression-performance

How do I make sense out of the seeming dilemma that the outlaw relationship is amazingly sexual with or with out intercourse? In the lifeworld, sexual expression and sexual behavior do not necessarily coincide. More than one hundred years after Freud gave us his gifts, western thought amazingly still equates sex with intercourse. But sexuality is broader than penis-in-vagina. Merleau-Ponty says that sexuality and existence are so coequal that it is difficult not to reduce one to the other. An outlaw relationship is a particularly preferred context for experimenting with the broad existential dimensions of human sexuality. One discovers that a mere glance into your outlaw's eyes or the refusal to go all the way to intercourse is equally sexually expressive. With your outlaw, you discover that a kiss could mean more than a climax or that the disciplined decision to decline sexual performance might be a qualitatively stronger expression of your sexuality than carelessly to yield.

The intertwined level

The outlaw relationship, like the chum and first love, exemplifies a developmental approach to social relations. Growth takes place not only as a result of biological maturation or psychological consolidation, but also as a result of interpersonal solicitation or provocation. The three dimensions, the involuntary, voluntary and interpersonal or intertwined, go hand-in-glove. Neither partner alone can make the relationship happen. It takes two. It is an arbitrary abstraction to consider either partner detached from the dynamic structure of their total bond. The partners make each other "be." They call forth each other. In this case, they summon each to actualize passionate sexual possibilities. Outlaws co-frame the "gateway to passion."

Transformation

Once again, it is a question of balance. It is not just raging lust that is at stake. The deeper level of outlaw anticipation and promise concerns transformation. The starkly sexual and downright spiritual come together. The dualistic split between them is nothing but arbitrary ideology. So the outlaw partners seek more than a new way to express their sexuality; they are looking for "redemption." Again, this is not a religious concept only. Literally, it means to "buy back." If you grant that the individual is ripe for an outlaw encounter precisely because she or he has recently undergone a loss, disappointment or failure, then the individual is seeking a "conversion." Again, this is not in the narrow sectarian religious sense, but as a "turning." In common parlance, one hopes for "a new lease on life." This is not orchestrating superficial "change" such as arranging for an in vogue "extreme makeover," the type of modification that mainstream psychology privileges. One seeks a deeper transformation or opportunity to "turn over a new leaf."

Context: neither accidental nor caused

Like chum and first love, the outlaw encounter is neither accidental nor caused. The two individuals are ripe for one another. Last month, last week, yesterday, they might have looked at each other and looked away or looked right through each other. Nothing would have happened. To understand in a psychologically scientific way the genesis of the relationship, we must pay attention to the context or total situation. What has changed in the person's existence that makes her ripe for an outlaw? The contexts are many. Each is unique.

But there are some "typifications."[130] He might be on the rebound from a painful ending of his first love. Now, he is on the prowl for something different, wild, exotic, and even dangerous. He seeks someone other than the girl next door. Chances are, if you asked him he would have no clear or concrete idea about what "strange stuff" he is looking for. But he is ready, primed even.

Her parents are going through an ugly divorce. Mom had an affaire. Dad found out by reading her email messages and went berserk. He couldn't forgive and forget; he opted to break up the family. So a big chunk of her innocence, like a broken ice shelf, has gone down the tubes. She is "pissed." She doesn't feel like acting in character or like being sweet, wholesome or debonair. She's ready for spice, for a touch

of the bohemian, for stretching the envelope, for walking on the edge...
or on the wild side.

One's orientation to the heterosexual other also might shift
dramatically in the face of death, whether in the family, of close friend,
or even of a cultural hero such as John Lennon, 2-Pac, the Kennedy's,
Janis Joplin, Martin Luther King Jr., Jimmy Hendrix, Malcolm X.
Being confronted within one's family with alcoholism, drug abuse, or
death-threatening illness also jars an individual such that he changes
direction in what he had considered the path of looking for love. Death
and loss, especially any loss of innocence, pluck chords of anger in us
all. In outrage, we are ripe for the outrageous.

To speak in a general sense, one is ripe for meeting an outlaw
whenever one is at a turning point in life, or going through a time of
transition, or experiencing a crisis, or come to one's breaking point. So
we come to the crossroads. We know where the limits are; we cross over
the line. On the other side of the border, we are open to an encounter
with a 'hunk' or 'beauty' from another "walk of life."

Psychological Reflections

She shines with her own kind of light

Within western rationalistic-dualistic thought, the bottom-line is
that the "Other" is unknowable. From the standpoint of academic
philosophy and psychology, the one we think we know is nothing but
an analog of self, our double, me outside of me. As soon as one accepts
the validity of this dualistic premise, it is like trying to punch one's
way out of a paper bag to prove that the other is really 'out there.'
You just quibble and quarrel with ridiculous abstractions in a morass
of rationalistic, dualistic logic. I reject such ivory-tower thinking and
adopt another philosophical vision, 180 degrees different. Within an
existential phenomenological vision, we encounter the other directly;
we do not see her in borrowed light. The true blue tenderness of the
chums, the blessed alchemy of the first love partners, and the reciprocal
desire and passion of the outlaws showcase a basic existential fact that
the mainstream paradigm cannot comprehend: the individual shines
with her own light.

Depth psychology: Sigmund Freud and C. G. Jung

Freudian psychoanalysis and Jungian analytical psychology pose a more serious challenge to this existential phenomenological perspective than naïve Anglo-Saxon pragmatism. In a nutshell, the proponents of both the personal and the collective unconscious ask this question: Is the other per se loveable? Does she shine in her light without the glow of my enchanting projections?

Freud on "finding an object"

Paul Ricoeur calls Sigmund Freud a "prophet of suspicion"[131] for his refusal to take anything for granted, for his disavowal of orthodox doctrine, for purifying idolatrous dogma, and for shattering social-cultural illusions. Since love is one of our most sacred cows, Freud cross-examines its premises. He queries how one finds an "object" -- or in what is the same question -- how does one establish a "bond"[132] and make love-connections? His answer is that our personal unconscious "projects" meanings on to the other who is always a duplicate version of an earlier parental edition. We look for and find someone who resembles in significant psychological ways an earlier love-object, most typically out of our family of origin. Freud privileges the Oedipus object. The other who attracts us and for whom we feel lust-love mirrors our father or mother. He describes two variations of this dynamic of "identification." We first know the other and find an object or attach through "narcissistic identification."[133] This is a process in which the self seeks and finds itself in an external other. In a moment of self-discovery, one of my adolescent clients crowed: "I luv me, I luv me! I wish there were two of me so that I can hang out with myself." Not surprisingly, he did find a willing partner. A narcissistic object-choice mirrors your ego or ego-ideal.

This second identification Freud names "anaclitic" from the Greek word for "to lean upon."[134]Anaclitic identification is the process of re-finding an Oedipal figure in a current environmental person. In the expanded sense in which Freud uses the sex-drive (trieb), this dynamo triggers falling in love. The environmental person wears our projections and satisfies our needs. But we don't have a clue of who she is in her own right.

Repetition

Freud's thought also sheds light on the outlaw experience of feeling "fated" or "destined" for one another. He insists there are no accidents in life. Taking this idea from the master, Alfred Adler puts it nicely. Unconsciously, we "arrange our fate."[135] In this context, Adler like Freud means two people attract one another based upon their past relationships and based upon what they think they want or what they unconsciously need. Adler's most relevant concept in this regard is the "counterfoil."[136] We seek and find a partner with whom we incessantly spar. We test our own strength against a "worthy" opponent. Adler bases the so-called "battle between the sexes" on the dynamics of aggression, compensation for weakness, striving for superiority and seeking control and power.

For Freud, the sharp affinity of sexuality and aggression that attracts us and prompts us to draw another close serves the "repetition compulsion."[137] We are doomed to repeat what we do not remember or haven't consciously assimilated. The bright aura of the outlaw that zaps us requires cross-examination. She might be the figure with whom I might be repeating a significant "bad" pattern, perhaps the very pattern pre-figured by my biographical predicament. The devil we know is easier to deal with than the devil we do not know. Seeking and finding the familiar because it is familiar might be just playing it safe by playing with the same old fire which we have learned to control.

Freud puts a more positive spin on repetition as well. The outlaw offers the opportunity for one or both parties to "work out" matters of the heart. We meet the one who confronts us with our cardinal issues and who will stay with us, struggle with us so that we might transcend them. Freud is clear. Every outcome hinges upon what we bring into awareness and then upon the choices we make. In Freud, the root issues which are sexual -- in the expanded sense -- are never narrowly sexual. He never espouses a pan-sexism.

Jung: The collective unconscious

Jung shifts focus to the anthropological or spiritual dimension. For him, the unconscious is not only personally rooted in one's biographical predicament but is anthropological also. He posits a "collective unconscious," the unconscious of the human race, the locus of primary ideas or "archetypes."[138] These are recurring images or powerful figures that mankind has dealt with from the time our species crawled out of the sea and began to mate. A poetic example may give a vivid picture of what Jung is driving at.

"Birches"

Take a young boy who has grown up in northeastern Pennsylvania with the woods more his second home than just a place to play. He and his friends would swing in the trees, bendy-bowing. Rima introduces Glowy to the activity before she introduces him to the kiss. The lad matriculates to university. His English Literature professor reads to his class a poem unknown to him, Robert Frost's "Birches":

> *When I see birches bend to left and right*
> *Across the lines of straighter darker trees*
> *I like to think some boy's been swinging them.*
> *But swinging doesn't bend them down to stay*
> *Ice-storms do that.*[139]

The teacher's voice mesmerizes him, transporting him out of ordinary time. In a flash, the poem steals his experience. He had believed that he and his pals invented bendy-bowing! But this rich and lovely depiction of it blows him away. He sinks into the hard uncomfortable school desk, as if it was a velvet couch, and he siphons the words into his soul:

> *Often you must have seen them*
> *Loaded with ice a sunny winter morning*
> *After a rain. They click upon themselves*
> *As the breeze rises, and turn many-coloured*
> *As the stir cracks and crazes their enamel.*
> *Soon the sun's warmth makes them shed crystal shells*
> *Shattering and avalanching on the snow-crust*
> *Such heaps of broken glass to sweep away*
> *You'd think the inner dome of heaven had fallen.*
> *They are dragged to the withered bracken by the load,*

And they seem not to break; though once they are bowed
So low for long, they never right themselves:
You may see their trunks arching in the woods
Years afterwards, trailing their leaves on the ground,
Like girls on hands and knees that throw their hair
Before them over their heads to dry in the sun.[140]

In his mind's eye, the young man remembers peeling the bark from one of the bent birches while sitting close enough to her to smell her... still... and yet still able to watch her gently pick twigs and leaves from her long thick curly hair. It seems like yesterday. He wipes a tear, wondering if anyone in the room had noticed. The teacher continues reading what seems like his self-portrait:

But I was going to say when Truth broke in
With all her matter-of-fact about the ice-storm,
I should prefer to have some boy bend them
As he went out and in to fetch the cows --
Some boy too far from town to learn baseball,
Whose only play was what he found himself,
Summer or winter, and could play alone.
One by one he subdued his father's trees
By riding them down over and over again
Until he took the stiffness out of them,
And not one but hung limp, not one was left
For him to conquer. He learned all there was
To learn about not launching out too soon
And so not carrying the tree away
Clear to the ground. He always kept his poise
To the top branches, climbing carefully
With the same pains you use to fill a cup
Up to the brim, and even above the brim.
Then he flung outward, feet first, with a swish
Kicking his way down through the air to the ground.[141]

The poem now gives him back his experience larger and more ample. When the finish comes, it takes his breath away: "One could do worse than be a swinger of birches." He is perturbed and excited. The tree, the girl and his life are interlocked and always will be. He is not sure now if he is sitting or climbing or swaying and bending. After a reflective pause, he reads the poem himself to take a second look, scanning to find Frost's words about love

> *I'd like to get away from earth awhile*
> *And then come back to it and begin over.*
> *May no fate willfully misunderstand me*
> *And half grant what I wish and snatch me away*
> *Not to return. Earth's the right place for love:*
> *I don't know where it's likely to go better.*[142]

His chest expands, his heart is racing: "Earth's the right place for love." He feels like jumping out of his skin. What is he doing in this silly classroom? He wants immediately to run back to his woods, back to her sitting on the rock... with lips eager to kiss him.

> *So was I once myself a swinger of birches.*
> *And so I dream of going back to be.*
> *It's when I'm weary of considerations,*
> *And life is too much like a pathless wood*
> *Where your face burns and tickles with the cobwebs*
> *Broken across it, and one eye is weeping*
> *From a twig's having lashed across it open.*
> *I'd like to go by climbing a birch tree*
> *And climb black branches up a snow-white trunk*
> *Toward heaven, till the tree could bear no more,*
> *But dipped its top and set me down again.*
> *That would be good both going and coming back.*
> *One could do worse than be a swinger of birches.*[143]

His mind is spinning; his heart is full. The poem gives him the immense satisfaction of knowing that he and his friends had participated in an action which is common fare of others; that it happened at least fifty years earlier in the mountains of part of his own country, in New

England; and that he had "met" a man who enjoyed it, a man he otherwise never would know. The poem somehow also gives him his "love" back -- everything except a lock of her hair. Time is endless and All is One. He has had an experience of a Jungian archetype.

Archetypes

Pertinent to love, the key archetypes are the "shadow" and the "anima" (feminine soul) or "animus" (masculine soul). Significantly, Jung affirms that to activate these latent images we must encounter another person in the lifeworld. In the case of the anima-animus, the contact is erotically or romance tinged.

The shadow

The shadow embodies my underdeveloped, unrealized self. We see it first in another person. In a flash, I detest him. Everything about her irritates me or turns me off and makes me recoil. He represents my weakness, Jung says, what I most fear about my own nature. Hence, I have an immediate visceral reaction. Observing his comportment and his style, I see my shadow. It spooks me. We are always, at least initially, afraid of our own shadow.

Perhaps I am deficient in what Jung calls a basic attitude. I am too "introverted." I almost exclusively use my own experience or ideas as the gold standard for judging the world. So I require balance. It behooves me to become more "extroverted" and open to influence by what is on the outside in the perceptual field. Or maybe I am over-developed in thinking as opposed to intuiting, in sensing as opposed to feeling. If I am a man, I have not cultivated my femininity; if a woman, I have not developed my masculine side. Jung's goals are individuation which requires balance, integration and wholeness.

The "hatred" I spontaneously, strongly, and irrationally feel for my shadow is potentially a gift or a blessing. Because why? In a word, be careful whom you are falling into hate with! Love and hate are not diametrically opposed; they are flip sides of the same coin. Kierkegaard puts it succinctly, "Hate is a love which has become its opposite, a ruined love. Deep down love is continually aflame, but it is the flame of hate."[144] Harold Searles[145] tells us that any strong, overt, visceral, emotional relatedness is love, whatever shape it assumes. Hate is love which is thwarted, twisted, scorned, unrequited, perverted. The notion is cross-cultural. In the Ewe tongue "the opposite of love...is not hate but rather disagreement and dissention which hurts feelings and compromises a sense of personal worth."[146]

What is the opposite of love-hate? It is unconcern, apathy, or indifference. Meeting your shadow, however, is never emotionally cold. The man or woman who you met in-the-world, who shoots alienating and revolting sparks at you from you-know-not-where, might eventually transform into your chum or your outlaw.

Animus-Anima

What is Jung making theme by his anima-animus concept? He affirms that I hold and prize a mental image of my ideal partner, my soul mate, the woman or man who most would complement my nature. The feminine figure is not my mother, or sister, or "kissing cousin," or nanny -- although "she" might resemble one or another of them. The same with the animus: not my father, brother or uncle but partakes of their significance. Jung believes we should first confront and come to terms with this unconscious collective image lest we carelessly, wantonly, and destructively project it onto some flesh and blood man or woman. But project it we do, he tells us with knowledge gained from bitter personal experience. That projective act forms the basis of romantic-sexual enchantment. Someone suddenly appears as my dream-woman or my knight in shinning armor, the one who I have awaited all my adult life. His presence overpowers me. She sweeps me off my feet. The Jungian possibility is that I am under the spell of an ideal image concretized in the woman I am staring at across the room; or my animus, living and breathing in the shape of this man standing before me with a lethal smile on his face.

Synchronicity

With his notions of anima-animus and shadow, Jung acknowledges an eruption of something beyond its link to the past. He opens to the future slashing into our lives like a bolt of lightening. In this context, encountering an outlaw coincides with one's readiness for newness and with the same readiness on the part of another. Jung's relevant concept in this regard is synchronicity. Synchronicity is an "a-causal"principle of meaningful coincidence. Two things happen at the same time and are meaningfully related but there is no cause-effect connection between them. Two people are looking for the same "thing." They are seeking precisely what they might find in and with one another. Therefore, they call out or summon each other from deep within, from deeper than roots, from as deep as one can touch the legacy of humankind within self. Not surprisingly, the person who seems to fit the bill and matches the heart's desire is experienced as someone sent by fate.

Synchronicity in the matter of love can be either positive or negative. The young woman's father in "Let Enter the Stranger" makes theme that paradise and perdition are nothing but a choice away. Two persons meet who both seek a miracle that would make life center for them. The timing is right. They make a match. The pieces fit. They start what develops into a very fruitful bond. They build a successful intimacy that defies all odds. It lasts a lifetime. Their grandchildren and great grandchildren look back at them as legends, defiant but loving and strong.

On the other hand, one might be conjuring up, unwittingly, one's worse witch or sorcerer. The minstrel tells the story: "If she looks like an angel, it's a perfect disguise. Everything 'bad' in me she brought it out; she was just no good for me."[147] Once conjured up, the 'bad' requires handling. It is the "weaker" one or the "innocent" one who is more at risk. She imagines her dreams are coming true; he is convinced he has met the woman who will "save" him. The fresh start at life that seems to be happening soon splinters like "crystal shells / Shattering and avalanching on the snow-crust / Such heaps of broken glass to sweep away / You'd think the inner dome of heaven had fallen[148]

In Jungian terms, whenever one is crushed or disillusioned as a result of being swept away, one must "depotentiate" the archetype in order to get one's soul back. The task is Herculean. There is no quick-fix; it isn't a time-lined process; it is a long and arduous journey of indeterminate duration. It is painful, too. It costs. Although it can be side-stepped temporarily or postponed, ultimately it cannot be evaded.

Comments of appraisal

Who can gainsay it? The Freudian and Jungian heuristics are powerfully insightful. Talk to any grownup that has had more than a little experience in love relationships. Everyday people know implicitly that we must silence echoes and chase or scatter old ghosts, if we are to establish intimacy. This is curious. In our social milieu, the guardians of the psychological order muffle depth psychology and denigrate it as not fitting into the straight-jacket of 19th century positive science. Nevertheless, humankind remains perpetually in debt to Freud and Jung for clarifying the less-than-conscious ground of our lusts, passions, and loves. Their point of view happily corrects the narrow superficiality of cognitive behavioral explanations which contribute nothing to the predicament of meeting someone who is the answer to my life-long prayer.

The psychological cluster of patterns and dynamics related to mommy and daddy do in fact loom large in our love life. And as soon as I encounter the woman who walks out my dreams, it would be best that I pause or rather stop in my tracks. It isn't as simple as "look before you leap." It isn't even a matter of being suspicious of what seems too good to be true. The "look" is good. I am experiencing a confluence of my deepest desire with the delectable power of the woman who just touched me. It is so good that it circumscribes the core problem. How will I ever extricate myself from this entanglement? With a critical eye, we must look beyond the looking. For Freud and Jung, hearthead criticism and analysis are the wholesome acts.

The archeological imperative

Freud and Jung teach us humility. They promote a necessary caution. Take nothing for granted concerning matters of the heart. Still, their ways of understanding love are also reductive. If we accept their basic premise, which I call the "archeological imperative," it traps us like quicksand and confines us just as the gobbledygook cluster of logical reasons of orthodox rationalism boxes us in.

Freud chases the elusive "first." He is convinced that every relationship has a prototype. His modus operandi is endlessly to trace back, find what came before this... and then what came before that. He is not satisfied until he finds the original trigger hidden within the orbit of the Holy Family. If you try to argue that he is wrong, that only tips off your fear-driven defenses and proves that he is right. There can never be any brand-new relationship. The love partners relate to each other on the basis of complexes already etched in granite.

Jung's archeology both digs deeper than Freud's search for personal roots and also reaches higher and farther. For Jung, love relationships roost within the collective family of mankind. Whatever 'little nothings' we whisper to each other in the dark, it all has been said before; whatever we do with our ingenious fingers, it already has been done repeatedly. In our sometimes feeble efforts to love, we dip into the pool of life and willy-nilly meet our ancestors and imitate their actions. If all the world is a stage and we are the players, as the Bard describes, then Freud sits us where we feel the warmth of the family hearth and where we play the Game of Triangles; Jung locates us in history's caves and caverns, huts and igloos, palaces and cottages. There we sit, reading the Tibetan Book of the Dead, laying out the Tarot Cards, or tossing yarrow stalks, and consulting the *I-Ching*.

When push comes to shove, Jung clings to "the eternal truth of the general similarity among men." For him, that is how our destiny is cast. In order to be able to cope with daily life, we must check and contain the collective images within us that unconsciously determine our fate in love. While shuffling the cards with the Queen of Hearts, we are blind to what is right before our eyes. The flesh and blood and bone woman fades, nay, is buried under images. Ideas, of course, are under our control. Such imaginative reverberations and intellectual elaborations diffuse the impact of the 'terrible other" so that we do not get swept away. At this point in history, we know that's how it happened with Jung. He never "fulfilled his love" for his anima -- the woman who co-created this concept -- Sabina Spielrein.[149]

It is foolhardy, nevertheless, to ignore this brilliant man who knows from experience about "poetry" with one's soul mate, about "thwarted" heroes and "wronged" heroines, and about creatures of destiny. Without doubt, Jung's picture of the anima fits many relationships that begin as two dream lovers destined to be, or as an amazing encounter with one's one-true-love. But as strongly as possible, I make a disavowal: the outlaw relationship manifests a different texture, a different density, and a different flow.

I clarify. There is a clear distinction between "projective identification," "mutual narcissistic mirroring," being overpowered by one's anima, and leaping towards an outlaw. The outlaw relationship qua outlaw cannot be reduced to imagined exercises, as if one is just indulging in empty infatuation or easily sexually hooked on "Mr. Right," or hankering after a woman that you simply must "have." My outlaw is no image that disappears as soon as I stop thinking about her. I cannot turn him off like a dripping spigot. If I blink, she won't disappear like last night's dream. My outlaw is there in the flesh, wish it or not. She has come of her own accord. She is irreducibly other. I did not conjure her up; I could not have made her come. It is impossible to awaken and say, "Today I am going to meet my outlaw." None of us posses such power. Two people must be ripe for each other and ready to risk and then make the leap. The outlaw is a unique flesh and blood individual whose powerful presence has turned my life upside down. Remember, she smells. She is an infinite other, the "terrible other" that western philosophy fears and tries to control.

Second sight

How did it happen that we fell in love and fell at first sight? How valid-valuable is the resulting bond? Every theory, because of the way we formulate our theories, comes with a built-in blind spot. Rational psychology and depth psychology share flip sides of the same flaw. Does not the glitch in thinking center upon the "terrible Other?" Levinas says that we are "allergic to the other" who therefore makes us nervous. D. H. Lawrence persuades us that passion and tenderness terrify western culture. Anxiety blurs and blinds human thinking. Arguably, anxiety and allergies underwrite both the denial in western thought that we ever encounter the other precisely as other, and its reduction of vibrant human dialogue to mere ventriloquism.

Weighted down with such philosophical baggage, mainstream viewpoints grant us only single sight. Laurens Van Der Post, borrowing the phrase from William Blake, names the white Christian masculine European the "one-eyed giant," a Cyclops.[150] Cognitive behaviorism, roosting on one side of the dualistic split, commands that we use reason in deciding about matters of the heart lest our unruly emotions deceive us. Psychoanalysis and its revisionists, privileging the other eye, believe our choices are determined by unconscious desires. One's mind has pitifully little to do with it.

Few of us would doubt that using either our head or heart alone in romance courts disaster. Because why? We want the person to be as we see them, don't we? We want them to meet our needs. The heart can be deceived; and the mind can be deceived too. In addition, the person who wants us to "love" him might fake it, thereby deceiving us by trying to "give" us what we want -- or at least what she thinks we want. Come then the woes.

Sometimes, we do desperately want to deceive ourselves. But we do not have to. If we crave authentic love-choices, we can use second sight. Because of the power of consciousness, we have the possibility honestly to see, listen, and pop questions to the person standing there before my eyes. Hearthead working together brings most truth to the surface.

I borrow from the artist: Picture a woman hitchhiking with her dog on Canada's transcontinental Highway. It's late at night. Fireflies are "buzzing 'round her head like candles in the fog."[151] Who wouldn't be looking out there for a ride through the night?

He's a trucker struggling to stay awake and too tired to make it through the night. Life has become just a job. He's tired of "writing letters to himself and living in the dark." The songwriter suggests they are ripe to meet, "bound for glory, bound for living on the edge.... She has a new way of living, a new way of looking at life... he's got an 84 International and two kids he left back home with his wife." It's outlaw. Whatever her marital status, he is married. They will have to violate the trading of at least one set of vows. "Two comets heading for a bed," they do negotiate the darkness. Then comes what I call the "the morning-after-the-night-before":

> *On the Trans-Canada highway, the sun came climbing up the cab. When it finally hit the windshield, they were waking up from what little sleep they had. When the heat hit the blankets,*

they were looking for love at second sight; staring at each other, finding it in the morning light.[152]

If love is blind, it isn't as myopic on second sight. Whether we let ourselves see the truth "in the morning light" -- no matter how disappointing -- or only see what we want to see in order to confirm what we thought we saw in the first place is our choice. Nobody has statistics or ever would or could get them to provide so-called objective information in this regard. It is a purely existential, qualitative matter. The "quantitative imperative" in psychology is bad joke waiting for a laugh when it comes to most of the issues treated in this book. Love relationships simply are of a different ilk than what numerical manipulation can generate. It will be absolutely one-in-a-row every time whether or not second sight succeeds in spying the grounds for a genuine relationship and finds it in the light of day. Second sight can also say, "I don't want to know the truth, I don't want to see the proof; "Tell me my lying eyes are wrong." "I never went to bed with a woman ranked # three on the scale of ten. But I woke up with a few."

It matters not whether genital sexuality punctuated the night in the cab. With daylight, a second look can give truth. The quizzical line, "I wonder what I promised her last night," make evident that eye-talk and body language would best move forward, not to ventriloquism, but to conversation. This is just one of the many places at which phenomenology, by privileging consciousness, escapes the dualistic trap of generating a theory which looks scientific but in terms of everyday life is rationally chaotic and useless.

Joy and gladness

By emphasizing the serious and transformative powers of the outlaw encounter, I have distinguished it from other intense or dramatic sexual relationships. But the partners don't sit on pins and needles twenty-four-seven. It isn't all doom and gloom. Outlaws laugh together, too, share tender moments, dance, exchange ideas about art, science, politics, and business, and cry over ordinary life events. Mostly, the partners do ordinary things and most of their interaction is ordinary. They go grocery shopping together, visit the Post Office, have too long discussions about which restaurant to eat in, attend concerts, do laundry, rent movies, eat popcorn, wash dishes, or load the dishwasher. In "moments," her chit-chat bores him; she tunes him out sometimes, distracted, when he pontificates about the evils of suicide bombers.

"Let enter" showcases the fine line between ambiguity and ambivalence in the relationship. Just as indicated in the reflections on first love, ambiguity laces all relationships. Things can be correct from more than one point of view; the same loving person who I find amazing is also imperfect. It is a challenge to learn to love and hate the same person at the same time. Ambivalence signifies the failure to meet the challenge. Instead, I capitulate and split. I idealize one and demonize the other. Henceforth, I vacillate from facts to suspicion, from truth to lie, from love to hate. Willie Nelson wrote it simply, "Sometimes its heaven; sometimes it's hell; sometimes I don't even know."[153] Ambiguity, according to Merleau-Ponty, is daring to stare ambivalence in the face.

In one "moment," the relationship feels like sure love, solid and firm, safe and secure, headed for permanency. In the next moment, it feels volatile -- in the words of the woman in the outlaw parable, "precarious" -- as if it is about to go up in smoke. Leonard Cohen makes the point poetically, "Love is like smoke, beyond repair."[154] Another man writes, "She knows all the best roads to Paradise; she also owns a detailed map of hell." In one moment, you crow, "I know where love is"; in the next, you feel despair that "love is past the point of rescue." Ambiguity melts down into ambivalence.

"Let Enter" also focuses on the destruction wrought by deception and cheating. But not every outlaw relationship involves treachery. Not all outlaws resemble the "blue blood lady and the ex-convict!" Run-of-the-mill flaws, foibles, and fragilities constitute the norm. Outlaws are everyday people who have to cope with, not an autistic child or changing dirty diapers, but with major differences that create obstacles to the very possibility of co-generating either a healthy or special needs child. The differences are exciting and stimulating; but they can also grate on the nerves and pull the partners to the end of their respective ropes. It all comes out in the wash, both the wine grapes and the juice grapes, both the laughter and tears. Only you can sort it out...for you. It takes honesty, courage, and resolve. But meanwhile, lots of smiles flash and fond hopes do blossom for the future. Waylon Jennings sings of the joy to come:

"Ladies love outlaws like babies love a bunch of stray dogs; ladies touch babies like a banker touches gold, and outlaws touch ladies deep down in their souls... One day I saw him staring and it chilled me to the bone, and I knew I had to see that look on a child of my own."[155]

CHAPTER 4

The Intimate Partner

"Come grow old with me, the best is yet to be."[156] Robert Browning

Intimacy is a phenomenon of maturity. Erik Erikson calls it the first task of adulthood. Mainstream developmental psychology makes achieving a sense of identity the prerequisite for the capacity for intimacy, the alleged outcome of a successful adolescence. It is a transition. It fits into a box, into the next psychosexual-psychosocial stage. This viewpoint meshes with establishment norms, mores, and conventions about love that are based upon traditional Judeo-Christian values about marriage and the family.

From this standpoint also, the theories "predict" that sooner or later most of us settle down, move in with someone, or get married. Often, the new arrangement is in service of parenting a child. We take a stab at permanent commitment. Usually, it means we have gone though some significant heterosexual experiences and have seasoned somewhat. It is no endpoint, however, and no final resting place. Although marriage, "housekeeping," or cohabiting constitutes an explicit or implicit promise of "growing old together," each arrangement is more truly a new beginning. We try to blend a psychosexual-psychosocial sense of oneness into a healthy sense of twoness. We live out the implications of the words "responsibility" and "commitment" especially since we are striding simultaneously into the world of advanced schooling or starting our career-trajectory. We are paying rent, too, wiping dirty bums, making car payments, buying life insurance, and maybe carrying a mortgage.

Is not the picture too pat? Just pencil into the picture a white picket fence and you have framed a vignette of the American Dream. However, it is possible to assess intimacy outside this tidy framework. Marriage, neither historically nor nowadays, is the only or best cradle within which to cultivate intimacy. Surely, many marriages give us shinning examples of enduring love; but not all do. This chapter, therefore, brackets any social structures which might embrace a particular relationship. Intimacy is a psychological achievement neutral with respect to any particular structural arrangement; it has everything and nothing to do with marriage or cohabitation. Marriage is neither the enemy of love nor its treasury.

True Love

> *I have been astonished that men could die martyrs for their*
> *religion -*
> *I have shudder'd at it.*
> *I shudder no more.*
> *I could be martyr'd for my religion*
> *Love is my religion*
> *And I could die for that.*
> *I could die for you.*[157] John Keats

Is it possible for a man to come into one's own? I came into my own with her. It's that simple. And that complicated. Oh, man, my tale is so complex it's convoluted. Before her, I made more mistakes than any man under the sun. I didn't only do it the hard way or go the wrong way, didn't just defy all the odds or defy gravity. I went straight to hell and back.

Ok! Go ahead, crack a smile. I know. My story is just one variation of the human struggle to love. We all feel that in romance we had it harder than anyone, don't we? After I was finally dwelling in the shelter of an intimate bond, I would say to anyone who would listen, "I earned every one of these grey hairs on my head and all the silver in my beard." Laugh if you want to, my man. Just the way your eyes dropped now, betrays it. You are saturated with confessional discourse. "True stories," jabbered on Oprah's and similar TV shows, embroidered with dramatic pain and the gain, glut popular culture. God alone knows how many tall tales have you've listened to in this very room. I'll spare you the gory details of my early woes, my dark and bitter past.

She's dead now. I almost said she died of natural causes, but that statement would be absurd. In whatever way we die, the cause of death is always...Life. Death is life's only true imperative. In the face of it, we humans live in such a way that we pick the path to our preferred demise. My Alexandra wore her heart on her sleeve. She had a big warm heart. Lord God Almighty, in certain moments of closeness, she would slip that heart into my hand and just as easily cradle my soul in her little palms. Such moments are so tender, so raw, and vulnerable that it is hard to explain them. It took my breath away each and every time. Sometimes when we would break an embrace, especially when one of us abruptly had to go somewhere to meet some reality demand, it would feel like an amputation. There is no better word for it. "How do we make sense of this?" I continually puzzled. "How can we understand the power of this touch?" Well, we talked about it. Every now and again, one of us would bring it up. But we couldn't find a satisfactory explanation.

One thing we did constantly was talk to each other, really talk. We talked full speech, not just chit-chat but intense talk, talk in which we challenged one another. At first, the picture of our hands trading soul and heart was the best we could come up with. Then one winter Sunday afternoon basking in the afterglow, when everything was so still the silence of the falling snow cut like a knife, she said: "Eureka! I got it. 1+1=1." I didn't even have to ask. I just said, "Roll over."

Alexandra's heart was always at risk.
For our first date, we met over coffee and tea on her half-hour lunch break in the mall where she worked. A mutual friend had connected us.

I emailed her and we made a date. Driving to meet her, my anticipation was sky high and seemingly way out of proportion. It was 17 November, snowing in Anchorage with the wind whipping from the north. Driving was hazardous. I was vigilant. And yet from out of the blue, the scene from *West Side Story* flashed before my eyes, the one in which Tony and Maria are about to meet for the first time. I hummed Leonard Bernstein's melody, "Something's happening. Something's coming" Then, I shrugged it off as foolish. "Don't go "bananas" over a woman before you even…peel her," I chuckled, immediately aware that I had prematurely pegged this encounter as a man-woman "thing." Then, while observing a car in front of me skid off the road I said under my breath, "Don't slide off no slippery slope."

Do you believe in "love at first sight?" When I saw her, immediately we smiled at each other. She was sparkling. Since she was dressed plainly, even subdued, it wasn't glitter that assaulted me. As if by magic or by grace, a double-showing mirror flashed her my way. The outer looking glass reflected her lovely face; from the flip side shone her insides, the love-rich and gorgeous core of her very soul. I know, that sounds corny, right off the wall. Years later, I stumbled upon a fifty dollar Greek word that captures it, "physiognomy." The word combines "nature" with the "one who knows." It fits. At first sight, I grasped her physiognomy. Ever since, she has been "woman" for me, all women wrapped into one.

I don't remember what we said for icebreakers. After she said enough for me to realize that she was incredibly intelligent, I mentioned the "glow." She blushed. I was savvy enough to know that if someone blushes like that, then she has nothing to hide. She is hanging right out there. Even as I was thinking about her blushing, my eyes spontaneously darted a time or two from her glowing cheeks to the other place where she was hangin' out. No surprise, she caught me looking and called me on it. I could feel my face redden. "You blushed too, Derek," she said. And she drew the vital conclusion, "I'm safe with you." I think I hemmed and hawed a bit, in agreement. Then she glanced at her watch. As I saw her gather herself together, I wanted to hold back the rushing minutes. That, too, became an oft repeated experience. We never had enough time. We still don't.

As we were moving down the hall, she walked briskly because we had over-extended the break-time. I reached to touch her shoulder.

She spun, as if on cue. Like a ballerina twirling, she danced into my arms, perfectly placed. It was as if we had been practicing endlessly to mesh and now we had got it just right. Just as effortlessly, she eased away from my arms. The impromptu pas de deux jolted me. I'll never understand how it happened. We continued another fifty yards or so and stopped at the foot of three stairs leading to the next landing, just outside her agency. We hugged again, just as spontaneously. This time, we went flush. I got hard immediately, uh, I mean I got soft immediately. I mean -- you know exactly what I am talking about! Yeah, you understand don't you, about the relativity of simultaneity in the Enfolding Universe? We broke this hug too, relatively quickly. There is no way I can even approximate the time of the "moment." Time stood still. Or it performed one of those saddleback tricks of Einstein, or a Heideggerian spiral, or some complexly folded synchronicity, or -- I don't know what I am talking about! But time as a linear sequence of before-now-after had surely ceased to exist. Whatever the hell Einstein had destroyed of Newton's tidy universe, I know that this "moment" contained all time forever and anon. I always knew this woman and always would know her.

I watched her as she walked up the few steps, memorized by the surprises of the last half hour and her lovely... ass. She turned to me one last time. We gazed into each other's eyes across some evolving Grand Canyon. She had a quizzical look on her face, the exact same puzzled look that I had on mine. Hell, I didn't need a mirror to tell me the truth of that synchronicity, even though suddenly everything was out of time and probably I was out of my mind. We were two hearts looking at each other. "How did we just do that?" our hearts spoke across the interval. "Where did the people we just were an instant ago go?" We had just changed each other's lives. Our second hug was lethal.

Throughout our relationship, I could never understand the power of our touch. Early on, I asked her, "What are you made of? Are you sure you're just flesh and blood and bone?" She just smiled, blew me a kiss and said, "I'm not the Bionic Woman, that's for sure! Come here, Derek. Feel me... No, not there... yes, there... down there... like that... yes.... more..."

Hell, we were always touching, just as we were always talking with one another, writing emails, and sending SMS messages.

Communication by touch and text was extensive and equally significant. Whenever we were moving about in the same room, we couldn't turn around without touching.

Intimacy is what you want me to discuss, my man, right? For me, the "way of the beginning" I just described is a metaphor of the whole. Everything was there: mystery, sensuality, honesty, vulnerability, and the blush. Each man-woman first encounter might carry such a valence. Either you become pregnant with intimacy, or else you botch it. If you don't like the way he smells, the sound of her voice, the quality of his thinking, or the way she carries herself, then the new beginning you wish to make is DOA -- dead on arrival. You initiate instead the beginning of the end. The Universe might have made an appointment for us because on that day snowflakes were descending like blossoms, the stars were properly aligned, and the Leonids were falling.

Driving across the bowl of Anchorage now really a mess with the snow, I kept chanting as if trying to write a song: "Time is a python / time and the tide / where is Einstein, the time-merchant, when you need him?" I emailed her as soon as I got back to my office. I needed to extend the time and was curious as hell to find out how she had processed the events. I didn't doubt that we had met, that's for sure, because I was still semi-hard. "What did we just do to each other?" I wrote, going right to the heart of the matter.

"I didn't know what to expect," she replied. "But everything felt natural, in spite of the blushing. The amazing thing, Derek, is that my heart feels at home already. I'll never forget that second hug. At your chest, I experienced a homecoming." I wrote back, "If I were you, Alexandra, I'd fall in love with me."

Well, my man, you and I can bullshit for hours about love. But when you boil it all down, our true love was just that: feeling whole and at home when we were together; feeling half and staring into a Black Hole without each other. We called it our "constant companionship."

About three months later, Alexandra wrote, "I am dizzy because I love you more than love." That captures intimacy for me. Love beyond love. At that point, I realized love is not a step to anything else in life. Love is an end in itself. In response to that particular email, I answered, "The whole world should think like you do." Even as I was writing that sentence, the thought came -- as if sent to me by Kierkegaard from beyond the grave, "If we would learn to love, we might learn to think." In the background of our lives then and there, spirals of revenge and counter-revenge worldwide were endlessly swirling. Terrorism and the terror of counter-terrorism, by shadowboxing, were killing thousands. I continued my message, "The collective rationalistic world cannot think its way out of a paper bag. Mercy must come first and then maybe rational thought might contribute something." "Since Lenin is dead," she wrote back, "Maybe you should run for president" She added three "smiley faces." At that point in time, we both knew that she was the only one of us with a revolutionary spirit.

The moment is etched in stone on my memory when it switched from the incredible beginning of a "good" relationship into true love. But you need a context.

I had had one protracted relationship before Alexandra. After grieving my painful divorce, I waited almost two years before "dating" again. Laura had no children. My twins, Chantal and Philip, were young teenagers. After a brief courtship -- ha, I keep talking like I am the purveyor of time -- we moved in together. The game of triangles is brutal: jealousy and rivalry are ugly phenomena; the compulsion to repeat is deadly. This particular horror lasted the length of two human pregnancies.

Laura's father's committed suicide. The total situation is important. She had defied him by taking out a student loan for university. He had wanted her to learn some marketable skill, like secretarial, that would prepare her immediately for the job market. The way she told me the story, it was an open wound between them. During her first return home, they skirted around it. It turned out she was the last one to talk with him before he hung himself. On this earth, the wound never had the chance to heal.

At her party for her fourteenth birthday, Laura got her first perm. She wore white and looked pretty. After the guests left, she wore her new muslin dress still, still unstained. By twilight time, her drunken mother passed out. With the TV blasting, she was sprawled on the couch in the living room, disheveled and wasted. In the lengthening shadows of the kitchen facing the dying light in the west, Laura stood washing the last of the dirty dishes. Her father came behind her, touched her and said with a faltering voice, "This is what men will want to do with you."

Stunned and quivering, both stared at each other with an unprecedented look. Each said, almost at the same time, almost as if the eyes of both had soared into the eye of the hurricane and had seen similar disasters in its wake, "No, 'it' won't work. 'It' would lead to no good."

When Laura told me the emotionally charged tale, I thought, "Cool! This woman understands. It should preempt any love-triangles, right?" Wrong! I discovered from her interactions with me and the kids, especially with Chantal, that she still ached inside. Instead of being satisfied about their choice, her father caved in to despair. Whatever had he wanted? What infinite desire killed him?

With me and my kids, Laura mounted a crusade. Chantal was just entering womanhood. The blush was on her. Laura's mission was to eradicate father-daughter passion. Like some kind of prophetess or avenging angel, she was an insufferable self-righteous superego on our backs. She was especially jealous of any time Chantal and I spent together.

I'm not perfect. So at first, my mind was open to her criticism. I wanted to be as good a father as possible. I considered as feasible her interpretations of my behavior. She accused me of being guilt-driven because of the divorce rather than authentically caring for my children. That, my man, cut not close but fatally into the juggler. She also insisted that my daughter's motivations "really" were manipulative, not sincere. It gave me headaches; it gave me nightmares. I started to feel more and more that she was misidentifying me and distorting the kids. I started to feel like I was caught up in her nightmare. I don't know how many times I said to her, "Who are you talking to?" She acted like I didn't know what I was talking about. In one interaction, when she was pitching a fit, I noticed her eyes. They looked …hungry. I said, "Laura, honey, what is it you need so desperately, tell me?" She shot back at me with venom, "I am not a needy woman. I know how to love. I-can-love-people-I-can." I shuddered and just zipped it.

In time, and it took too much time, I realized I couldn't live with someone who mistook and treated me like somebody else. When

I tried to talk to clarify the issues, she insisted she had the superior vantage point to see "my" family dynamics. I was just being defensive.

Years later, Chantal told me Laura resented her and Philip. She also said she was trying to be a superior version of their mother and punished them because of the impossibility. The situation was a vicious circle. It went from bad to worse.

When I was at my wits end, I dreamed one of those dreams in which I dreamed I was dreaming. Trapped within the swarming life of Jerusalem, I was an actor on location for Mel Gibson's *Passion of Christ*. Until the last moment, I did not know if I was to play the role of Saint Peter, Pontius Pilate, or Judas Iscariot. Suddenly, the makeup-wardrobe woman, a big Scandinavian wearing a "Hooter's" tee shirt with no bra, began to attach to me a fiery tongue and a long tail. I was to play the dragon that Saint George soon would slay. In the dream, I screamed, "You're making a mistake! You've got the wrong man!" She refused to listen to me and without flinching zipped me into the scaly costume. "I'm wearing somebody else's clothes," I wailed again, "Let me out of here!"

Whoever knows for certain when you're driving uphill or when you are going down, when you're coming or when you're going, when it's the beginning or when it's the end? Let me assure you, my man, this dream was the beginning... of the end.

Why am I telling you this? Your question is about intimacy, right? Well, I'm not just a jag-off who after his divorce stumbled into love with a brilliant woman, a political radical whose ass is a song [158] and moved to la-la land. This ordeal with Laura taught me harder lessons than even my divorce about what intimacy is not. Misidentifying the other poisons the roots of love. That leads to dumping a load of shit on someone and expecting them to carry it. The charade only lasts as long as the two parties collude, one acting the "container," as C. G. Jung[159] names it, and the other the "contained."

I started to tell you about the "moment" when I recognized indubitably that it had become true love. I don't know what you mean by "intimacy." I don't particularly like the word because almost everyone's first association to it is "into-bed-to-jump-the-bones." I prefer to say "enduring love," or "true love." True love involves heart, head, and genitals. Ya' gotta like the one you love, love the one you like, and get horny for the one you both like and love. Ha, now you expect I'm going to stumble around with that weird terminology of spirals, synchronicity, or "string theory," right? No. But there used to be a popular phrase, "Get your shit together." Well, maybe the bona fide saints like Jesus and Gandhi can consolidate their shit using their own steam, but most of us ordinary flunkies need the push and pull of others. We can't learn to love alone. What you are calling intimacy, my man, takes two. The cliché it takes two to tango in Paris contains a sliver of wisdom. Laura's conviction that she taught herself to love and worked her own "program" until she got it right is both self and other-deceptive. Friedrich Nietzsche,[160] that ole shit-kickin' stick of dynamite, shows us that the difference between a "conviction" and a "lie" is zilch, is nada. Funny, but when Laura and I said our parting words to each other, although I wanted to end with dignity and with both of our egos intact, nevertheless I let slip out, "You lied to me even when you were telling me the truth." That ambiguous line covers all the bases.

Alexandra, on the other hand, embodied for me the true way to love. The strength of a willow is precisely that it can bend. You don't stand there, dig in your heels, spread you toes, and grit you teeth saying, "I-can-love!" You bow; you open both your hands; you reach out to touch; you surrender.

Alexandra and I had been together for nine months but living separately. Gun shy, I wanted it that way; she concurred with my caution. By now, Chantal and Philip were finishing adolescence; her son by her previous marriage was just reaching it. Not only had we met each other's kids, but had included them in our relationship and were routinely doing things together. Don't construe these words to mean we re-created a small "Brady Bunch," but we felt like a family. All the pieces were starting to fit nicely. I asked her to marry me.

I asked her over a meal at out favorite Indian Restaurant. I asked her after we had supped on poppadums and dall, on sag paneer and tandoori chicken with naam and rice. When I popped the question and gave her the ring, she didn't screech, squeal and do cartwheels. And I didn't get down on my knees, babble like a schoolboy, or piss my pants. The moment was more a completion, restful and solemn. Slipping on of the ring was like stroking in the last arc of the circle we had been drawing for so many months. We celebrated with a mango lassie and spiced tea. Since she had a flight early the next afternoon to attend a week's seminar, we left early and went back to my place to make love.

Making love that night wasn't sex anymore. I mean it was sex but something else besides. It was like we were playing music or creating art. It was holy! It felt like we were kissing each other inside a cathedral, the way I imagine some medieval church I had read about in Paris, Rome, Cologne, or Trondheim. It had become genuine worship. I fell asleep still inside her.

When I awoke, she was sitting by my side wearing only a sheer blue shawl over her shoulders, richly embroidered. And she was rubbing my belly. "Don't you recognize me?" she teased. Her question was as soft as cotton baton. I squinted and tried to focus my sight. It was a shock. She never ever had awakened in the morning before me. In some curious way, everything felt band-new. I reached to touch the flesh and bone I was sure about. Warmth circulated between us. Our fingers were knitting our hands together, making them one. Our fingers played at turning the ring on her finger, moving over and under and over again, twisting and thereby choreographing its symbolism: 1+1=1. Our warm fingers were restless and vibrating. Our two separate hands kept slipping away, too, shifting from one holding position to another, still detached yet in concert. I felt tenderhearted. "If you were plastic and not skin," I joked, "or putty not flesh we'd be fused together by now, melded into one." On a back track the thought kept percolating, "How can ordinary flesh and blood hold such power over me?" I had full breath, but I was dizzy. I cupped her breasts. As I rolled her nipples between my thumb and index finger, I realized they were eyes that saw me, saw me through and through. It was delicious and unnerving.

And all the while, she waited. She waited and gazed at me with her nipple-eyes searching unhurriedly, seeing all of me. She waited with her fingers dancing. Her skin was warm butter changing into liquid ivory and it smelled, I swear, of the spices of the Indian food we had eaten, the curry and garam masala.

"If I were a fly, you could break me easily," I said, only marginally conscious of death's approach.

"No argument there," she said, sounding soft and ordinary.

151

"But I have a heart," I said, feeling raw. "You can break me worse."

Calmly, she said, "Nobody could ever hurt you like I can, Derek. But I will never hurt you."

Still she waited, touching me and suffering my meandering migrant fingers. There was no rush. We were creating the "now" between us. We were weaving the future. It was the beginning of the world. There is no hurry at the beginning of the world. When it is the beginning of the world, in sufferance and holy patience we wait.

In that "moment', she was the dawn breaking. Like Edvard Grieg, who wrote the music of being present at an absolute start, she orchestrated the dramatically beautiful sunrise, purple lavender red and orange. Only music can express the amazement of it. Alexandra was sitting there rubbing my belly and spreading light and beauty around us. And she was humming.

The sun was coming up bringing heat and light. We sat there holding hands, bathed in the colors of daybreak, alternately looking at each other with wonder, and kissing each other as if in the kiss alone was the breath of life.

So now, it was one more new beginning. Now, it was my final beginning. If it was hers, too, I could not know for certain. Then we made love.

While I was cooking breakfast, she dug out Lawrence's book of poetry *Look! We Have Come Through*. She chimed, "Listen to this from "First morning,"

> *Everything starts from us.*
> *We are the source.*[161]

If she didn't have to fly solo imminently, we would have flown united one more time right there and then, on the floor.

After breakfast, I drove her to the airport. The cold stone diamond of the engagement ring shot rays of warm love between us. "I never experienced making love like we did last night," she said. "This ring has mystical powers. Our souls were one." "Without you, it's just cold metal." I answered, knowing without doubt it was the truth. Then I grinned and uttered some Lawrence, "You are the call and I am the answer." "Yes, it's us," she said. "We put the heat in the fire." As I pulled into the parking area, as she was wont to do, she pulled out of her briefcase Dag Hammarskjold's *Markings*, quickly flipped to the right page and read his priceless lines:

> *This happiness is here and now,*
> *In the eternal moment of co-inherence.*
> *A happiness within you—but not yours.*[162]

By the time we got to the security checkpoint, we were both dreading the departure. "I picked a piss-poor time to give you the ring," I said. "It all feels too abrupt." Through sobs, she managed to say, "We are together, darling, no matter where we are. Our presence defies absence." Then waving to me, she disappeared through security without a beep. Too late, I noticed that she left her multi-colored sweater on the seat. I just held it and sniffed it, not practicing to be a full-blown fetishist mind you, but just to savor the scent of my woman.

Driving home, I was in a twilight zone. I remember bearing down while driving, making sure I was alert. When I got to the empty house, it hit me like a comet crashing with another rock. Sitting at table over an espresso, with her in the air somewhere en route to New Orleans, I felt a strange fear crawling. "Oh, shit," I complained to myself. My life is finally coming together. I had not bargained on this."

You look puzzled, my man. Don't you know what I mean? Do you think I, too, was invaded suddenly by a politician-preacher's contrived "war on terror?" No. And it wasn't just the idea of marriage that assaulted me either, although in honesty I can't rule out that interpretation completely. Don't you see? The Mystery had brought us a love-beyond-love. It followed naturally that now she was wearing my ring. But I wasn't expecting the encroachment of this other thing. Mr. All-American All-Pro Anticipation Personified! I didn't see it coming. I didn't foresee that I would worship her. This was outside what I had ever known and beyond anything I could have bargained for.

Whatever else we were doing that night, it was adoration. Now, I could not picture my life without her. Without her, I would be "half" for the rest of my life. The whisper of death terrified me. Hell, no, not a soft whisper! Death was shouting at me, "I have just pronounced on you a life sentence. I have sentenced you to death. From this, there is no exit." With or without her, it would be permanent.

The feelings did not subside. They got worse. All week, it was unbearable without her. Not to have her by my side for the rest of my life emerged as intolerable. Suddenly, simple things like going grocery shopping, falling to sleep with her in my arms, and waking up with her by my side seemed the most precious things in the whole world. I panicked at my raw vulnerability.

The second night after she was gone, I saw a dream. I was a little black ball, the size of a pea or maybe of a ball bearing. A giant wave of putrid smelling orange ooze buffeted me about. I was struggling, unable to surface and unable to drown! The medium turned into the ocean first, probably the Gulf of Alaska because ice floes were drifting like monks holding up their hands in prayer. Then the ocean started sinking and I was sinking with it. I couldn't stop the descent. I had nothing to hold as a handle. I remember screaming within the dream, "How in the hell can the ocean sink?" While I was struggling, chunks of a glacier were breaking off, so it must have been the Columbia near Valdez. The ice chunks were pouring into the seawater with a magnificent roar. I was bobbing and weaving, trying to dodge them as if I were a prizefighter, a hostage to the roaring crowd while fighting desperately to win the Heavyweight Crown, or boxing with my Destiny. Yeah, shadowboxing with sinking silhouettes!

I woke up in the middle of the night from this one. I could see the darkness. Inside, I screamed, "How can I put out the dark?" I had no idea what I meant. Two years earlier, I had stopped believing in love, period; I gave it up as a "bad job." Now I believed in a touch that would not end and faced permanent longing. Unconsciously, I was scared shitless of ultimate darkness.

Do you ever wonder about commonplace experiences that no psychologist ever writes about, or very few ordinary individuals discuss? How about when both men and woman have a sexual tryst with someone other than the soon-to-be-spouse the week before the wedding? They might even "fly united" with a stranger the night before they tie the knot? There are no stats about this "ballgame," excuse my pun. In fact, our polite establishment-society doesn't even want to acknowledge that the phenomenon regularly occurs. And your close friend is not apt to walk up to you and say, "Let me tell you what I did the night before my wedding!" But we all have heard a spate of stories.

What's going on? I am talking about upstanding sincere people, a man or woman who will be true blue to their partner for the next forty years! What's the dynamic? Does the terminal phase of engagement carry with it a case of corruption? Or is this temporary insanity? No. It is death stalking us, my man! Before the solemn pronouncement, "Till death do us part," Death pays a visit to some cheap hotel, even if it is the Hotel Astoria, and turns down the sheets. The routine bachelor and bachelorette party pays lip service to the "last night of freedom," making the matter light. But by sleeping with someone after the "party," one takes it far beyond funny and extends, too, the locations on the anatomy that the lip service... serves.

To know what it takes to be intimate, you gotta crawl up the asshole of death, my man, feel the womb of fear and face it.[163] Dwelling in this "moment of destiny," you live your whole life. You realize you have only one life to lead, one only. It is the zenith. You recognize that you are in the "place" where you are meant to be, even though probably you would never have chosen it. You recognize, too, that all your previous choices, good, bad and ugly brought you here. What remains is that you find the courage to "leap." Like Nietzsche challenges us, we must affirm it all and wish everything to return back again in exactly the same way it happened... with no additions and no subtractions.

By the time Alexandra got back from the "Big Easy," I had grown up. We went all the way. We traded vows.

For a "moment" there, we had a full house. It wasn't a perfect round; but it was warm and life felt centered. We just did normal, ordinary, usual things. Much of our life revolved around the activities of the kids, their sport, ballet, and school activities. Alexandra and I both read a lot, listened to music, enjoyed the theatre, concerts, and a good movie -- which for us was not Hollyweird's usual fare. I'm not saying we were "culture vultures," you know. We had picnics and snowball fights; we frequented flea markets and regularly walked hand and hand by the water; on certain occasions we jumped into the Jeep to go find the best site to view the Northern Lights.

We also shared everything equally. Cooking, cleaning and doing dishes. Sometimes, uh, she'd be on top and sometimes I would. I'm not talking about the kind of equality demanded by low-grade shrieks and squalls who want to erase the differences between the genders! Hey, look, my man! I'm for equal pay for equal work and for equal social, educational, economic, and political opportunities for all genders, races, colors, and creeds. From where I sit, however, that will never happen in my lifetime. During this run-up to election 2008, it is dubious that the USA will tolerate a woman calling the shots for Uncle Sam. France, Germany and Little Britain condemn the Muslim women's burka. Even as we speak, "Junior" is building a racist wall between Mexico and the Big Mac. No. I'm talking about deep eyeball-to-eyeball equality between a man and a woman that shelters togetherness and solitude. A woman isn't more of a woman, when she becomes more like a man; a man is less a man, if he refuses to face his feminine side.

Early in our relationship, this issue of woman-man equality surfaced over one of her short lunch breaks. She mentioned that D. H. Lawrence wrote about the nonsense of trying to equilibrate a ruby and a rose. Later, she sent me an email:

> *Dearest Derek,*
> *After you left, Lawrence visited me. ☺   He shared two lovely*
> *images of authentic gender equality. Mutual love is a flame*
> *between wax and air. A disproportion of either ingredient creates*
> *a god-awful mess. The flame goes out and the union disappears.*
> *Two stars in the sky need space between them to cast towards*
> *each other their bright light, imperial beauty, and warmth. Take*
> *away the distance between them, and the ensuing collision would*
> *create a destructive conflagration. Thus space between stars both*
> *connects them and sets them at a distance. Our love is not in-*
> *you or in-me, it is between-us. We must shepherd with supreme*
> *gratitude the mystery given to us.*
> *Much Love,*
> *Alexandra*

Oh, man, was I ever glad to hear that we saw this one eye to eye. I simply responded, "We kill love with either a craving for individuality or the yen to merge, right?" Tell me I was surprised when she simply wrote back: "1+1=1."

What's a vow, my man? Does it signify just dried ink on a legal document? No. A vow is a promise. It is a love-letter to the future. With true love, you must renew the pledge everyday. By daily renewal, you keep the promise. Commitment and responsibility fall into line. It can be a delicate juggling act between duty and desire in any committed love relationship, marriage or not. These two "Big D's" never are arranged in a pattern of pre-established harmony. You gotta work at it. Sometimes, you gotta go "whole hog" to sustain the balance. Go all the way. For Alexandra and me, too deep, and too far, and too high were never enough.

My man, now it's my turn to smile. We had no perfect intimacy. I never canonized St. Alexandra in life and won't now, now that she is dead. "All the way" for us meant walking barefoot on some rocky roads. We had "moments" of recoil, of snapping back to our own solitary singleness in anger and frustration. Sometimes the recoil bordered on stubborn selfishness and false pride. But we worked at it; we did what I could never do with Laura. We put a barometer to our storms and talked them through.

    You want some "for instances," eh? Fine, well, let's see. Ok. We never argued about money, my man, or over the children. I'd say one bone of contention would best be subsumed under the rubric, "Who owns the time?" Personally, I think every couple has to deal with this one. If you are going to blend two lives into one, there are issues about what time do you eat dinner, retire for sleep -- ha, wait, this is a better way to express it, "the politics of the bedroom." Do you turn the heat high or open the window for the night? Do you leave a light on, a lamp or a nightlight, or do you, uh, grope for each other in the dark? Do you buy separate twin beds? Or buy a Queen size, in which you can wrap and twist each other's legs into one warm pretzel? Or purchase a King size, in which you each can get comfortably... lost? The issue Alexandra and I used to hassle about, however, was making love in the morning. That was my favorite time. I am an early riser. I joke that if I ever write my autobiography I'm going to title it *Woes of an Early Riser*. I wake up... up, if you catch my drift. Alexandra awoke like a flower, slowing unfolding. She did not appreciate my restlessly chaotic fingers going on an "explore" in her... uh, geographical vicinity. That's why the morning after our engagement was so unprecedented. You remember, don't you, that she asked me if I recognized her? Anyway, I was touchy about the matter. It wouldn't matter that we made love every other hour on the hour day and night (smile), but I would be irritated that she'd roll away and grumble when I poked her at seven A.M. She just got frustrated with the intrusion and doubly perturbed by my touchiness. It triggered a battle royal or two. Damn, Einstein and his warped notions about time! Hey, my man let me tell you: in terms of woman-man intimacy, nobody owns the time.

But by far and away, the issues that make the Grand Canyon look small—well, it started with the illegal invasion of Iraq. Now, I never bought any of the Neocon's lies about the weapons of mass destruction, my man. Give me some credit! But I thought it was ridiculous to see people marching all over the known world with Bush's picture decorated with a mustache that made him look like Hitler. Alexandra tried to make me understand the world's "truth," namely that Uncle Sam is the self-appointed patriarch of the world.

"The USA controls everything from behind curtains," she stated with a large sprinkle of sarcasm.

"Alex, come on. Most countries want the Uncle Sam involved. They want his muscle and money."

"No, Derek. The USA feigns non-interference even as it meddles, bribes, and then sabotages the world's governments. Eventually, it punishes those who won't kowtow. Usually, it bullies the world community into imposing sanctions on its foes. Or it threatens force. This time Bush is flipping the finger at the whole world and illegally invading."

"There are other countries going along with us: Britain, Japan, Australia and Poland."

"Listen, this is no genuine coalition. 'Preemptive diplomacy' and 'preventive war' are Hitler's tactics."

"Oh, Stalin was a walking living breathing saint, was he? Is that why he assassinated Trotsky?"

"I'm not defending Stalin."

"I'm not defending Bush."

"Who are you defending?"

"Nobody, I just want our country to be safe."

"Don't lump me together with these gutless countries who are obeying Uncle Sam's commands. I'm not joining the 'us'. I dissociate myself from this unholy ...what, you can't even call it a 'war'! If the girl scouts from Missouri played the Kansas City Chiefs, would you call it 'competition'?"

I started shouting that "we" had to stop the "butcher of Baghdad" and prevent Iran and North Korea from developing nuclear weapons. She screamed that Bush wants to be the butcher of Baghdad and that the USA is the only country that should not be allowed to have nuclear weapons because it is the only nation that has ever used them to destroy people. I zipped it at that point because I could not defend my country's hypocrisy concerning dropping the atomic bomb, not just once but twice. It ended a stalemate.

Every cold war smolders. This one simmered white hot. Our argument degenerated into a seething renewal of the struggle between Super Powers. Alexandra and I, living sap dab in the Last Frontier where oil is king, had to put the damper on. We didn't make love that night. I crashed on the couch. At least, I didn't have to worry about dreaming about a Mushroom Cloud or about black slaves in chains being shipped to the Big Mac. A least, I didn't have to worry about awaking early; I never fell asleep.

When I told my grandfather on my mother's side I'd gotten engaged to Sonya my first wife, he blurted out spontaneously lines of conventional wisdom: "Kiss and make up," Derek. Then he elaborated. "Never go to sleep with an argument because that's who you'll wake up with. And never argue about religion or politics." I smiled. I didn't take the advice seriously. The kiss-last-thing-at-night-and-first-thing-in-the-morning, well, that's a charming idea. But I was too young or naïve or both to realize that adults come to hold views so centrally and so deeply they would divorce over or die for them.

Some personal convictions are as intimate as sex, my man. It matters little on a one night stand, does it, whether or not you and your bedmate might eventually stand on the same platform and look to see, if not the same things, at least a convergence of negotiable matters? It is a matter of integrity. Sometimes, it is necessary for would-be lifetime lovers to sacrifice all for love. Sacrificing when integrity is at stake happens on a different level than giving up one's vibrator or starting to use a condom. It takes courage. When push comes to shove, the basic irreconcilable differences and genuine grounds for divorce are tucked within the fold where sexual compatibility and the meeting of the minds should cradle the couple... but fail.

Alexandra was born and raised in St. Petersburg, so she had a different set of peepers for viewing the Red White and Blue. She argued that the entire "war on terror" was contrived. "It's a transaction in the politics of oil, a business venture with blood the currency." She emailed me:

> *Dearest Derek,*
> *I love you, you 'old fart' don't you know it? You are the smartest man I know. But come on! Wake up and smell the roses! 'Freeing the world for democracy' is just a code phrase for spreading capitalism. The military-industrial combine wants endless war not the end of conflicts. Ever since the USSR collapsed ending the cold war, the Big Mac has craved a replacement to fill its capitalistic coffers. War generates profits impossible to make by selling three billion hamburgers. Enter the terrorists. They gave the excuse. That's why the USA military let 9-11 happen, just like it knew in advance about Pearl Harbor but deliberately didn't stop the attack. It was the lead-pipe excuse for the military-industrial complex to enter the war. It is insidiously brilliant, my darling. While the American taxpayers foot the bill for war and reconstruction, the money makers rake in billions, hand over fist. The oil pipeline sucker president is basically big business's publicity agent. Tonight, Derek, lets not go cold and isolated. Let's go hands over fist, ok?*
> *So much love,*
> *Alexandra*

Hey, my man! I just saw your eyes dart off with a bored look on your kisser. Does this mental fencing over global-political issues irritate you? Don't you get the big picture? You don't want to hear, do you, that what the USA does best is promote slavery, pollute the environment and drop atomic weapons? Are you just a brainwashed academic "brain-fart" who can't comprehend the connection between love and war? Why not just make up one of those ridiculous quantitative questionnaires? Yeah, frame the questions you think are important and, damn straight, you'll get the answers you are looking for. But love doesn't fit on the ding-dong bell curve, understand? And it isn't hiding away in some Platonic world of ideal forms either. Nor is it some lovey-dovey kissing of the petun-y! Everything in life is interrelated. Is your social science "club" ever going to stop chopping up everything into neat little artificial boxes and then selling the contents as science? Shit! Love is lived everyday against the backdrop of how the local football team had fared, the weather report of ten inches of snow, the church bizarre held next Thursday and Friday, and marching downtown tomorrow to exercise our right of political dissent. So unless you want to terminate this discussion immediately, stick lying statistics up the place where the sun never shines and listen up. Love is in everyday life, not in your psychological theories!

The matter of Abu Ghraib both disgusted me and revealed the deep-seated racism of my people. Soon after, Condoleezza Rice waltzed across Europe singing the deceitful tune of 'extraordinary rendition" to cover up USA illegal transports to torture chambers. Next, the west committed a heinous crime against humanity. It cut off vital survival funds because, in one of the freest and fairest elections in recent history, the Palestinian people elected into power Hamas. The west preferred a puppet-government and thus punished an already occupied, locked-in and beleaguered people. Predictably, it provoked inter-factional fighting. Pop goes the weasel!

While Alexandra and I were on holidays in Prague during 2006 July, it was the last straw. We watched the horror on prime time TV. Instigated and supported by the USA and Britain, Israel demolished Lebanon. The world watched, too, and in spite of eloquent pleas in Rome from even the pro-business Prime Minister Fouad Siniora 'they' did nothing to stop the devastation and murdering. Both the European

Union and the United Nation's were too chicken-shit to stop the bullies. It was pathetic. The world has never witnessed anything as barbaric.

The ton of bricks finally hit me. I apologized to Alexandra for my pig headed-ness. She just said to me, before she put her tongue in my mouth to end our cold war, "I guess our love was just dying to live. Now come inside me."

Fidelity to vows requires truth, courage, and the willingness to sacrifice. Oh, yeah, and the capacity to say "I'm sorry" and to mean it. As far as I'm concerned, our love was a marvel because we never allowed the chords of untoward circumstances to strangle our love. In spite of our respective flaws foibles fallibilities stupidities, we kept our pledge. Instead of dwelling in love-killing withdrawal, we snapped back from each snapping away. After we unwound the knot, we re-lighted the candle and re-arranged the stars in our sky. We surrendered. That made all the difference.

Then in an eye-blink, home was empty. My twins trekked off to university in the Lower 48. The only time they came home that autumn was for Thanksgiving. Tragically, an avalanche killed Bruce, Alexandra's son while he was on Christmas holidays with his father in Sweden. Bruce died before the bizarre hanging of Saddam. The year 2006 was not a seller year for the Lebanese people, for Saddam, or for us.

It was a phenomenological death for my Alexandra. I lost count of the times I heard her say, "I wish it had been me and not him buried under ice and snow." I was savvy enough to know grief is a killer. I worried. But when I saw that she got out the tears, expressed her agony, rage, and disgust for her careless ex-, I figured she was out of the woods. She would find a place for this. We'd laugh again in our empty home; there would be sunshine again, rainbows, and the Northern Lights.

Sorrow kills, too. Maybe by having such a big heart, Alexandra cradled too much of it. Cooped up within her warm heart, sorrow spontaneously combusted and took blaze. On May Day, she died of a broken heart. The "half-assed" doctors say she died of a heart-attack. Who cares that I can't comprehend how Einstein's theories destroyed Newton's idea of absolute time, or understand what happened the first time that woman and I touched, or why the second hug was lethal? I know why she died.

Death is the only true imperative in existence. When Alexandra obeyed the law and gave back to Life the Death she owed it, for me the world that usually goes round and around went upside down. Einstein is correct, no absolute space. And time stood still, too. He is right again. The measurable concept of linear time that dominates western thinking is bankrupt. In 1933, Einstein and Freud exchanged correspondence published under the title, "Why war?"[164] It is so timely that it could have been written today or yesterday or tomorrow. They did not live to witness the Holocaust Hiroshima Mai Lai Rwanda Darfur Iraq Lebanon.... But they both knew they were up against a cauldron of destruction. As Nietzsche trenchantly demonstrates, western thought devalues time in favor of eternity, demeans this earth while looking to heaven, and denigrates the body while privileging the soul. Platonic Christendom's violent greedy racist nerve cheapens life and renders individuals expendable, especially the poor, the disenfranchised, and the disadvantaged masses.

But it was precious, this life of my beloved Alexandra. Her death broke my heart. Excuse me, if I want to scream and ball my eyes out. Excuse me, if I prefer livingness to any mechanical, technical alternatives. Pardon me, yeah, if I cry out for mercy, forgiveness, and love for all humankind.

On her death bed, she was conscious long enough for us to say "good-bye." Some things never change. I could feel her mentally juggling our marriage of two hearts and minds so that I might be clear what belonged in her hands and what would be left in mine ever after. To share my feelings in the most beautiful words, I read her parts of a Lawrence poem:

I have been so innerly proud, and so long alone,
Do not leave me, or I shall break.
Do not leave me.

What should I do if you were gone again
So soon?
What should I look for?
Where should I go?

What should I be, I myself
'I'?

Do not leave me.

What should I think of death?
If I died, it would not be you:
It would be simply the same
Lack of you,
The same want, life or death
Unfulfilment
The same insanity of space
Think, I daren't die
For fear of the lack in death.
And I daren't live.

Do not leave me.[165]

And some things never do change. With tears rolling down both our cheeks, she reached out her tiny hand and touched me. She spoke softly. This is my Alexandra in a nutshell. She did not say what most might say, "I love you." No. She said, "Thank you for loving me... so well." I could have died on the spot.

Bobby Lane, the legendary quarterback from the State of Texas, played most of his professional career for the Detroit Lions. He didn't have pure athletic ability and wasn't a graceful passer. But he was a tenacious leader. A quarter-century after he played, members of the Pittsburgh Steelers were still repeating words he reputedly spoke to fellow Texan, Doak Walker, one of sport's glamour boys, "I never lost a game, time ran out." Søren Kierkegaard says the same thing differently, "Live as if you are already dead."[166] That's how I came into my own. Nothing frightens me now. What else can possibly hurt me? "I wasn't afraid to be born," Garcia Lorca responded to an interviewer, "Why should I be afraid to die?"[167] I lost Alexandra but I never lost the freedom she helped me to win. She gave me the finest gift in the act of dying. She affirmed my love. I lack wisdom, but I seek it. If its high cost is perpetual longing, take the price tag off.

She is dead. Time stopped. I ponder it a lot these days. Time, our elusive cunning enemy is what everybody knows, but which nobody can explain. Probably, that's because it is so completely fused with our individual being. My coming into my own was my homecoming. When you come into your own, you permeate time; when you come home, you infiltrate the "moments" of your life. I'm only sure of one thing about time. It melts down. Yesterday now forever liquefy into one. And as far as relativity goes, I'm the last person on the globe to monkey around with Einstein's unfinished revolution. All I know is this. His account of the universe we live in unmasks mainstream's psychological theories as pathetically and hopelessly mired in a Newtonian universe which is passé. I cannot swallow relativity hook, line and sinker. About Alexandra, I sing with the ole possum George Jones, "There's nothing better once you've had the best."[168] That's pretty absolute. But it's my story, and I'm sticking to it. However, I do go along with Einstein 100% about the fluidity of time. Like right now I'm clear. We're talking, my man. And it's today. The day I met Alexandra was... yesterday or tomorrow or everyday -- every new day.

With her, every time felt like the first time.

Analysis of the Intimate Partnership

Two eagles, each strong and powerful in their own right, have flown their respective perches on the cottonwood trees along Resurrection Bay in Seward, Alaska. They circle the grey autumn sky. These proudest of creatures, holding up and supporting one another, are making love in mid-air. Each depends on the other, but each is infinitely strong in themselves.

The image is D. H. Lawrence's; it parallels what Alexandra in "True love" mentions: two stars with space between them; and wax and wick balanced such to shelter a quivering flame.[169] Lawrence continually strains the limits of his fertile imagination and stretches the plasticity of his English language to its breaking point to express his life-giving, love-enhancing insights. He says it in yet another way:

> *A woman is a flow, a river of life, quite different from a man's river of life: each river must flow its own way, without breaking*

its bounds; the relation of man and woman is the flowing of two rivers side by side, sometimes mingling, then separating again, and traveling on. [170]

Here's the rub. Lawrence's way of thinking runs against the grain of western psychology's perspective on intimacy. Mainstream thought makes the phenomenon an outcome of an alleged developmental process. If one does not first experience self as a source of strength and power in her or his own right -- so the story goes -- it is impossible to enter into an authentic intimate bond. Attaining a sense of identity is the precondition for intimacy. One-ness must precede two-ness. To be dubious and shaky about one's identity and where one fits in impedes intimacy. At first blush, it sounds not only brilliant but true, not only true but wise. With second sight, however, it shows as only a partial insight aligned with pragmatic behaviorism. It displays the myth of rugged individualism, the insistence that self-reliance best generates positive outcomes or results -- and to name the bottom line, financial profit. So the mainstream bias about the capacity for intimacy reflects the American way of life, packaged and exported to the world. Like any partial insight, surely it has value. At first, it suits to elaborate its positive contribution. Then I will come back to Lawrence's vision.

The lack of a sense of identity and feeling at home creates two loveless outcomes. Closeness is either so threatening that one shies away from it or else one hops on the back of the perceived stronger one and, as Gail Sheehy describes it, tries to "piggyback" into the world of adult love. [171] Stated somewhat differently, either one is terrified of losing oneself and one's bearings, or one becomes a psychological parasite. Not infrequently, a male and female click and form a bond precisely because they perceive the possibility of feeding off each other. In a psychotherapy session with a young couple contemplating marriage but struggling mightily in their day to day being together, an image flashed as I listened to them pulverize each other's weaknesses. I saw a precarious balance of two crutches leaning against each other without any people under them to support or hold them up. This image spurs the strong conclusion that the collusion of two weaknesses never adds up to a single strength. Simone Weil describes the logical and phenomenological consequence of such symbiotic relatedness: "We hate what we are dependent upon, and we become disgusted with what depends upon us." [172]

Flip it over. Women and men are who grounded, individuals in their own right, are able to enter a relationship as equals, both separate and related. Intimacy halves their weaknesses and doubles their strengths.

Is attaining one's self-power, therefore, adequate for attaining intimacy? Does lack of it forecast love's derangement? I suspend belief in taken-for-granted orthodox western thinking and, therefore answer, "No." Identity is the necessary but insufficient condition for intimacy.

Stern and Marino describe the limitation of making identity the prime issue by showing it needs deepening: "Learning to love another human being is the greatest challenge in human experience because it makes the most fundamental moral and psychological demands"[173] Put differently, requisite for establishing and maintaining an intimate partnership is precisely going beyond self. Enter Lawrence. To his vision, I now return.

D. H Lawrence poignantly experiences the deadness of clinging to one's individuality. His *The Fox* addresses the grave demand to shed it. His words ooze with pain, "It had seemed so easy to make one beloved creature happy. And the more you tried, the worse the failure."[174] How come? What is lacking? Lawrence's diagnosis contests normative thinking. "Our dual worship of individuality and love in the same breath is absurd and elicits mockery... To love, you have to learn to understand the other more than she understands herself, and submit to her understanding of you."[175] The precious prancing ego must exit stage left.

Since the dawning of the modern world, Lawrence believes "We live in an age that believes in stripping away relationships."[176] From then until today, insofar as information technology increasingly blankets our life-space, we dwell in T. S. Eliot's "wasteland," living as "hollow men."[177] Lawrence has no patience for it. Western women and men, in their quest "to find themselves," to have their own personal space to "do their own thing," etc., have snapped all connections with the natural world of sunbeams, rainbows and the northern lights, severed vital contacts from friends and neighbors and smothered down the passionate touch-sparks of love to empty and blank.

167

Lawrence turns it 180 degrees, reversing the western preoccupation with individuality. Not separation, but the relationship between people is the primary given in life.

> *Everything, even individuality itself, depends upon relationship...*
> *Apart from our connections with other people, we are barely*
> *individuals, we amount... to next to nothing. It is in the living*
> *touch between us and other people... that we move and have our*
> *being. Strip us of our contact with the living earth and the sun,*
> *and we are almost bladders of emptiness... Our individuality*
> *means nothing.*[178]

Intrinsic to life are the sparks that flicker and glow between man and woman. Paramount is the quickening of their bond. Attachment comes first. It is not something a woman adds to her person, or a man enters into from without as he comes to her. All man-woman commitments and contacts build upon a fundamental natural link, a warm-hearted and compassionate life-flow. Lawrence considers the love between a man and a woman "the greatest and most complete passion the world will ever see... because it is dual, because it is of two opposing kinds... the perfect heartbeat of life, systole and diastole."[179]

> *Man is connected with woman forever, in connections visible and*
> *invisible, in a complicated life-flow that can never be analyzed...*
> *The woman... sends forth to me a stream, a spray, a vapor of*
> *feminine life that enters my blood and my soul, and makes me*
> *me. And back again, I send the stream of male life which soothes*
> *and satisfies and builds up the woman.*[180]

Women and men find their true individuality and their distinct being in this deep "warm flow of common sympathy" between them.[181] Radical healing for what ails us consists of the "livingness of woman-man touch. The couple's embrace is the most important touch, the veritable hinge upon the door both to individual health and to social sanity. Using the shrill voice of an Old Testament prophet Lawrence bellows and roars, "Touch or die."

Who is going to create peace in the world? Will it be our ambitious politicians, beholden to their wealthy campaign donors and worrying about their legacy in the history book? David Herbert Lawrence mocks the idea. This earth-bound mystic, to the contrary, insists that the tender passion of the lovers' caress alone can save the world. And he isn't kidding. This living touch, Lawrence insists,

> *is sex. But it is no more sex than sunshine on the grass is sex. It is a living contact, give and take: the great and subtle relationships of... man and woman. In this and through this we become real individuals, without it, without the real contact, we remain more or less nonentities.*[182]

What do you make of this debate? Is the mainstream correct? Do we follow a blueprint directing us to step from one box into another and from one stage or phase to the next? Is standing alone a precondition for standing together? Is growth the result of intra-individual, intra-psychic integration? Or do we grow by love-sparks, by the quickening of vital connections, by the beating of our living heart? Lawrence's alternative is that we grow as a result of interpersonal provocation and solicitation.

It is a question of balance, both-and not either-or. In trying to understand the simplicity and complexity of love, we must appreciate the subtle, pervasive, and ineluctable relationship between integrity, individuality, and self-surrender. We find our identity in loving and not the other way around. "Once you've known what love *can* be," says Lawrence, "sticking up for the love between a man and a woman," then the touch and the recoil, the coming together and the going asunder of love pre-empt "disappointment" and preclude "despair."[183]

Deus caritas est presents a view of man-woman love that converges with Lawrence. If we would love authentically, then we must get outside of and beyond our narrow self. "Love is 'ecstasy'... a journey, an ongoing exodus out of the closed inward looking self toward its liberation through self-giving, and thus toward authentic self-discovery."[184]

Sexual intimacy and psychological intimacy

"I love thee that I can go into thee," Mellors says.
"Do you like me?" Connie says her heart beating.
"It heals it all up, that I can go into thee. I love thee that tha
opened to me. I love thee tha I came into thee like that."[185] D.H.
Lawrence

As Derek in "True love" voices it, the ready-to-hand association to intimacy is sexual indulgence. Although sex is most often a constituent of mature psychological intimacy, it is not the whole story and not its kernel either. Obviously, being intimate in a sexual way can and usually does precede personal or psychological intimacy. The former is a physical event that can be impersonal; the latter is a preeminently personal achievement. Intimacy is more than just sexual. Its essence is lived out within many different lifestyles and ways of life. For example, a virgin or celibate that vows to foreclose on sexual performance still might develop the capacity for intimate relating. On the other hand, sexual acrobats, who prefer "one night stands" to nurturing long-term relationships, may fail to develop psychological intimacy. Because why? Intimacy is the act of getting outside of self, of losing self in another precisely to find oneself in the surrender. Self-abandonment, which may or may not necessarily involve sexual performance, is crucial.

This discussion brackets any value judgment concerning casual or recreational sex, or any bias in favor of marriage, virginity, celibacy or heterosexuality. It is unrelated to whatever happens in the process of accumulating many and varying sexual partners, or of preserving your virginity, or of staying together with one partner for fifty years. Unlike animals, instinctively programmed in the exercise of sexuality, we humans make choices. From within phenomenological brackets, a difference between an affaire or marriage, between a gay or lesbian partnership and celibacy is just a difference. Differences are not deficits. One chooses one's sexual activity, even if she feels she does not have a choice; and then one lives with one's choices.

A straightforward way to address physical-psychological intimacy is this. It is easier to undress the body than it is to undress the mind, spirit, or soul. Taking off ones clothing once makes it easy, except under certain circumstances, to strip again. But to let someone into the hidden recess of self is never a simple matter. An intimate flow requires the sharing of ideas, dreams, and desires that are tucked away in the hidden country of one's mind. Ex-posing the forward edge of one's thinking to one's beloved, hallmarks intimacy. It is sharing my "moving thought" and offering him my "word on a wing." Such exposure of our just-formulating-thoughts, still unborn and in no way yet understood, necessitates an intimacy that is more revealing than physical nakedness. Merleau-Ponty distinguishes between originating or constituting talk (*parole parlant*) and constituted speech (*parole parlé*).[186] The language of the streets variously calls the latter "canned speech," "recipes," or hackneyed "lines." Using a recipe simply repeats what has already been said to no-matter-whom. There's little risk; it's safe but insipid.

Originating speech, on the other hand, is our spontaneous arising thought that Alan Watts[187] insists is more carefully hidden than anything. Our body is never so carefully and deliberately concealed. Fashion always partially reveals and even highlights some zone of our flesh. It especially selectively unveils a woman's body, either showcasing her beauty, seductively promoting her career, or selling a spate of commercial products.

Children and poets have the corner on originating speech. Stephen Spender's poetic line goes, "Within our nakedness, nakedness still is the naked mind."[188] R. D. Laing tells us that one ceases to be schizophrenic when known by another; that "one who is brokenhearted... will mend... if we have the hearts to let them."[189]

Rumi captures the gist of this notion in a few stanzas:

A mouse and a frog meet every morning on the riverbank.
They sit in a nook of the ground and talk.

Each morning, the second they see each other,
They open easily, telling stories and dreams and secrets,
Empty of any fear or suspicious holding back.

To watch and listen to those two
is to understand how, as it's written
sometimes when two beings come together,
Christ becomes visible.

171

The mouse starts laughing out a story he hasn't thought of
In five years, and the telling might take five years!
There's no blocking the speech-flow-river-running
All-carrying momentum that true intimacy is.

Bitterness doesn't have a chance
With those two.[190]

Bodily surrender is always more than bodily. To make that statement, I bracket what it means to purchase sexual pleasure-release-play-punishment from a "sex worker," our latest politically correct term for a prostitute. For the purposes of this book, I unfold the meanings of man-woman interaction when romance, Eros, or love is at stake, especially when someone is trying to build a long term, enduring relationship. With that in mind, the issue of intimacy emerges as a dialectical phenomenon of sexuality and spirituality, of duty and desire.

Our western dualistic language hinders us at the juncture, just as it makes dealing with all the themes of this book cumbersome. "Spirituality" is a word that conjures up a plethora of meanings, as peculiar to each reader as her fingerprints. I detach the term "spiritual" from any religious credo or ideology. Spirit translates the French *l'esprit* and the German *geist*. Spirit names the distinctively human about us. It is life itself cutting into life, in Nietzsche's apt sentence.[191] No beaver awakens and decides not to build a damn dam that day just because it is raining. A female cat in heat does not choose to refrain from mating lest she become pregnant. We humans make choices about our sexual activity. Choice is of the spirit. Spirit is that whereby we relate to our life, not just live it. Spirit is the relationship we have to our work, play, prayer, sexuality, and death.

If we don't grant that this spiritual dimension is part and parcel of the human love-sexuality drama, then we must provide another explanation of the various meanings sexuality holds for an individual, and for the many ways sexuality is used. In "True love", sexuality partakes of the holy. But sexuality can also be used as a bargaining chip, a tool for seduction, or a weapon.

Be that as it may, until one attains the capacity for intimacy, or if he fails to achieve it, loneliness, isolation, or the tendency to withdraw fills much of the individual's life. One is growing old alone. Stephen Spender describes the gesture:

> *They have fingers which accuse*
> *You of the double way of shame.*
> *At first you did not love enough*
> *And afterwards you loved too much*
> *And you lacked the confidence to choose*
> *And you have only yourself to blame.*[192]

The crisis of intimacy

Intimacy reverberates. "True love" details the power of love to change one's political hearthead. Alexandra and Derek deal with antithetical political stances. East meets west. They borrow each other's eyes. It opens their own. New horizons appear. The challenge is almost overpowering. Handled honestly, it promotes growth.

Carlos Castaneda understands it as freedom from "distraction" which promotes a new mode of awareness that he calls "seeing."[193] One no longer merely sees, but beholds. The new vision is all-encompassing because everything about human existence is interconnected. In-sight into the geopolitical situation that the parable showcases is merely a qualitative algebraic example. Everything from religious beliefs to child-rearing practices is grist for the mill of altered perception and viewpoints.

The major life-turning insight pertaining to intimacy is that I have only one life before me. Because we typically flinch in the face of death, I repeat it. We really do only have one life to lead. By committing to one man or woman, some choices become definitive and irrevocable. They are not fluid and disposable like the individual acts of buying a new car, a cell phone, or roller blades. Important and weighty matters confront us. Largely depending upon how one grew up, for example, buying a house might be a piece of cake. Or it might smack of a lifetime commitment. Take the individual, for instance, who lived in one family home throughout his or her formative years;

or consider someone who lived in apartments all her life and never in a house. For either, purchasing a "home" might be a big deal.

Even more significantly, issues such as an unexpected pregnancy demand a choice 180 degrees different from picking the Pontiac you will trade in next September. Such choices as whether to marry, become pregnant or to abort are frightening in their consequences because apparently final.

Arguably, coping with ambiguity characterizes the shift from adolescence to adulthood. Arguably, too, it is the capacity to deal with ambiguity that hallmarks the mature adult. What do I mean? Ambiguity is the realization that something can be correct from more than one point of view. One must let go of absolutistic thinking in order to tolerate ambiguity. The Robert Frost poem, cited earlier, vividly showcase the fork in the road created by the necessity to choose. We are condemned to choice. De-cision is literally a cut. We can't have it both ways; we can't have our cake and eat it too. Death enters the picture because we prefer to think that, concerning choices, we have lots of time. We can put it off until tomorrow. Let's take it one day at a time, ok? Why hurry? Why act impulsively? So we postpone. We defer. We cogitate and stall. We procrastinate. We form a romantic attachment that comes equipped with a built-in out. Waylon Jennings uses a bouncy mischievous voice to make the point, "When it comes to women, boys, I like to keep one in reserve."[194]

In part, this is our run-of-the-mill death-denial. "My number isn't up yet." But Kierkegaard smiles and clobbers us with the most blunt of instruments, truth "What if death is so treacherous as to come tomorrow."[195] We live on borrowed time. Death is just a heartbeat away. We know not "when" or "how" we will die, but we know definitely "that" we will die. Choice coils within this ultimate ambiguity of definite that and indefinite when. Procrastination is preeminently comprehensible. But in consternation, sometimes, the decision that either will kill or create intimacy must be made in the proverbial New York minute! An unplanned pregnancy confronts the individual. "We can't wait a week!" Or one reads an email from an ex-lover saying, "I want to meet... and try again....to see how we will feel... and what we will do." You can only pretend your system is down for a day or two. The sender wants soon either a Yes or a No.

I use emotional algebra to describe such "moments" that we both crave and simultaneously dread. Remember. Starting with first love, "forever" and the beauty of commitment haunt us. Consequently, in part we seek the razor's edge of love. The idea of "growing old together" presents us with a two edged-sword. I must give myself over to my one and only life and shut the door on wider horizons and "greener pastures." I must commit myself to one future with all its ambiguities and with no guarantees. The double blade is this. The exciting and stable possibilities found within an intimate partnership make me feel complete and help me to come into my own. They make me feel at home, too. The price tag, however, is giving self over to one's finitude, limitedness, and to one's inevitable death. To become convinced that I want to live the rest of my life with this one woman or man is to embrace my own death. Martin Buber expresses the wonderful possibility of relating as I-Thou with my whole being rather than as I-It in a partial way. "But it is here that the fate of the relational event rears up most powerfully," he writes. "The more powerful the response, the more powerfully it ties down the Thou."[196]

Being tied down is not exactly the script advanced by western media, entertainment, or education. "Keep your options open" is the usual chant. Some relationships start with an evident escape hatch. Such equivocation or ambivalence confounds the delicate balance between what is freedom or license in terms of involvements and commitment. As Eric Fromm depicts it, that which feels free might be an "escape from freedom."[197] The minstrel sings, "It look like freedom but it feels like death."[198]

It's a death-defying culture we live in. The implications for intimate partnership are awesome in their gravity. It would be speculative in the extreme to ask if the way death-denial mangles love is cross-cultural, cross-historical, a result of our modern-postmodern culture, or a manifestation of human nature. But in this millennium, it becomes increasingly more difficult to commit oneself to one's one and only life, to one's one and only body, to our family, and to the very person with whom we have found intimacy. The propaganda runs counter to self-limitation. Keep options open; get a major "make-over." There are two or three or four million potential mates Online just waiting for your message of interest. Isn't more better and the latest or newest best? Shouldn't we always be "shopping?" Capitalism and death are bitter enemies. The only death capitalism relishes, as Derek and Alexandra debate in the parable, is war. Or "shop till you drop."

Bracket whatever is the convoluted relationship in our times between intimacy, capitalism, and death. Nevertheless, in daily life we have to come to terms with our finitude. Baudrillard has likened the massive "simulation" of our postmodern world to the construction of society as one gigantic Disney World.[199] But we cannot exist indefinitely as Peter Pan, Wendy and Tinkerbell in Never, Never Land. We have to grow up. We cannot ward off death. Whether or not that means we make promises and keep them, trade vows and stay faithful, forge permanent ties or refrain from making commitments, the following holds true about contemporary love: the crisis of intimacy shows in the tendency to flee from it. What forms the underbelly of our tendencies to disorder in romance and Eros, of our high divorce rates, of our indulgence in cheap thrills, and our pseudo-intimate action? It is the specter of our abiding permanent partner: Death.

Hyper-Reflection or Reflections on the Reflections

In this section, I reflect upon the narratives and upon the reflections based upon the narratives. The purposes are to draw out explicitly what might be too implicit in them, to clarify what might still be hazy, and to express theoretical implications.

Focus on the Relationships Themselves

No serial relationships

First and foremost, I decidedly and clearly am not proposing that the chum, first love, outlaw, and intimate partner coalesce to form a normative and predicable series of relationships. They are merely possibilities and not inevitabilities. They happen. I depict them. They might happen again but not necessarily. The most I claim is that an actuality for one person is a possibility for all. And although I present four distinct pictures or gestalts embedded in four separate stories, I am not proposing that they comprise a serial progression as if one builds upon the other or grows out of it. If someone experiences all four, they need not even be in the shape of four different persons. One and the same person might embody them all. I have a chum. Our relationship turns romantic or erotic. It converts into my first love. We marry. We are raising a family, growing old together as intimate partners. One day I awaken, maybe after our last child had "flown the coop," and find a stranger in my bed... my wife, my outlaw. I discover a something about her I never knew or realized. It is like seeing her as if for the first time. Ah, like finding the world's last four leaf clover!

The finite relationship

What is the farthest reach of generalization about the chum, first love, outlaw and intimate partnership? They are "infinite" relationships. I borrow the notion from Emmanuel Levinas.[200] What does this super-ordinate idea communicate? What exactly distinguishes a finite from an infinite relationship? In capsule, a finite relationship is self-centered; an infinite relationship is other-centered and relationship-constellated. This statement requires elaboration.

Finite refers to the self-centered quality of a bond. It bespeaks an over-arching attitude of coiled concern with one's own needs that blurs the radiance of the other qua other. I am wrapped up in myself. In terms of friendship, I am mostly looking out for myself, still experimenting and preoccupied with my social position within the group, relating to someone out of convenience, or using the other to gain some specific advantage. It is a "self-contentment containment absorption."[201] The language of every day life calls this "selfish."

In young heterosexual love, "falling in love with love" exemplifies the finite possibility. Insofar as I am infatuated with another, I am dazzled by the exciting idea of romance. The person with whom I am enamored matters little. Rather, I veer toward the image of that person or what filters through the distorting lens of my needs. Love! I want to be "in" love; I want to be loved.

A few descriptions of finite interactions serve to illustrate the concept: "Having a boyfriend was a status symbol. To be needed and liked by a boy and to be popular at school were actually more important to me than my boyfriend." "Dating her was my form of insurance against being alone." "My life revolved around having that one boy who made me feel special." "When our relationship ended, I discovered that he had been using me for our swimming pool, our snowmobile, and my body."

The finite possibilities within an outlaw relationship are legion. Anyone can seize upon the eruption of sexual arousal to manipulate the other. One male, aware of using his sexual prowess to orchestrate "idolatrous affairs," writes:

> *My ego seems to act like a stomach on occasions. It gets hungry; it needs food. To be blunt, when it gets most hungry, I go on a "pussy mission." Then I feed it with juicy succulent sixteen year old girls who adore me. My ego has a strong preference for this young and eager food. The girls want to run the gambit of sexual possibilities, or need to be handled a little roughly. I oblige. But I have to confess. What is ego-gratifying does not satisfy the heart.*

In such finite interactions, the other whom I allegedly love or desire is more accurately designated as an extension of me. His reality pales beneath what he represents. My ideas mask her face and my needs and intentions muffle her voice. I want him to notice me, admire me, rave about me, gratify my sexual urges, or play the fool. In brief, the finite other shines in the "borrowed light" of my ego-boasting needs for social prestige and self-esteem. A finite tie is an ad hoc situation of self-appeasement and bilateral adjustment. It lasts until the new wears off and the conquest made, or the pleasure traded. "Someone's gonna get hurt before you're through," Waylon croons, "Someone's gonna pay for the things you do."[202]

The infinite relationship

An infinite relationship, to the contrary, is other-centered and relationship-constellated. The other "overflows" my ideas or images of her. At each instant, she "undoes the form she presents." There is always more to her inexhaustible richness than what meets my eyes. She comes as an epiphany who shines with her own kind of light, radically "other" and outside of me. She brings into my life new surprising sights and sounds.

For chums, a newborn "us" becomes a source of absorption. Insofar as their friendship is balanced such that both are "in it" equally reciprocally, they manifest the capacity genuinely to share and care for each other. The infinite nerve in the bond is that they summon another to be-come. In the words of *The Velveteen Rabbit*, they make each other "real." In the language of *The Little Prince*, they tame one another. Glowy in "True blue" names the transformation a "transfiguration," a "dawning of creation," a "moment" of joining the human race. It is Harry Stack Sullivan's miracle.

First love also pivots around the person of the partner as other than a fantasy projection or a correlate of my needs or intentions. Insofar as the relationship is balanced, the two persons are informing and orienting presences. The relationship is a coming out for both. The two experience a psycho-spiritual debut. Like existential alchemists, she calls out the burgeoning man he is becoming; he calls out the woman blossoming in her. It is an enduring situation of self-realization and mutual coordination. Even if it ends, it is unforgettable and never profaned. Its ending leaves the gentle melancholy of a beautiful sadness. "Once you love someone," Waylon croons, "you always will....You'll remain a part of me, like a song that I can't sing, a love song I can't sing anymore. You're a love song I can't sing anymore."[203]

The passionate intensity of an outlaw bond is also infinite. The chum calls me to "become... real"; the first love to "come out" as a man or woman; the outlaw who draws out the height, depth, and breath of my sexuality. She takes me to the gates of passion. The call however, is not given in the tone of fun and games, but of challenge. Sometimes, the invitation comes within the context of menace. Sexuality with one's outlaw simmers over with danger. It is not hazardous in the potentially lethal way of engaging in sexual intercourse without protection. With or without a condom, sexuality with one's outlaw shakes your life from pillar to post.

Cheap thrill and pseudo intimate sexual relationships

The finite alternatives cast infinity into sharp relief. One might be ripe for an outlaw (e.g., at the end of a first love; significant death in the family, etc.), but instead the individual takes a less perilous romance-path. He starts a pseudo-intimate relationship with a "built-in out"; or she gets involved with a man "to have sex just for the sex of it." Again, who can gainsay it? It is a choice. From within phenomenological brackets, the meaning of each act is held in abeyance. But it is also clear that pseudo-intimacy, or what the culture calls "cheap thrills," is not random or careless behavior. It is possibly a defensive evasion of the intensity and personal challenge of an outlaw relationship. The lines of demarcation, however, are permeable and thin. The thrill may be cheap, but it is never free. We are whole people not only sexual organs. The possibility and actuality that one has a purely sexual relationship without involvement of the greater self is close to zero. Sexual action always gives us both more and less than we bargain for. It starts out light breezy and causal; it then turns intense; finally it blows a hole through your living heart.

Core Phenomena: The Pivots of the Pivots

This section is a synthesis. It brings together ideas about love's core phenomena that are embedded in but not limited to the parables. The reflections express what is important about what is important. The purpose is not pragmatic in the one-dimensional way of pinpointing what might work to make love relationships better. The reflections aim instead at second dimensional depth and even third dimensional height. If Kierkegaard is even half right, then knowing our own hearthead is the precondition to knowing the other and knowing what matters when love is at stake. What follows explicates the pivots around which the pivotal relationships spin.

Trust

Except for the innocent youngsters in "True blue," one character in each of the other parables moans and bristles that their partner has been lying even while telling the truth. The statement is qualitative algebra about deceit. It stands for multiple different expressions of the same complaint. As such, it addresses an essential component of every love-bond. Trust is a sine qua non of loving. As soon as trust dies, love dies. The relationship might end abruptly; it might linger on and on, going through various and sundry shifts; or it might last another forty years. To survive, cope, or hang on, one party typically plays a secret psychological game. Or both might collude in ways that obscure the lie and shelter it. But without trust, something vital is lacking at the core of one's promise or vow; authentic intimacy is dead.

The notion of an ontological "moment" along the life spiral frames best the importance of the matter of trust. Remember, the drive for fidelity is our most dominant one in the matter of love, romance, and Eros.

What is more fragile than trust? Trust always totters on the razor's edge. In every instant, trust is vulnerable to the possibility of treachery; every moment of loyalty carries with it the possibility of disloyalty. The act of trust, in the full Kierkegaardian sense, is a leap into the unknown. Trust, Alfonso Lingis insists, is not logical and not produced by knowledge: "One attaches to someone whose words or whose movements one does not see."[204] The intoxicating energy of trust, therefore, binds us to another with an upsurge of tremendous strength. "Trust is a break," Lingis writes, "a cut in the extending map of certainties and probabilities."[205] It is a commencement or birth that defies clarity, consistency, or coherence. Once it takes hold, trust feeds on itself, compounded by a qualitative geometry. But once trust is shot down or treachery besmirches it, it goes with the wind.

"Who's first?" and "Let Enter the Stranger" each depicts situations of deception that cut the ratchet out of trust. How does the human being bounce back in the face of lies, deception, or adultery? How to forgive blatant betrayal? Since fidelity is our most basic drive, healing must touch the matter at its heart. Superficial patchwork is not enough. Put slightly differently, cognitive homework that negotiates "contracts" concerning adjustment, coping, and negotiating another start merely touches the tip of the iceberg. Restoring trust is a matter of integrity. It takes courage. In the case of the man, trust centers on virility. In the case of the woman, it is a question of grace or elegance.

What do I mean? Firstly, I make a disclaimer. Virility does not equal machismo.[206] The stereotypical masculinity that we admire in athletes, military commandoes or even our plant foreman is not virility. Virility or manliness is what we hope to find in our friend and our mate, either heterosexual or homosexual. Alfonso Lingis writes that virility defines outlaws. Of course, he is first of all acknowledging the excitability of passion that spontaneously flashes in a context of provocation or unexpected sexual allure. Virility, however, has much more to do with "beauty and flair and style." There is a slang saying that goes, "The size of your dick doesn't make up for lack of balls." Virility means that you are your own man. You do not "cave in" to peer or group pressure; you do not "sell out" to the whims of the "club" to which you belong or aspire. You decide on the basis of your own hearthead and then act without alibis. "Manliness... is to not take anybody's shit. It is also not to shit on another, not to let anybody shit on others."[207] At bottom, such manliness is innocent. Manliness, that is, is imbued with a sense of justice, a thirst for truth, and an ache for compassion. The truly virile man whom we trust is an "unwobbling pivot." Lingis again: "We see another's courage by feeling the pounding of that very courage in us. Our trust then is not as assured dependency on his courage but a surge of courage in ourselves."[208]

What is the womanly counterpart of virility? It is a symptom of our western way of life that our language lacks a parallel word. Inherently and deeply, western culture remains a patriarchy even after a century of women's rights movements and women's liberation. We need to use several words about her, therefore, to match the meaning of virility.

In everyday parlance, the phrase that would capture the same sense is "She's a 'real' woman." Above, I mentioned the words grace and elegance. We don't trust the glitter and dazzle of a fashion model nor the "come hither look" of the Playmate. We don't trust the wily seductress either, do we, or the woman easily seduced? Self-indulgence in a female or a hankering after comfort breeds trust neither. A woman's strength resides precisely in her combination of steadfastness and suppleness. Derek describes Alexandra in the parable as a strong willow tree that can bend with pliancy. A woman's strength is graceful. Elegant fits, too, because it captures the beauty and the ripeness of a woman who moves roundly and smoothly. Graceful elegance in a woman also betokens her intelligence. No female who is dozy and dull can exude grace and charm. The graceful woman evokes trust because her brightness enthralls. She generates an aura that is soothing and reassuring. You don't feel tricked or manipulated by gloss. You feel enraptured. Substance, not surface sheen, grips you. Whether this woman is a large package or a small slight whisk, it is well nigh impossible to blow her over or blow her away. That tenacity manifests her courage. She is not about to sell herself for money, position or power. She exudes mature emotions and a made up mind. You trust her. There is no forgiveness without trust.

The body

The experience of feeling amputated at the moment of physical separation from a kiss or a hug is also qualitative algebra. The expression signifies the importance of the living body in a loving relationship. Another book will be forthcoming to elaborate more fully the fleshy phenomenon of the kiss, the hickey, the blush, the reach, the touch, and the caress. But in what follows, I do present the importance of those phenomena to the relationships that this book has unfolded.

Yukio Mishima depicts the ache of the psychological amputation that follows the end of a "transformative" kiss:

The moment when a kiss ends—it was like awakening reluctantly from sleep, struggling drowsily against the glare of the morning sun as it struck their eyelids, as they yearned to hold on to the fragment of unconsciousness left to them When their lips parted, an ominous silence seemed to fall, as though the birds had suddenly stopped their attractive song.[209]

The kiss starts a lot for us. It is an initiating act. "In the beginning was the kiss." Take the time we are not thematically aware of romantic feelings for a person until we "surprisingly" kiss. But here we are, lip to lip! We break the moment; we open our eyes. Now, our mouths are agape. We look at each other. We both know it. It will never be the same. We have just changed each other's lives. D. H. Lawrence puts it this way: "…he kissed her on the mouth, gently, with the one kiss that is an eternal pledge… He had crossed over the gulf to her, and all that he had left behind had shriveled and become cold."[210]

During adolescence, our first kiss was a revelation whether it surprised, shocked, or revolted us.[211] We did not know how to do it "right"; we did not even know how to do it "wrong!" "Where do the noses go"? "How long should it last"? "What do I do with my hands"? Kissing romanticizes our total body in both the anatomical-physiological and lived senses. Body parts, especially lips, tongue, the genitals, and the anal area transform into potential "zones of interaction."[212] After tasting another's lips, we all wanted "more". "More please" we said, perhaps under our breath. We didn't even know what more we ached for; but we found out.

The first two and then the third kiss between Rima and Glowy mark the climax of their relationship and its turning point. It also expresses its essence. Glowworm admonishes the 'Sir' who is his presumed listener that he better not profane the relationship by reducing it to sexuality. He insists instead that tenderness graced their bond, the very gentleness that was to haunt him for the rest of his life. The outlaw relationship in "Let enter the stranger" also starts with kisses outside the church hall, one soft and tender, and the other unprecedented. The woman in 'Who's first?' reiterates that kissing was more central to her first love than intercourse.

Kisses also end "things." The missing passion or tenderness of a relationship gone "dead" is manifest in the kiss. I can "mouth" all the "right" words that tell you I love you and even mean it. But if I stiffen and kiss perfunctorily, then the truth-in-the-kiss belies the verbal-lines-lies.

The kiss is a true symbol insofar as it signifies precisely what it is and does. Kissing joins and mingles. The kiss fuses. Two become one flesh. About intimately shared kisses we say, "You take my breath away." "Your kiss is holy water for my lips." "I can't get enough of you." "I want to eat you up." "Such kisses that they must kiss each other for ever."[213] Pause a moment. Conjure up your romantic-erotic partners. Remember the place that kissing held within the economy of any or all of your relationships. See what I mean? The way we kiss each partner existentially diagnoses our relationship. It detects truth.

Kissing is more intimate than sexual intercourse. It surely can mean more than a climax. During sexual intercourse, a man can easily feign emotional responses. Similarly, a woman can pretend climaxing. Their intercourse might be sheer coupling performed without passion or tenderness, without union of hearts, bodies, minds, and souls. But during kissing, there is no place to hide and no way to camouflage heartfelt emotions. One cannot fake a kiss. Either you are in the act or it is empty and cold. The kiss is a "lie detector."[214]

The blush

Picture a young girl sauntering down the spiral staircase in her home. A moment ago, she was priming and primping in the mirror, pretending to be a grown woman. It was still child's play. In an oft-repeated moment, she enters the living room where her older brother and his best friend are sitting watching TV or playing video games. This time, her developing body and pretty face spontaneously evoke "the once over." The boy glances at her, by no means innocently. Catching the look, she blushes.

What does the blush signify? Sexuality has entered her existence. She knows… that he knows…and he knows that she knows. Like an "atmosphere," sexuality is now part of her experiential world.[215] Last month, last week, or even yesterday, the boy might have leered at her in the same invasive way. She did not understand a "second look." She looked right through it. It meant nothing to her. Now, she understands it and feels it. It warms her; she blushes. In an eye-blink, she has reached a new level of existence.

Phenomenological reflection elaborates the happening. What does it take to blush? We are skin. If there would be an angel, an angel could not blush. Secondly, consciousness is necessary. The flesh recognizes itself as sexual with sure but ambiguous awareness. Mark Twain pens a pithy one-line gem: "The human being is the only creature that blushes, or that needs to." Thirdly, the blush requires a complex social membrane, an intercorporeity, and shared consciousness that connects us to a shared erotic field: I-know-you-know-we both-know. A "barrier of blood" both hides and broadcasts fledgling sexual desire; one recoils at being gazed upon as a sexual object while simultaneously wanting to inhabit the desired eroticized flesh.[216] In the existential rhythm of the parable, the blush acts as a natural diagnostic sign for both Derek and Alexandra. It is a concrete and evident phenomenon that speaks volumes. It is uncontestable evidence. If one blushes, especially in the adult years while talking to the other on a first date, her emotions are out in the open. The blush promotes trust or, as Alexandra says it, with Derek she immediately felt safe.

The caress

Under the lurking shadow of death, we sense that there is
someone who waits for our kisses and caresses....We sense we have
in our hearts and in the sensuality of our hands a love to pour
upon someone like no love ever poured forth.[217] Alfonso Lingis

The power of touch is a major theme in the relationships. Like the blush, the meanings and values that cluster around it happen at the involuntary level. The caress is the movement of intimacy par excellence. It is an ambiguous double of material and immaterial contact. "Touch me on the outside and make me feel it on the inside." Unless I specify what I mean when I say, "you touched me," I leave you in the dark. Did I mean on the outside, inside or both? As I indicated when analyzing touch as part of the outlaw relationship, perhaps it is only touching someone on the inside that authorizes touching her on the outside.

My caressing hand is not an anatomical appendage reducible to muscles, bones, and nerves. My caressing hand is not an instrument, a tool, or a weapon. The caressing hand reaches. As Ron Cornelissen beautifully puts it in a personal communication, "Longing is the heart's reaching, just as reaching is the heart's longing." (January 21, 2007). I reach for what always slips away or for what always escapes my grasp. Even when I do reach my beloved, she remains more than flesh stretched out at my fingertips. So one's reach searches blindly, daringly, restlessly beyond the tangible. Whenever I reach for an elusive feeling, it is without knowledge or plan. The caress craves absence, craves the future which cannot come quickly enough. The caress seizes upon nothing. Fingers stretch and the hand aches for her who is inexhaustible.[218] "You're just out of reach of my two empty arms."

But solicitation is playful, too. The caress is complacent. It enjoys. Carnal intimacy relishes the nearness and accessibility of my beloved. During moments of tender fondling, I touch soft, smooth skin, silky hairs, and hot thighs with the light friction of reverence. Sensible flesh communes with sensible flesh. With largesse, the beloved couple shares with one another more roughly too, with the priceless gifts of biting and sucking; with squeezes and hugs; by sniffing and tasting; with nibbles and licks; by cooing, snuggling, and cuddling: "This is my body! With this body I love every part of you. Give it to me". It is an act of donation. Skin against skin, locked in an embrace, chest to chest feels like home! Nothing feels more natural. Lovers swoon in surrender...

The hand that caresses is my hand. The fingers are mine. I have my hand in lots of ways. "This is my loving hand." When I softly and gently rub my beloved and then rub her more forcefully and probe, my actions express far better than mere words: "My heart is in my hands." "This is my very soul." Sometimes, "This is my entire life."

Under the caressing hand, I am vulnerable. Paradoxically, by surrendering I create. I evoke unprecedented emotions and bring ordinary miracles to pass. Is it not amazing what one touch can do? It arouses her, summoning passion, and engendering tenderness.

She asks, "How do you want this touch to end?" "I don't want it ever to end," he answers. "I want your touch to be first, last and only." In one simple sterling sentence, D. H. Lawrence "nails" it: "I could die for the touch of a woman like thee."[219]

Time

Time is a python, squashing and swallowing us; time is a careless thief; it is our cunning enemy. Time heals all wounds. And on and on and on! Some words of time are not just mundane utterances, but what Federico Garcia Lorca calls "deep song:"[220] "remember when?" or "yesterday!" or "our anniversary!" In first love, always, never and forever are imperative. Derek, in the intimate partnership parable, drags Einstein off and on into his conversation with the "man" who is his presumed listener. And the choice is not arbitrary. Like a chant, lovers say what Derek says and what outlaws always say, "It feels like I have always known you." Lovers also say, most especially when there is a large chronological age gap between them, "It feels like we are the same age; age is relative."

Then, too, there is the question of never having enough time. Derek says lack of sufficient time punctuated his relationship with Alexandra from the get-go. In a radical sense, time is never on our side. It's always over too soon however much we have been granted. Since Death is life's only true imperative, the finish of a love relationship is never well-timed, whether that ending is by death or by break-up.

The one who experienced rejection complains, "You picked a fine time to leave me... just when I needed you most..." We could multiply the expressions, but it all boils down to a basic truth. There is no good time for the ending. Every one of us knows at least one of the... worst kinds!

Of course, there is the ending that won't go away. Memories! How can we speak about love and time and not mention memories? The woman in "Who's first?" lives out the complicated drama of letting go and of finally ending "it." Memories haunt her. They come back at the most inopportune time. Memories of her first love plague her even during sexual trysts in her bedroom. Isn't it amazing how, of all the places on the planet, "old memories" just seem to have a penchant for finding their way into the bedrooms of the world? How come selected memories always find the "wrong" time to come around to call? We have to laugh in ridicule, don't we, over mainstream psychology's neglect of the personal and subjective, over its dismissal of experience and meaning in favor of objectified measurable behavior, over its reduction of the power of memory to mere "memory-traces?" Our own very individual personal meaning-matrix, not biology or conditioning, creates my memories.

Claude Lebouch's movie,[221] *A Man and a Woman*, depicts a poignant scene. For the first time since her husband's tragic death, Anouk Aimee is naked, on her back, moaning and holding a man. She loved her husband. There is nothing to regret except that his passion for Formula # 1 car racing killed him. What does she do? Dry up? Or now, will she finally come back to life as a woman? Naturally, making love to another for the first time brings to the foreground the ghost that she is letting go of. So her memory shows her a collage of pictures of her and her husband even while her body bucks, opens and liquefies. Memories to cling to, they are, and memories to let die.

About memories coming back at the wrong time, the balladeers complains, "Don't your memory have no pride at all?"[222] Or, the songwriter hypostatizes memory's recalcitrance: "I know you're hiding there in the darkness, and it's got me running scared and blind. Since you walked out of my life, out of my world, please walk on out of my mind."[223] But no! His lover has left footprints all over his memory that he cannot erase no matter how hard he tries. One male says, "Time stood still when she said 'good-bye'. How in the hell can time 'slip away'?" So what has happened to those so-called "healing hands"? Isn't time supposed to cure all wounds? We are always advised seemingly wisely by family, friends, and those trained to help us, "'In time' you'll forget and get over it." "Ha," we laugh and then shoot a rejoinder, "Tell me what to do about today!"

Repetition is one of time's favorite games. Is there a "second chance" at love? Will I get my princess back? Is love better the "second time around" allegedly -- as the song goes -- "with both feet on the ground?" Both "Who's first?" and "Let enter the stranger" end as the respective former lovers of the women return and want to try again. It is a normal disease, this wish to pick up the pieces and this need to rake through ashes hoping against hope to find the missing spark. After a relationship ends, it is only a matter of time when we remember the "good times." And we ache to go back to "the way we were." We humans don't find it easy to "throw it all away," especially when with 20-20 hindsight and in regret we are painfully aware that throw it away was exactly what we did in the first place. "Give me another chance," we plead. "Aren't you and I worth it?"

Whenever the invitation comes to start over, time is of the essence. A decision about "Let's try again" might have to be made relatively quickly. As often as not, "It's now or never." The woman in "Who's first?" either must call back soon, even that day, or else drop it. The woman in "Let enter the stranger" hums her cocksure conviction that this decision is a snap and not like the difficult task of quitting smoking. For both women, soon it will start again; or for the men soliciting them, it will soon be "too late."

Why don't we realize the values of what we have in a relationship until we lose it? What is it about the way we have been thought to think in the western world that we cannot anticipate what someday in retrospect we will see with blinding clarity? Is it that we hedge our bet against the limitedness of life, keeping our options open, keeping death at bay? Or, as Derek voices in "True love," is there simply a fatal flaw built into western abstract rationalistic thought-patterns?

Truly, there is a flawed approach to thinking in our politics of love. It seems absurd, does it not, to conclude that it is human nature to throw away something precious and then want it back? It is obvious, however, that out of such mulling and fumbling the saddest words in the English language surface: "Too late."

Jealousy [224]

Jealousy is not the 'Green Monster'; envy is. But if jealousy isn't the 'Black God' what is? Let's just compromise on terminology. Daily, the green-eyed black monster rears its ugly head and destroys love-bonds. If we are going to surmount jealousy, either to prevent destruction or survive it, then compromise must be the name of the game.

Fledgling tenderness is fragile. The collision of tenderness with romance and lust originally occurs within the delicate cocoon of first love. There and then, it is particularly raw. So our young loves are apt to be possessive. They are jealousy-prone, too.

To state it in terms of what we have already discussed, first love belongs to the discovery phase of the ontological revolution. For the first time ever, the growing individual has endorsed with intellectual fervor and with wholehearted sincerity fundamental values of devotion and commitment. Trust, promise, and vow now signify something both intensely personal and mystically transcendent. The young woman or young man trusts fiercely. In all innocence, he or she is convinced that no power on earth can destroy love. Their daily absolutely innocent and perfectly pure emotional connection seems solid. Their many-splendored love seems endless. But the young people have not yet learned that taming-being tamed demands the correlative capacities to loosen and set free. They have not encountered or coped with the cold hard facts of life. They are unaware that fidelity, jointly promised with silvery sighs, verges on bursting into nothingness. But in the shape of an interloper, the outside world trespasses into heaven on earth and both wrecks our rapture and ravages our divine dream. Jealousy is one of several common heralds of the loss phase of the ontological revolution, the phase of pain.

The betrayal of love and the breach of trust are adjudged a perfidy and a felony. The lessons to be learned are that a vow made indefinitely and once and for all requires daily renewal; every promise commits to a future that harbors no guarantees. Facing this loss phase of the revolution places the individual on Kierkegaard's dizzying cliff of anxiety. One fellow captured his experience in a poem: "First vows brittle/ first vows frail/ vows with flair / with a sent of deception/ with an odor of doom."

"Who's first?" is one woman's tale of the struggle to attain closure on her first love relationship. Her "old time love" haunts her field of consciousness like a festering presence. Especially at those wrong times her "old flame" intrudes into her love-life. At one level, the story demonstrates that self-deception and other-deception are interrelated. At the start, she disclaims knowing why her present boyfriend is upset. What's his problem? She has spilled the beans about her first love! He should be glad she hasn't held back much. As the story unfolds, however, it dawns on her gradually that her verbal assertions do not square with her actions or with her heart. But the parable does more than depict her private journey. Her actions also provoke her current boyfriend's jealousy. Knowing that her "first" man is always in the back of her mind affects him tremendously. The echoes he does not hear and the shadows he cannot see nevertheless spill into the life-space between them. They make him uncomfortable, irritated, and nervous. He is running scared.

The ready-to-handle explanation is that he is the jealous-type or has either an over-active imagination or an over-developed male intuition. But from a more radically interpersonal understanding of psychological happenings, her irresolution co-creates his jealous malaise. She is carrying the torch. Smoke curls between them. He sees the smoke getting into her eyes. Even before he could put them into words, he lives the fearful questions: "What will she do if her 'old flame' returns?" "What if he still wants her?" "What if she still wants him? Her act of asking the rhetorical question, "Guess who's back in town?" discloses the searing question that always has been hovering over both parties, maybe over all three: "Who's first?"

"Let enter the stranger" showcases blatant deception. The woman must come to terms with the arch soul-thief of cyberspace. Although she discounts as the definitive issue jealousy concerning Mona, nevertheless she must cope with the disillusionment of breached trust.

In an authentic emotional algebra, what emotion supplants this necessary "moment" of disenchantment? It is another one of Lorca's deep song words: sorrow. Jealousy-triggers have fired. In the face of disillusionment, sorrow remains. It is the season of grief; it is "blues time;" perhaps I will sing the "lovesick blues."

Sorrow fits the situation because the object of the blues is external, visible, important, and consciously concerns my central core. The threat to my absolutely perfect love-bond cuts to the quick and breaks my heart. The existential reality and power of a third party to bring doom into what I had believed to be my reward and destiny terrifies me. The healthiest response to this devastating resistance of the world is the outward flow of my intensity: my aggressive jealousy. The sharp, aggressive bite of jealousy signals that I want to keep what is most precious. Aggression, at root, means to "step out." The intensity of aggression is necessary to heal. Sorrow, therefore, springs the trap on distorted memory, one that ultimately would lead to bitterness and regret. Sorrow aims at renewal, at authentic forward-oriented repetition, at coming to terms continually with what persists and what in its persistence demands that we keep coming to terms with it, wholeheartedly. I might then see the whole affair from a new angle in which it appears comprehensible, endurable, and livable. Absolutes now look just relative. I still pursue truth; hope abides; I regain the capacity to recognize any new phosphorescence of radiant innocence.

The weave of jealousy, sorrow, and aggression teaches me that my personal drama is a metaphor of human existence and also a metaphor of self. My struggle through love-jealousy is my destiny. Like every crisis, this drama presents equally opportunity and danger. It is a chance for me to work through issues about loving that most bear my own fingerprints and to grapple with my most basic character flaws. It behooves me to grasp in whatever way I, partly, have orchestrated the drama. Likewise by tapping roots, I understand how the legacy of my father or mother visited the event upon me. If I authentically do tap roots, then I open a crack to forgiveness. Then, I can really get on with my life.

Jealousy teaches other important lessons also. It tells me about the quality of my own love. What is the rock bottom threat to love? According to Kierkegaard, it is despair. If someone makes me doubt the goodness of my love, I am in despair. My love is not good enough; it hurts; it destroys; it kills the one I love. Radical cure for this despair is radical humility. Neither my love nor my lover need be perfect. I both love and hate the same person at the same time. To repeat, it is the very one I depend upon, who is gentle and generous is also infuriating and under certain circumstances vicious.

And me! Arrogance, the original sin of pride, insists that I be loved because I am lovable or deserve it. In Kierkegaard's eyes, this is merely love that wants to be loved back. My heart is not even open to receiving. Arrogance reduces love to a tradeoff between two egoists. The struggle to surmount jealousy teaches the simple humility to allow ourselves to be loved as a gift. Not loved with or in spite of imperfections, but loved precisely because we are flawed, fallible, and undeserving of life's greatest gift. This is the point of authentic resolution of the jealousy-drama. I show forgiveness; therefore I tolerate and accept myself. "There is a crack in everything. That's how the light gets in." 223

Addendum: THEORETICAL Digressions

The substance of the book is complete now. The reader, who is not intrigued by or even interested in its theoretical underpinnings, might wish to turn to the last page where I come full circle and reach closure by transitioning to what might follow.

The purpose of the book is to reveal four faces of love. I have done that in a way neither clinical nor coarse. Using heartlines, my approach "smells neither of the laboratory nor the sewer."[226] My writing appeals equally to the reader's heart and head. I count upon each individual in the living present to recall whatever is central to her love life and to feel the wide-range of emotions connected to it. Hopefully, you have re-visited by-gone days, remembered someone you had cared for, dwelt long upon your feelings, and now look to the future with insights you have gleaned from my words. The book is relationship-centered. It is about our experiences with love and what they mean to us.

In the preceding section, I accented key ideas that arch over all the issues of love. Deliberately, I minimize psychology's two sacred cows, theory and method. Because why? Ideology or theory only should orient a work; method is simply the way or road from a research starting-point to its destination. Both are dialectically interrelated with content or subject matter which, after all, is what we seek knowledge about. Therefore, this book balances what is out of whack. Mainstream psychology is obsessed with theory and addicted to method. It ignores or overlooks, as if too trite or trivial, the cargo of heartlines wherein our love-lives reside.

I include them. I trump them up. In order to execute the studies that comprise this book, I switch focus. My work both leans upon a different philosophical and theoretical standpoint and uses a different method. Put simply, I eschew positivism and neo-positivism in favor of an existential phenomenological approach. And I jettison quantitative methodologies in favor of qualitative ones. The key ideas that motivate this switch are basic to this work. They constitute the framework around the frame of the pivotal relationships. An existential phenomenological approach fundamentally alters the way love is typically studied by western disciplines, particularly by psychology.

For some readers, even those committed to mainstream social scientific theory and methodological practices, these discussions might shed light upon or even open cracks in the staid and monolithic wall of positivism. For many readers, however, they are digressions or extra reflections of little interest. Grasping the meaning of the love relationships does not depend upon reading about my conceptual concerns. In what follows, I tease out some implications of this book for the academic and therapeutic disciplines, in particular. For me, the implications are radical. For the ordinary reader, the one to whom I have pitched this book, this theoretical digression is gravy.

Platonic Christendom

The fatal flaw in western thought starts with Plato.[227] Nietzsche rails against Plato's cowardly other-worldly orientation, decadence-values, and also his nihilistic "hostility against life" According to Nietzsche, Plato's writings about love, the body, Eros, and sublimation are contrived.[228]

Platonism expresses horror for the good earth, this patch of ground upon which we live and die. Earthly life counts for nothing; be-coming has no real existence; time is merely the moving image of eternity. Ideal, eternal forms constitute the privileged "real." Our pre-existing souls, trailing clouds of glory, plop into our bodies and crash land into a cave. With our legs and necks chained so that we cannot move, we face a wall. Behind us, a fire blazes. On a raised ledge, a puppeteer shows marionettes. As the parade marches, the world's veritable panorama flickers as shadowgraphs on the wall. Unable to turn to see the light, we cast our own shadows also. Our lying eyes deceive us; the beautiful scene we think "real" is merely simulated.[229] Ideas, grasped through reason, are superior to actual, concrete, material, corporeal things.

Our individualized mortal flesh is nothing but a contemptible, corruptible shell, a container of darkness and lust that imprisons the eternal spirit. In Plato, it is reduced to carrion and filth.[230] Life is cheap and expendable. In the *Republic*, Plato justifies as perfectly fine the brutality, murder and torture of war. He gives us as our task to escape our temporary abode in dank dungeons of soil and motley flesh, and to seek eternal light beyond this vale of tears. Our true home is elsewhere, somewhere beyond our environmental prison. Deconstructionists from Nietzsche and Heidegger to Derrida and Foucault have unmasked this way of thinking as racist and violent, and as a white western masculine European Christian chauvinistic metaphysics.

This discussion is not just an exercise in the philosophy of science. It goes to the heart of the matter of love relationships. The work of Luce Irigaray[231] gives one example of the Herculean task of getting at the nihilistic root of western thought. She has dug into Plato's myth of the cave to show that it contains the seminal ideas that have demeaned not only this good earth, existential time, and the body, but also a woman. Plato's patriarchal ideology, his "hystera," is anti-feminine, anti-life, and anti-love.

Levinas: The Phenomenology of the Face and Carnal Sexuality

One set of prejudices especially pertains to the content of this work. Western rationalism denies the originality of the other, denies that consciousness is a phenomenon in its own right, and denies that speaking is original and creative. Levinas offers the radical alternative, an "infinitizing" way of thinking that honors the originality of consciousness, privileges the individual while simultaneously demonstrating that the face to face relationship between individuals is the basic human reality.

For Levinas, we do not infer the other is there, but we look at her as she stares at us. We speak and touch and smell and taste one another. The other is outside of me, not reducible to me, not just an alter-ego, or my double. I know her in the immediacy of the glance and the touch and words. I know her in the vocative not objective case. She is not subsumed by my ideas or images. When you and I talk, our speaking is active and determinative. It is by no means just ventriloquist's monologue. When our touch joins us and we make love, we make babies. Our child is of us but outside us, radically other. Only a strange and warped abstract bracketing holds life in abeyance. This putting out of play of the lifeworld, Platonic-based and Descartes-reinforced, sustains the denial of genuine presence and co-inherence.

Nothing is more naked than the eyes. "They are more naked than flesh without pelt or hide, without clothing."[232] Everything else is naked by analogy to the stark naked vulnerability of human face. Whenever two people exchange glances and lock eyes, both are exposed. If they do not avert the eyes out of anxiety, guilt, shame, or racial hatred, then speaking ensues. I meet the other in a primary way in the vocative mode. Naked, defenseless eyes appeal to me, "Look at me; above all hear me." This invocation is also imperative. It shakes me out of my own sphere and contests my living at home (*chez moi*). It is an ethical demand.

Concerning Eros, Levinas then makes a revolutionary "move." He insists that blatantly exhibiting the bare body does not banish "the chase nudity" of the visage or of risk-talk. The nakedness of face and flesh, authentically understood, are two sides of the same coin. Simply put, both the face and the body equally are carnal and erotic. For Levinas, the standard for measuring carnal eroticism, for pinpointing what makes Eros precisely human, is the confluence of the hand and eyes that gracefully caress.

Mainstream Psychology

It has never abandoned its roots in modernity, in 19th century natural science. The "quantitative imperative" rules psychology.[233] Dichotomies litter its texts: heredity-environment, nature-nurture, biologically determined-socially constructed, sexuality-spirituality, emotion-reason, etc. It caters to pragmatism which is the biased conviction, "If it works, it's true." In our contemporary context, this prejudice holds sway by making sacred cows of what are only slivers of existence, namely behavior and especially cognitive behavior. In the same vein, it demands that the criterion to assess the value both of research and treatment be "outcomes."

The 19th century belongs to Charles Darwin. He cast a long shadow over orthodox social science as well. His evolutionary bias co-rules the mainstream. Psychology theorizes on the basis of his misguided notion that human life is based on instincts.[234] These are presumed to operate for the good of the individual and the species. Psychology also sadly accepts Darwin's struggle for survival as the mechanism that spurs growth. In addition, it embraces the warped notion that only the strong survive—an ideological bias that legitimizes cutthroat competition in education and the business sector as well as colonialism, imperialism, oppression, racism, and violence.

I reject the entire natural scientific program as inappropriate and inadequate for studying the person. I use instead a "human scientific psychology."[235] For such thinking, the ordinary events of each day are interrelated, intertwined, and embroiled. The connections between them are existential and qualitative and not numerical. Our commonly accepted dualisms are arbitrary and false. Practicality is certainly a value; but it is a merely a minor one. Behavior and cognition deserve no privileged status. How one behaves is less than half the story in matters of the heart. To understand love, not merely explain it or explain it away, we must balance behavior with experience and meaning. Thus this book does not feature strategies and techniques. It is not dotted with "do's and don'ts," "plus versus minus," "how-to-do-it," formulae, ratings from one to ten, or color codes from red hot to ice cold. It is holistic. It welds together emotion and reason and head and heart. In daily life, choice and the "leap" trigger the important "moments" of human development, change, and transformations. Instinct applied to humans is a misguided metaphor. Human life is based upon consciousness and inter-consciousness.

Identity

Identity is a totally normative concept, excessively conventional, and tied to the conceptual baggage of the 19th century natural science paradigm. Deconstructionist approaches dismantle the notions of "presence," "efficient causality," and 'linear time" They also de-center the concepts of self and identity. The mainstream also links identity to the simplistic Darwinian assumption that an evolving person eventually progresses into a loving partner. Only be strong enough to survive; then you will adapt; soon you will make the transition to a new stage of development. Based on instincts, mainstream normative thinking presents a neat, tidy developmental progression: early stages and phases result in a solid sense of identity that overflows to intimacy that in turn spills into procreation. Instincts serve the good of the individual and the species. The strongest survive, win the princess, mate, and propagate the species. This theoretically posited progression aims to safeguard the individual, the family, the society, the culture, and the geopolitical community. It supports establishment politics.

However, the vision hardly squares with lifeworld experience and with the world we live in that is divorce-riddled and war-ridden. It is sheer abstract theory, the left-over wine of the 19th century optimistic belief in unlimited progress, "Every day in every way we are getting better and better." As Derek in "True Love" rails, since the dawn of the 20th century western thought has generated one disaster after another: the Holocaust, the Mushroom Cloud, Black Rain, Mai Lai, Rwanda, Darfur, Iraq, and Lebanon. A fatal flaw nests in the heart of western rationalism.

Building blocks

An allied rationalistic prejudice is the stale belief in stages and phases. The bias is typically expressed as an "epigenetic principle" which purports that we develop through a predetermined unfolding of our personalities in stages such that our progress through each stage is in part determined by our success in all the previous stages. The view is simply trucked in from biology and manifests one more time the fraudulent Darwinian influence on psychological theory.

For a rose bud to unfold, each petal opens up at a certain time and in a certain order which nature through genetics has determined. If we interfere in the natural order of development by pulling a petal forward prematurely or out of order, we ruin the development of the entire flower. Human growth and development, however, do not follow such a naturally preprogrammed and inevitable progression. The chum, first love, and outlaw do indeed serve us in our personal-emotional-sexual-spiritual seasoning. Negotiating and living through them affords a tremendous gain. But they do not provide the necessary building blocks for authentic intimacy. Such a notion is hopelessly Darwinian, and conventionally western. Growth happens because life is not pre-arranged. Time is spiral, not a line; nothing adds up. "Moments" are discontinuous, indeterminate, and sometimes absurd. There is no psychological recipe, no master plan into which we should fit. Social existence is a dynamic network of evolving relationships that you and I orchestrate and create. The creative "product" is not the result of some pre-existing pattern. It springs forth, leaps. and jumps. These leaps are future-beckoned, will-inspired, and require courage.

The social sciences still also theorize on the basis of Newton's absolute universe. Space pre-exists like a gigantic container or big box. Within it are stages and phases, little boxes. These are pre-arranged as part of a wonderful design within which every thing hangs together orderly and coherently. Developmental psychological literature thus treats us to the assumption that each box holds a specific achievement, a building block, and furthermore that the series of achievements add up to some Grand Finale. This view also presumes that time is linear, that events are additive, and that everything we experience somehow puts in another ingredient of the necessary meat, potatoes, carrots, celery, and spices that when we apply heat cooks into stew. After Einstein, such thinking is hopelessly out of date. It is a philosophical bias that borders on a religious conviction. It is by no means a psychological science. It is the prevailing viewpoint of the "Club" that holds the power and the purse strings in science.

Intimacy

We ripen, season, and grow up. There is no recipe, however, for an intimate love bond. Intimacy is not an apple that ripens and falls off the tree as a wonderful gift of nature's vegetative processes of rain and sunlight, plus a bit of pruning, fertilizing, and insecticide application done by the hands of man. It is the main refrain of this book that life and love hinge on individual choices, on taking risks, and making leaps. Everything is one-in-a-row. In whatever way you have successfully negotiated adolescence, still it takes finding a new resolve and new courage to create intimacy. I borrow the words of the songbird: "All of your history has little to do with your face."[236] None of the phenomena in this book fix and freeze. First lovers have to deal with the ambiguities of daily existence and with the "cold hard facts of life" lest their bond decays into a withered love-cocoon. An outlaw relationship, as a protracted episode, either runs its course, ends -- often badly -- or else it converts into an in-law relationship and optimally into an intimate partnership. There comes a point along the developmental spiral at which "playing with fire" would not so much constitute "outlaw" dynamics as it would be cheating or even adultery. Intimacy is a new adventure and not a transition. We prepare for it; but to seize it we have to reach far beyond our preparation. Intimacy is a promise renewed daily. At bottom, it means accepting and embracing one's own death. I have only one life; will I share it with you? Or will I regret for "the remains of my day" what I failed to do for love's sake? "The proof is in the pudding," the old saying goes. The modern one is "what goes 'round comes 'round." Failure results in perpetual loneliness, ache and perpetual longing.

The Alternative to Concepts

Daily life swarms with music and movies, with photos and footage of actors, sports heroes, and TV personalities. Lyrics, images, and words flood our consciousness and fill our conversations. We relate to, absorb, and identify with certain artistic or "pop culture" heroes. Likewise, philosophers, novelists, poets and visual artists donate us ideas, words, and images. We fiddle with the Tarot cards, consult the *I-Ching*, and read our horoscope. We visit fortune tellers. We read popular science articles about "string theory" and about the general and special theories of relativity. Every now and again, a leading periodical like *Time* prints one more article "killing" Freud for the umpteenth time, or killing once more Nietzsche's "death of God" pronouncement. We frequent the theater and go to the ballet, even if it is only to enjoy our precious little girls dancing as a mouse and garden-sprite in *Cinderella*. These preoccupations or distractions encircle and fill our daily lives. It is impossible to imagine going through a day without them. It's hard to imagine a conversation in a fitness center, a bar, or a beauty salon that will not include animated discussions about politicians, banter about baseball players or soccer stars, and gossip about some Hollywood starlet whose photos are plastered on *People* magazine or *Cosmopolitan*. Our youth, in particular, watch MTV and chat about who's dating whom, who's pregnant, or who's getting divorced. Is not such daily conversation and inter-commerce grist for the mill for knowledge about love and its derangement? Pathetically, social science uses theoretical concepts and models to elbow them out of its studies. Mainstream orthodox psychology bristles at a genuinely descriptive approach to knowledge. Inevitably, it bars from its corpus the free and spontaneous utterances of everyday people and the poets or songwriters who come from among them. Such neglect manifests that academic research on love is situated in "ivory towers," not "in time" and not "on the ground." Here too, I upset the apple cart. In order to be faithful to the way people lead their lives and discuss their existence with others, I litter my book with the prattle that makes up everyday interaction: two philosophy students debating Heidegger's role in the Third Reich; two Southern kids passing the time of day by discussing the ambiguous role of technology in our postmodern world; two young woman sharing the words of the poet Rumi when at stake is longing over a lost love; a married man and women having a battle royal about the geopolitical predicament of post 9-11 planet earth. In such normal matters, we find genuine psychological material, not in the textbooks that make the money-makers a fortune. And so it is that I sprinkle this book with everyone from William Shakespeare to Zora Neal Hurston; from Emmylou Harris and Edvard Grieg to Robert Frost, from Anne Frank and Leonard Cohen to D. H. Lawrence, from Garcia Lorca and Anais Nin to Søren Kierkegaard, from Dag Hammarskjold and Simone Weil to Waylon Jennings.

Winding towards a Transition

All we have in life are moments. Some are one-in-a-row and once only. There are moments of tenderness and passion that congeal the entire spiral of our entire life, past, present, and future. Such moments also galvanize the edgepoint of our ultimate relationship, the

> *moments in lovemaking when one has the certainty of having been born for this love, the nerves of one's organs and the recesses of one's brain made for this passion, moments when all the craving, abandon, hope, adoration one is capable of are emptied, moments when one reserves nothing for the morrow or for another lover, as thought there will be nothing after, as though one could or would die in this transport.*[237]

> *"I was born to be here, in your arms, I could die now."* [238]

"Gamble everything for love," Rumi prods us, "If you're a true human being... Half-heartedness doesn't reach into majesty."[239] And then he points beyond finitude towards our infinite home:

> *To a frog that's never left his pond the ocean seems like a gamble. Look what he's giving up: security, mastery of his world, recognition! The ocean frog just shakes his head. "I can't really explain what it's like where I live, but someday I'll take you there."*[240]

Endnotes

[1] Blaise Pascal, *Discourse sur les passions de l'amour* (Paris: Mille Et Une Nuits, 1995).

[2] Søren Kierkegaard, *Works of love,* trans. Howard Hong and Edna Hong (New York: Harper Torchbooks, 1962), 23-24 ; "First love," In *Either/Or: Volume I*, trans. David F. Swenson & Lillian Marvin Swenson (Princeton: Princeton University Press, 1971), 229-277; "Diary of a seducer," In *Either/Or: Volume I*, trans. David F. Swenson & Lillian Marvin Swenson (Princeton: Princeton University Press, 1971), 297-440; *Either/Or: Volume II, trans.* Walter Lowrie (Princeton: Princeton University Press, 1974); *Concluding unscientific postscript*, trans. David F. Swenson & Walter Lowrie (Princeton: Princeton University Press, 1974); *The concept of anxiety*, trans. Reidar Thomte (Princeton: Princeton University Press, 1980); *Stages on life's way*, trans. H. Hong & Edna Hong (Princeton, New Jersey: Princeton University Press, 1988.

[3] Alfonso Lingis, *Dangerous emotions* (Berkeley: University of California Press, 2000), 63; 81; *Excesses: Eros and culture* (Albany: State University of New York Press, 1983); *Libido: The French existential theories* (Indianapolis: Indiana University Press, 1985); *Deathbound subjectivity* (Bloomington, Indiana: Indiana University Press, 1989); *The community of those who have nothing in common* (Indianapolis: Indiana University Press, 1994); *Abuses* (Berkley: University of California Press, 1994); *Foreign bodies* (New York: Routledge, 1994; *The Imperative* (Indianapolis: Indiana University Press, 1998); *Trust* (Minneapolis: University of Minnesota Press, 2004.

[4] Lingis, *Dangerous emotions, 60.*

[5] Lingis, *Dangerous emotions, 60-61.*

[6] Lingis, *Dangerous emotions, 141.*

[7] George Jones, "How proud I would have been," On *Country Heart* [LP]. Nashville: Musicor Records, 1966; "There's nothing better once you've had the best." On *The grand tour.* [LP]. Sons of Polygram, BMI, 1972; recorded (1974).

[8] William S. Cook, "You can have her," [Waylon Jennings]. On *Waylon live: The expanded edition* [CD].Grove Park Music, 1964; Distributed by BMG Heritage, 82876 51855 2. (2003).

[9] Friedrich Nietzsche, *The gay science.* trans. Walter Kaufmann (New York: Random House, 1974); "The antichrist," In *The Portable Nietzsche*, trans. Walter Kaufmann (New York: Penguin Books, 1982), 639-40; "Twilight of the idols," In *The portable Nietzsche*, trans. Water Kaufmann (New York: Penguin Books, 1982), 558-59; 572; 574).

[10] Sigmund Freud, "Note on the unconscious in psychoanalysis," In *General Psychological theory* (New York: Collier Books, 1966), 66; *Beyond the pleasure principle: a study of the death instinct in human behavior* (New York: Bantam Books, 1963); "Contributions to the psychology of love," In *Freud on sexuality:* Vol. 7, 1977, p. 249ff; *Three essays on the theory of sexuality* (New York: Avon Books, 1992).

[11] Teilhard de Chardin, *The phenomenon of man* (New York: Harper & Row, 1961) 265. In stunning contrast to the naturalism, mechanism, racism and violence built into Darwin's view of evolution, Teilhard de Chardin shows that love is at the heart of the evolutionary processes of building the earth and creating a future for mankind.

[12] Gloria Vanderbilt, *Reverie Pure.* This quip appears on a post card that I stumbled upon in *3-T*, a fitness center in Trondheim, Norway.

[13] Esther Vilar, *The manipulated man* (New York: Bantam Books, 1978), 132-33.

[14] Kierkegaard, *Works of love*, 33.

[15] Emmylou Harris, "The pearl," On *Red dirt girl* [CD]. Nonsuch Records, 79616-2, 2000.

[16] Alfred Lord Tennyson, "I*n Memoriam: XXV11*," In *The Poetic Works of Alfred Lord Tennyson* (Collins Clear-Type Press, London and Glasgow, 1849) 7. (The volume I cite here is bound in musty leather, a treasure the owner is proud to possess).

[17] Virgil, *Eclogues*, (New York: Penguin, 1984), Ecalogue X.

[18] Jalal al-din Rumi, *The essential Rumi*, trans. Coleman Barks (New York: HarperCollins, 1995), 229.

[19] Ibid., 42.

[20] Ibid., 270.

[21] James Hillman, "The fiction of case history: A round," In J. B. Wiggins (ed). *Religion as story* (New York: Harper and Colophon, 1975), 169; *Re-visioning psychology*, (New York: Harper Perennial, 1976), 236.

[22] "Moment" is the cardinal concept of the book. Throughout, I keep it in quotes. Moments are all that we have in life. Any given "moment" might die on the vine in an eye-blink; or it might build into an encounter, become a genuine meeting, evolve into a relationship, even a lifelong one. The "moment" is living, immediate, concrete and specific--180 degrees opposite abstract theoretical concepts, constructs, and models. It is connected ineluctably with individuality and uniqueness, with decision and choice, with hope and anticipation about the future, and with "inwardness" and the "leap" which creates change, transition, metamorphosis, and personal transformation. It is a "psychological" psychological concept, not a behavioral one.

[23] "One-in-a-row" is the second key notion of the book. It signifies also the uniqueness and irreplaceably of us and of our experience. "Once only" is a phrase of the same ilk. Unlike orthodox psychology stuck in the 19th century, contemporary physicists thoroughly understand that often they experiment with an event that never will happen again. In this book, "one-in-a-row" and "once only" fly in the face of our psychology's obsession with measures of central tendency and demand to replicate, predict, and control. It opens for freshness, newness, and spontaneity. It respects and honors the here-and-now, this good earth, and this, the time of our lives.

[24] John Keats, *The poems of Keats* (London: Longman Group Limited, 1970), 537.

[25] William Shakespeare, *The tragedy of Hamlet Prince of Denmark* (Baltimore, Maryland: Penguin Books, 1957), Act 1, Scene 3, 46.

[26] Harry Stack Sullivan, *Conceptions of modern psychiatry*. (New York: W. W. Norton, 1953a), 41; *The interpersonal theory of psychiatry*, New York: W. W. Norton., 1953b).

[27] Francis Bacon, "The quotations page," http://www.quotationspage.com; Accessed 25 March 2005.

[28] Anne Frank, *The diary of a young girl*, trans. Arnold J. Pomerans (New York: Doubleday 2003).

[29] Kahlil Gibran, *The prophet* (Alfred A. Knopf, New York, 1980), 58.

[30] Margery Williams, *The velveteen rabbit: Or how to become real* (New York: An Avon Camelot Book, 1975), 16-17.

[31] Sinead O'Conner, "Scorn not his simplicity," On *Universal mother* [LP]. Asylum Records, Ensign / Chrysalis, 1990.

[32] Antoine De Saint-Exupery, *The little prince*, trans. K. Woods (New York: Harecourt, Brace and Company, 1943), 64-71.

[33] W. H. Hudson, *Green mansions* (New York: Random House, 1944).

[34] James Taylor, "You've got a friend," On *Mud Slide Slim and the Blue Horizon* [LP]. Warner Brothers Records, 1971.

[35] Paul Simon and Art Garfunkel, "Bridge over troubled waters," On *Bridge over troubled waters*, [LP]. Columbia Records, 1970.

[36] Gordon Lightfoot, "You are what I am," On *Gord's gold* [CD]. Reprise UPC 075992722520, 1967.

[37] Horace, *The Odes of Horace*, trans. James Michie (New York: Washington Square Press, 1963).

[38] I used this "stimulus-item" in my research project in order to elicit written descriptions of the best friend.

[39] Since my analyses intermingle material from the parable and the qualitative research data, my work is interpretative or hermeneutic, not purely phenomenological.

[40] Freud, *Three essays on the theory of sexuality*, 70.

[41] Erik Erikson, *Identity and the life cycle* (New York: International Universities Press, 1959), 86; *Identity: Youth and crisis* (New York: W. W. Norton & Company, Inc., 1968).

[42] Sullivan, *The interpersonal theory of psychiatry*, 127.

[43] Martin Buber, *I and Thou* (New York: Charles Scribner's Sons, 1958).

[44] Sullivan, *The interpersonal theory of psychiatry*, 246.

[45] Gabriel Marcel, *Being and having: An existentialist diary* (New York: Harper Torchbooks, 1965).

[46] Jean Piaget, *Origins of intelligence in children* (New York: International Universities Press, 1992).

[47] Jean-Paul Sartre, *Being and nothingness*, trans. Hazel Barnes (New York: Washington Square Press, 1956).

[48] George Herbert Mead, *Mind, self and society from the standpoint of a social behaviorist* (Chicago: University of Chicago Press, 1963).

[49] Edmund Husserl, *The idea of phenomenology*, trans. W. P. Alston and G. Hakhnikian (The Hague: Martinus Nijhoff, 1973).

[50] Immanuel Kant, *Critique of pure reason*, trans. Lewis White Beck (Indianapolis: Bobbes-Merrill, 1956).

[51] Martin Heidegger, *Being and time*, trans. John Macquarrie & Edward Robinson (New York: Harper & Row, 1962).

[52] Albert Camus, *The rebel* (New York: A Vintage Book, 1956).

[53] George Simmel, *The sociology of George Simmel*, trans. Kurt H. Wolff (New York: Simon Schuster, 1985).

[54] Alan Jackson, "Where were you" [Live Video]. *You Tube*, http://youtube.com August 2006; Accessed 13 March 2007.

[55] Heterosexual relationships constitute the theme of this book. However, I have data that shows the essential similarity between gay, lesbian and heterosexually-oriented individuals concerning the experience of each of the four pivotal relationships. The mater demands an article or book of its own.

[56] Radley Metzger (Director), *Therese and Isabelle* [Film]. Audubon Films, 1968.

[57] Sullivan, *The interpersonal theory of psychiatry*, 162.

[58] R. D. Laing, *The divided self* (Harmondsworth, Middlesex, England: Penguin Books, Ltd., 1965); *The politics of experience* (New York: Pantheon, 1967; *The politics of the family* (Toronto: The Hunter Rose Company), 1973).

[59] Rumi, *The essential Rumi*, 229.

[60] Boris Pasternak, *Doctor Zhivago* (New York: Ballantine Books, 1997).

[61] Jimmy Webb, "All I know," [Art Garfunkel]. On *Angel Claire* [LP]. Sony Music Entertainment, 1973.

[62] Marguerite Duras, *North China lover* (New York: The New Press, 1992), 125.

[63] Roy Orbison, "It's over," On *Only the lonely* [LP]. London 1960.

[64] Irini Spanidou, *God's snake* (London: Secker & Warburg, 1967), 200.

[65] Rumi, *The essential Rumi*, 16-17.

[66] Ibid., 20.

[67] Buck Ram, "Enchanted," [The Platters]. On *The Magic touch Platters anthology* [CD]. Polygram, 1991.

[68] Theodore Isaac Rubin, *Coming out* (Markham, Ontario: Pocket Book, 1977) 9.

[69] F. Scott Fitzgerald, *Tender is the night* (New York: Bantam Books, 1962), 74-75.

[70] Richard, J. Alapack, "Adolescent first love," In Christopher .M. Aanstoos (ed.), Exploring *the Lived World: Readings in Phenomenological Psychology* Carrollton: West Georgia College, 1984, 101-117; "The Outlaw relationship: An existential phenomenological reflection upon the transition from adolescence to young adulthood. In Amedeo P. Giorgi, Constance T. Fischer & Edward Murray (eds.), *Duquesne Studies in Phenomenological Psychology*, Vol. II (Pittsburgh: Duquesne University Press, 1975, 182-205); "The Outlaw relationship as an intertwining of two identity crises: A phenomenological, psychotherapeutic reflection upon female awakening at late adolescence and male rejuvenation at mid life," *Journal of Phenomenological Psychology*, 17, 1986, 43-63; "No life to spare: A scientific phenomenological study of being on parole," presented to the meeting of the *American Psychological Association*, Division 32, Atlanta, GA, August 1988; "Home free: A human scientific study of release from prison," presented to the *Seventh International Human Science Research Conference*, Seattle, WA, June 1988"A phenomenological approach to recidivism and relapse", presented to The Ielase Institute/Mon-Yough Forensic Retreat, Wheeling, WV, November 1989; "Adolescent first kiss," *The Humanistic Psychologist*. 19 (1), 1991, 48-67; "Jealousy in first love: Unwitting disclosure," In Anne C. Richards & Tiparat Schumrum (eds.), *Invitations to dialogue: The legacy of Sidney M. Jourard* (New York: Kendall/Hunt, 1999), 91-106; "Sketches on human love, sexuality and sensuality, *Psykologisk Tidsskrift*, 1 (4), 2001.

[71] Duras, *North China lover*, 113.

[72] Sonny James, "Young love," On *Young love: The collection* [CD]. Razor & Tie Music, 82150, 1997.

[73] Jean Miles and Paul Robi, "One in a million" [The Platters]. On *The Magic touch Platters anthology* [CD]. Polygram, 1991.

[74] Pasternak, *Doctor Zhivago, 398.*

[75] Hillman, *Re-visioning psychology*, 236.

[76] Duras, *North China lover*, 72.

[77] Aldo Carotenuto, *The secret symmetry* (New York: Pantheon Books, 1984), 96.

[78] Pasternak, *Doctor Zhivago, 534; 550.*

[79] Duras, *North China lover*, 223.

[80] The matters of longing for and grief over lost love will be of the themes in a forthcoming book.

[81] Sartre, *Being and nothingness*, 86-112.

[82] Alexander Solzhenitsyn, *Cancer ward* (New York: Bantam, *1972)*, 346.

[83] Ibid.

[84] Ibid., 346-47.

[85] Anais Nin, *The journals of Anais Nin: Volume five* (London: Quartet Books, 1976), 33.

[86] Ibid.

[87] Adrienne Rich, *Diving into the wreck* (New York: W. W. Norton & Company, 1973), 22-24.

[88] Ibid., 23

[89] Jacques Lacan, *Ecrits: A selection*, trans. Alan Sheridan (New York: W. W. Norton & Company, 1977). (Lacan says that one suicides because one is in love with death).

[90] Alapack, "Adolescent first love," 113-14.

[91] Bernard J. Boelen, *Personal maturity: The existential dimension* (New York: The Seabury Press, 1978), 92ff.

[92] Piaget, *Origins of intelligence in children.*

[93] Kierkegaard, *The concept of anxiety*, 81.

[94] Erikson, *Identity: Youth and crisis*, 233; 235; 256.

[95] This concept helps Erikson understand the rise of the Third Reich. His passion therein abides. Hitler appealed to the German youth's highest human possibilities in order to accomplish the basest goal, genocide.

[96] Diederik F. Janssen, "First love: A note on the science, discourse and anthropology of propaedeutic concepts"; *Growing up sexually*. Volume I: World reference atlas (Victoria Park, W. A.: Brooks Reborn, 2003); "The body as (in) curriculum: On wars, complexes and rides," *Pedagogy, Culture & Society,* (forthcoming).

[97] Janseen, "The body as (in) curriculum: On wars, complexes and rides."

[98] Kierkegaard, *"First love,"* 252.

[99] Ibid.

[100] Kierkegaard, *"Diary of a seducer,"* 327.

[101] Laing, *The politics of the family.*

[102] Alapack, "The outlaw relationship: An existential phenomenological

reflection upon the transition from adolescence to young adulthood," 182. (I asked participants-subjects to respond in writing to this item: "Please describe a romantic or erotic relationship with a person who was significantly different from you or your background").

[103] Buck Owens, "Tall dark stranger." On *Tall dark stranger* [LP]. Capital Records-ST-212, 1969.

[104] Billy Joe Shaver, "Black rose" [Waylon Jennings]. On *Honky tonk heroes* [CD]. Buddha, 1973.

[105] Ron Cornelissen is the actual writer of this haiku. I am grateful that he allows me to use it.

[106] Herman Raucher, *Summer of '42* (New York: Dell, 1971), 6.

[107] Jane Olivor, "Daydream," On *Jane Oliver in concert* [CD]. Columbia UPC074643793827 Sony Distributors, 1988.

[108] Merle Haggard, "Always wanting you," On *Always wanting you* [LP]. Kingfisher Records, 1996.

[109] David Bowie, "Word on a wing," On *Station to station* [LP]. RCA Records 1976.

[110] John Steinbeck, *East of Eden*, (New York: Bantam Books, 1974) 524.

[111] Martin Heidegger, *Being and time,* 166.

[112] Vern Gosdin, B. Cannon & D. Dilon, "I guess I had your leaving coming" [Vern Gosdin]. On *Chiseled in stone* [CD]. CBS Records Inc., 40982, 1987.

[113] Sullivan, *The interpersonal theory of psychiatry,* 86-91; 118; 121, 166.

[114] I worked first with criminals on parole in 1986 in Pittsburgh at the Ielase Institute, directed by Richard Asarian, Ph. D. Then, In the wake of the Exxon Valdez oil catastrophe, 1989, I directed the Seward Life Action Council, Seward Alaska. We ran an out-patient drug and alcohol programs and also mounted the program at Spring Creek Correctional, the only prison—and a maximum security prison-- in Alaska. There and then, men and women told me their stories of life and love. Recidivism, all recognize, is the scourge of the criminal justice system. I addirm that the three "snakes" which potentially compromise a parolee's successful re-entry to society are a woman (or man), money-unemployment and legal-illegal chemical substances. I present the structural-dynamic issues about the ex-con as 'outlaw' in Richard J. Alapack, "No life to spare: A scientific phenomenological study of being on parole"; "Home free: A human scientific study of release from prison"; "A phenomenological approach to recidivism and relapse."

[115] Vern Gosdin, "Do you believe me now?" On *Chiseled in stone* [CD]. CBS Records Inc., 40982, 1987.

[116] Alapack, "The Outlaw relationship as an intertwining of two identity

crises: A phenomenological, psychotherapeutic reflection upon female awakening at late adolescence and male rejuvenation at mid-life," 43-44.

[117] Waylon Jennings, "I'm living proof," On *A man called Hoss* [CD]. MCA, MCAD-42038, Universal City, CA. 1987.

[118] Diane Ackerman, *A natural history of the senses* (New York: Vintage Books, 1995), 68.

[119] Emmanuel Levinas, *Totality and infinity, 66.*

[120] D. H. Lawrence, *Look! We have come through!* (Marazion Cornwall, England: The Ark Press, 1959); *Sons and lovers*, (New York: Viking Press, 1961); "The horse dealer's daughter, In *A Modern lover* (New York: Ballantine Books, 1969); *The Virgin and the Gipsy* (London: Penguin, Ltd., 1972); *Lady Chatterley's lover*, (New York: A Signet Book, 1959); *The fox,* (New York: Bantam Books, 1973; *Fantasia of the Unconscious / Psychoanalysis of the unconscious*, (Harmondsworth, Middlesex, England: Penguin Books, 1974); *Phoenix: The posthumous papers, 1936* (Harmondsworth, Middlesex, England: Penguin Books, 1978); *Phoenix II* (Harmondsworth, Middlesex, England: Penguin Books, 1978); *Lady Chatterley's lover* (Toronto: Bantam Books, 1983).

[121] Alapack, "Sketches on human love, sexuality and sensuality." 6.

[122] Zora Neal Hurston, *Their eyes were watching God* (New York: Perennial Classics, 1990), 12.

[123] Henry Elkin, "Love and violence: A psychoanalytic viewpoint," *Humanitas*, 2 (2), 1966, 165-182.

[124] Johnny Paycheck, "For a minute there," On *20 Greatest Hits* [CD]. Deluxe, 1994.

[125] Robert Frost, "The road not taken," In *The Poetry of Robert Frost*, Edward Connery Lathem (ed.), (New York: Henry Hold and Company, 1975), 105.

[126] The western countries have a narrow and distorted understanding of "JiHad." Its root meaning is "to work hard" or 'strive." This fertile word combines "ability, power, energy, zeal and fatigue." And as "JaHaDa," it means to fulfill religious duty, including, if required, a fighting for the faith against infidels: c.f., William R. Polk, *Understanding Iraq* (New York: HarperCollins Publishers, 2005), xvi-xvii.

[127] Robert Frost, "Death of a hired hand," In The *Poetry of Robert Frost*, 38.

[128] Alapack, "The outlaw relationship: An existential phenomenological reflection upon the transition from adolescence to young adulthood," 191.

[129] Ibid., 192-93.

[130] Alfred Schutz, *Collected papers, Vol. I: The problem of social reality* (The Hague: Martinus Nijhoff, 1973), 59f.

[131] Paul Ricoeur, *Freud and philosophy*: An essay on interpretation, trans. Denis Savage (New Haven: Yale University Press, 1977).

[132]Freud, "Contributions to the psychology of love," 249ff.

[133] Ibid.

[134] Ibid.

[135] Alfred Adler, *Individual psychology of Alfred Adler: A systematic presentation in selections from his writings* (New York: HarperCollins, 1958).

[136] Ibid·

[137] Sigmund Freud, *Beyond the pleasure principle: a study of the death instinct in human behavior* (New York: Bantam Books, 1963), 65.

[138] C. G. Jung, "Marriage as a psychological relationship," In J. Campbell, (ed.), *The portable Jung* (New York: The Viking Press, 1974), 163-177.

[139] Robert Frost. "Birches," In *The Poetry of Robert Frost*, 121.

[140] Ibid., 121·

[141] Ibid., 122.

[142] Ibid.

[143] Ibid.

[144] Kierkegaard, *Works of love*, 49.

[145] Harold Searles, *The collected papers on Schizophrenia* (New York: International Universities Press, 1965.

[146] N. K. Dzobo, *African proverbs: The moral guide to Ewe proverbs, Guide to conduct Vol. II* (Accra: Bureau of Ghana Languages, 1997), 73.

[147] Waylon Jennings, "No good for me," On *Waymore's blues (Part II)* [CD]. RCA, 07863 66409 2, 1994.

[148] Frost, *Birches*, 122.

[149] Aldo Carotenuto, *The secret symmetry.*

[150] Laurens Van Der Post, *The dark eye in* Africa (New York: William Morrow & Company, 1955).

[151] Neil Young, "Bound for Glory," [Neil Young and Waylon Jennings]. On *Old Ways* [CD]. Geffen Records, A Universal Music Company, 069 409 705 2, (2000).

[152] Ibid.

[153] Willie Nelson, "Heaven or hell" [Waylon Jennings]. On *This time* [CD]. Buddha, 1999.

[154] Leonard Cohen, Cohen, "Say a prayer for the cowboy," On *Recent songs* [LP]. Recorded: April–May 1979, A&M Studios, Hollywood; *The future* [CD], Sony Music Entertainment. Columbia records, Original Release Date. Released: September 1979: November 24, 1992.

[155] Lee Clayton, "Ladies love outlaws," [Waylon Jennings]. On *Waylon live: The expanded version.* [CD]. Grove Park Music, 1964; Distributed by BMG Heritage, 82876 51855 2. (2003).

[156] Robert Browning, *My last duchess and other poems* (Mineola, New York: Dover Publications, 1993).

[157] John Keats, "Love is my religion." In *Letters of John Keats to Fanny Brawne* (The Netherlands: Maastricht, 1931).

[158] Roger Vadim (Director), *And God Created Woman* [Film]. Home Vision Cinema, Chicago: Ill., 1956. In the film, the words are evoked to describe Brigitte Bardot's fluid derriere.

[159] C. G. Jung, "Marriage as a psychological relationship," In *The portable Jung*, 163-177.

[160] Friedrich Nietzsche, "The antichrist," In *The Portable Nietzsche*, 639-40.

[161] Lawrence, "First morning, "In *Look we have come through*, 32.

[162] Dag Hammarskjold, *Markings*, trans. Leif Sjoberg & W. H. Auden (New York: Alfred A. Knopf, 1970), 38.

[163] Robert Alley, *Last Tango in Paris*, (New York: A dell Book, 1973), 170.

[164] Albert Einstein and Sigmund Freud, "Why War?" In *An International Series of Open Letters. Vol. II*, trans. Stewart Gilbert (Paris: International Institute of Intellectual Cooperation, 1933).

[165] Lawrence, "Humiliation." In *Look we have come through*, 41-42.

[166] Søren Kierkegaard, *Concluding unscientific postscript*, 141.

[167] Federico Garcia Lorca, "Conversation with Bagaria, In *Deep song and other prose* (London: Marion Boyars Publishers, Ltd., 1982), 129.

[168] George Jones, "There's nothing better once you've had the best." On *The grand tour*.

[169] D. H. Lawrence, "Love was once a little boy," in Phoenix II, 445.

[170] Lawrence, "We need one another," In Phoenix, 194.

[171] Gail Sheehy, Passages: Predictable crises of adulthood (New York: Bantam), 1984.

[172] Simone Weil, "Friendship," In *Simone Weil: An anthology*, Sian Miles, Ed. (New York: Weidenfeld & Nicolosson, 1986), 269.

[173] E. Mark Stern and Burt G. Marino, *Psychotheology: The discovery of sacredness in humanity*, (New York: Paulist Press), 1970), 55.

[174] D. H. Lawrence, *The fox* (New York: Bantam Books, 1973), 100.

[175] Richard Aldington, *D. H. Lawrence* (New York: Collier Books, 1967), 148.

[176] Lawrence, "We need one another," In *Phoenix*, 193.

[177] T. S. Eliot, "The waste land"; & "The hollow men," In *Collected poems: 1909-1962* (London: Faber and Faber Limited), 1963.

[178] Lawrence, "We need one another," In *Phoenix*, 190.

[179] Lawrence, "Love," in *Phoenix*, 153.

[180] Lawrence, "The real thing," in *Phoenix*. 198.

[181] D. H. Lawrence, "The state of funk," In *Phoenix II*, 569.

[182] Lawrence, "We need one another," In *Phoenix*, 191.

[183] Richard Aldington, 129.

[184] Benedict XVI, *God is love: Encyclical letter of the Supreme Pontiff* (Boston: Pauline Books & Media, 2006), 9.

[185] D. H. Lawrence, *Lady Chatterley's lover*, 165.

[186] Merleau-Ponty, *The phenomenology of perception* (London: Routledge & Kegan Paul, 1962). 179; 197; 389.

[187] Alan Watts, *Nature, man and woman*, (New York: Random House, 1991).

[188] Stephen Spender, "from Explorations," In *Selected poems* (London: Faber and Faber, 1975), 64.

[189] R. D. Laing, *The politics of experience* (New York: Pantheon, 1967), 90.

[190] Rumi, *The essential Rumi*, 79-80.

[191] Nietzsche, "The Antichrist," In *The portable Nietzsche*, 640.

[192] Stephen Spender, "Double shame," In *Selected poems*, 55.

[193] Carlos Castaneda, *Teachings of Don Juan: A Yaqui way of knowledge* (Berkeley: University of California Press, 1985).

[194] Waylon Jennings, "Waymore's blues," On *Waymore's blues (Part II)* [CD]. RCA, 07863 66409 2, 1994.

[195] Kierkegaard, *Concluding unscientific postscript*, 148.

[196] Buber, *I and Thou*, 11; 132.

[197] Eric Fromm, *Escape from freedom* (New York: Henry Holt & Co., 1994).

[198] Cohen, "Closing time," On *The future*.

[199] Jean Baudrillard, "Disneyworld Company," In *Liberation* trans. Francois Debrix (Paris, 4 March 1996).

[200] Emmanuel Levinas, *Totality and Infinityy: An Essay on Exteriority*, trans. Alfonso Lingis (Pittsburgh: Duquesne University Press, 1969), 67.

[201] Theodore Isaac Rubin, *Coming out*, (Markham, Ontario: Pocket Book, 1977), 43.

[202] Waylon Jennings & Don Bowman, "Just to satisfy you," [Waylon Jennings]. On *Waylon: The RCA years* [CD]. BMI Master: WWA4-2076, 1968; Distributor, BMG, 1993.

[203] Waylon Jennings, "A love song," *On A man called Hoss* [CD]. MCA, MCAD-42038, Universal City, CA. 1987.

[204] Lingis, *Trust*, 64.

[205] Ibid., 65·

[206] This discussion contributes to dismantling the normative biases about masculinity and femininity that rule in western culture--both those supported by the Patriarchy and the alternatives instigated by so-called feminists. D. H. Lawrence's vision shows how women and men might relate with one another after a successful deconstruction of the traditional western patriarchy. How? With genuine equality: eyeball-to-eyeball, back-to-back, and belly-to-belly.

[207] Lingis, *Trust*, 80.

[208] Ibid., 79.

[209] Yukio Mishima, *Spring snow, trans.* M. Gallagher (New York: Pocket Books, 1973), 85.

[210] Lawrence, "The horse dealer's daughter," In *A Modern lover*, 331.

[211] Alapack, "Adolescent first kiss," 49. (I asked participants to "Describe your first 'real' adolescent kiss, the one that was not just a 'peck on the cheek").

[212] Sullivan 1953, 62-75.

[213] Lawrence, *Lady Chatterley's lover*, 143).

[214] S. Weitman, *On the elementary forms of socioerotic life.* 71-110. In Mike Featherstone (ed.), *Love & Eroticism.* (London: Sage, 1999), 76.

[215] Merleau-Ponty, *The Phenomenology of perception*, 168.

[216] J. H. Van den Berg, *Different existence: Principles of phenomenological psychopathology.* Pittsburgh: Duquesne University Press, 1972), 70-71.

[217] Lingis, *The imperative*, 154.

[218] Levinas, *Totality and infinty*, 257-258).

[219] Lawrence, *Lady Chatterley's lover*, 135.

[220] Lorca. *Deep song and other prose.*

[221] Claude Lebouch (Producer and Director), A *Man and a Woman* [Film]. Allied Artists Pictures, 1966.

[222] Merle Haggard, "Ain't you memory got no pride at all?" [Doug Stone]. On *From the heart* [CD]. Sony Music Entertainment, 1992.

[223] Red Lane & Wanda Jackson, "Walk out of my mind," [Waylon Jennings]. On *Love of the common people* [CD]. Recorded August 30, 1967, BMG Distribution. Buddha Records, 1999.

[224] Alapack, "Jealousy in first love: Unwitting disclosure." I asked participants, "If you had a 'bout' of jealousy while you were involved with your first love, please describe your experience and what it meant to you."

[225] Cohen, "Anthem," On *The future.*

[226] Ronald Barthes, *The pleasure of the text* (New York: The Noonday Press, 1989), v.

[227] Plato, *The Republic*, trans. B. Jowett. In L. R. Looms (ed.), *Five great dialogues.* (Roslyn, N. Y: W. J. Black, Inc., 1942), 215-495.

[228] Nietzsche, "Twilight of the idols," 558-59; 572; 574.

[229] Plato, *The Republic*, (398-402).

[230] Ibid., 114-117.

[231] Luce Irigaray, *Speculum of the other woman*, trans. Gillian C. Gill (Ithaca, New York: Cornell University Press, 243-364.

[232] Lingis, *Foreign bodies*, 171.

[233] Joel Mitchell, The quantitative imperative: Positivism, naïve realism and

the place of qualitative methods in psychology, *Theory & Psychology*. 13 (1), 5-31, 2003.

[234] I eschew Darwinism as irrelevant for psychology and damaging for understanding love relationships. My standpoint has nothing to do with the right-winged Christian terror that Darwin destroys the Biblical account of creation. My critical rejection roots in philosophical thinking. Nietzsche scathingly denounces Darwinian and all Anglo-Saxon philosophy as bankrupt naturalism, mechanism, materialism, empiricism and pragmatism. *The origins of the species*, spliced as it is with massive empirical evidence, is perhaps history's prime example of a speculative treatise trumped up and paraded as science. The zeitgeist simply was ready for ideas that Darwin supported, but surely did not create! Especially Social Darwinism, with concepts of dog-eat-dog competitiveness and "survival of the fittest," enshrines British smug arrogance and warped sense of superior "breeding." It metaphysically legitimizes and justifies its colonialism, racism, imperialism and greedy thirst for conquest. Cf., Charles Darwin, *The origins of the species* (New York: Gramercy Books, 1979).

[235] Amedeo Giorgi, *Psychology as a human science*, (New York: Harper & Row, 1970).

[236] Joan Baez, "Love song to a stranger," *On Greatest hits* [CD]. A&M. Original Release Date: May 7, 1996.

[237] Alfonso Lingis, *Deathbound subjectivity*, 32.

[238] Lingis, Dangerous emotions, 107.

[239] Rumi, *The essential Rumi*, 193.

[240] Ibid.

Author Bio:

Richard Alapack, Ph. D. is an Associate Professor of Psychology at the Norwegian University of Science and Technology (NTNU). Power fades; money vanishes; fame is fickle; ambition is foolish; only love endures. Most importantly, therefore, Richard is father to three splendid children, Nicole, Richard and Orion, and the grandfather of two bright and beautiful girls, Sophie and Olivia.

His principal disciplinary areas are love and death approached from existential, phenomenological, hermeneutic and psychoanalytic points of view. His original research includes such topics as first love, first kiss, the outlaw relationship, flirting on the Internet and the hickey, and tender-erotic touch. A stint as clinical-community director of the Seward Life Action Council in Seward, Alaska, expanded love-matters to included death-themes; and a concurrent visiting lectureship at the University of Pretoria-- when Apartheid ended in South Africa-- triggered ongoing teaching and research both on natural and manmade disasters and on global political themes. Currently, he also researching the phenomena that cluster around peace: humiliation, violence, revenge and their cures: forgiveness, compassion, mercy.

Richard hails originally from Pennsylvania. During his career, he has held appointments at all the major human scientific and humanistic psychology departments in the USA: Duquesne University, the University of Dallas, Seattle University and the State University at West Georgia. For fourteen years, he held a joint post at the University of St. Jerome's College and the University of Waterloo. Since 1990, he has been a visiting professor at the University of Pretoria, South Africa, and continues to advise its doctoral students. He is also affiliated with the California State University at Northridge, CSUN in Los Angeles.

Does love have a future?

Love definitely has a future. The future lives in our children. Environmentalists remind us that we did not inherit the earth from our ancestors, we borrowed it from our children...and our children's children. I close this book on love with images of innocence, hope, and beauty. Instead of tattooing it with photos of my three beautiful children, Nicole, Richard, and Orion, I present to you the small one's, the youngest generation, Nicole's contributions to Light, Life, and Love: Sophie and Olivia.

Printed in the United Kingdom
by Lightning Source UK Ltd.
122480UK00001B/184-234/A